A Spelling Dictionary

By Patrick McLaughlin
with Iseabail Macleod

Schofield & Sims Ltd
HUDDERSFIELD ENGLAND

0 7217 0670 3
Net Edition 0 7217 0671 1

First printed 1993

Spelling Dictionary Exercises
ISBN 0 7217 0675 4

A separate book of exercises is available which aims to set out a system for the easy diagnosis of spelling problems with the appropriate follow-up.

Design and Artwork by Armitage Typo/Graphics Ltd., Huddersfield
Printed in Great Britain by The Bath Press, Avon

Notes on the use of A Spelling Dictionary

All of us from time to time, if not more frequently, have the need to check the spelling of a particular word. This can be done, of course, by using a general dictionary but it is a cumbersome and time-consuming task for such dictionaries serve many more purposes than simply giving the spelling of a word. The beauty of a spelling dictionary is that this is its sole purpose.

A good spelling dictionary should have three main attributes: it should be *extensive*, that is to say it should have a sufficiently large vocabulary bank to cater for a wide range of users; it should be *comprehensive*, that is it should include all the words formed from a given root plus all acceptable variants; and it should be *user friendly* in allowing easy identification of the particular word which is being sought. This is what **A Spelling Dictionary** sets out to do.

Extensive

The range of users envisaged for this dictionary is from upper Primary to adults. Only very simple words, such as 'dog', and highly specialised or technical terms have been omitted. Great care has been taken to reflect the multi-cultural nature of modern British society and so many words have been included, like 'Rastafarian', 'kosher' and 'Ramadan', which are now part of the speech currency of the whole community. The effect of this incorporation of minority cultures in the national mix is seen most clearly in the way our eating habits have changed to include dishes once thought exotic which are now part of our national diet. Our dictionary acknowledges this by the inclusion of such words as 'tandoori', 'chapatti' and 'poppadom'. Modern attitudes to health and the environment dictate the inclusion of words like 'aerobics' and 'biodegradable'. Computer terms are also included to represent the importance of computers at all levels in our society.

Language is a living thing; new words are constantly coming in or losing their currency. We have tried to reflect currently acceptable usage in our selection of words for the dictionary. On the whole we have veered towards inclusion rather than exclusion of marginal words.

Comprehensive

All words are shown in their complete form, including those formed from a particular root, for example,

> 'clear cleared clearer clearest
> clearing clearly clearness'.

The only exceptions to this are nouns which in the plural simply add 's', and verbs which add 's' in the present tense and 'd' in the past; these are not given. Thus 'watches' is given as the plural of 'watch' but 'farms' is not shown as the plural of 'farm'.

Where a plural is the same as the singular we indicate this, for example,

> **'deer**   *plural* deer'.

Where there is an acceptable alternative to the spelling of a particular word we give both spellings separated by an oblique stroke with the commoner usage placed first, for example,

> 'lovable/loveable'.

This is also the way we deal with those words where a shift in favour of a simpler spelling appears to be taking place, for example,

> 'anaesthetist/anesthetist'.

We have chosen to do this because we have been at pains to reflect current usage rather than to be in any way prescriptive.

User Friendly

The whole point of a spelling dictionary is that the user should find the word she or he is looking for with the minimum of difficulty. A book with tens of thousands of words in it can be quite daunting for most people. Of course, the alphabetical arrangement cuts down this difficulty right away. However, even within most letters of the alphabet there are still a large number of words to cope with. What we set out to achieve was a handy means of subdividing within each alphabet letter to allow the user to home in quickly on the word they are looking for. After considerable research we found a novel way of doing this which clearly works.

We found that most people with uncertainties in their spelling can manage to get the first two or three letters of the word in question. It is thereafter that their lack of confidence leads to confusion.

What was needed was a means of sub-sectioning the lists of words so that the user could go swiftly to the area where the word they sought would be found. This is based on the first four letters of each word. Where this group of letters is different to that in the previous word, the whole word is in bold type. Subsequent words with the same first four letters are put in ordinary, non-bold type. Here is an example.

abhor	abhorred abhorring
abhorrence	
abhorrent	abhorrently
abide	

This segments the text of the dictionary so that the eye of the user can focus quickly on a particular section where all the words with the same first four letters are to be found. Once within that segment it is just a matter

of looking for the particular word amongst a comparatively small number of likely candidates. Pleasingly, we found that the segments so created are within highly manageable parameters, usually around ten to thirty words at most. It is much easier to find the right word in thirty than thirty-thousand.

The only exception to this is where there is a very large number of words starting with the same first four letters, such as the words beginning with

comm-
over-

In these cases we simply use bold type for the first **five** (or even **six**) letters on their first appearance, for example

comma etc.
commemorate etc.
commiserate etc.

If this book makes it easier for people to correct their own spelling and therefore encourages them to take more pride in their writing and themselves, then it will have fulfilled all our hopes for it.

Appendices

The Appendices to **A Spelling Dictionary** (on pages 217 to 250) give in clear detail the rules which govern the spelling of English. Each rule is accompanied by examples and a list of the most common words which follow or are exceptions to that particular rule.

Acknowledgements

We would like to acknowledge in particular the contribution made to our research by the staff and students of the People's College, Edinburgh, and Leith Walk Primary School, Edinburgh. We are grateful also for the invaluable contribution of Lizzie Harkin who typed the manuscript.

abacus abacuses
abandon abandoned
abandoning
abandonment
abate abating
abatement
abattoir
abbess abbesses
abbey
abbot
abbreviate abbreviating
abbreviation
abdicate abdicating abdication
abdomen abdominal
abduct abducted abducting
abduction abductor
abeyance
abhor abhorred abhorring
abhorrence
abhorrent abhorrently
abide abiding
ability abilities
abject abjection abjectly
abjectness
able ably
abnormal abnormalities
abnormality
abnormally
aboard
abode
abolish abolished abolishes
abolishing
abolition abolitionist
abominable abominably

abominate abominating
abomination
aborigines aboriginal
abort aborted aborting
abortion
abortive abortively
abound abounded abounding
abrasion abrasive abrasively
abreast
abridge abridging
abridgement
abroad
abrupt abruptly abruptness
abscess abscessed abscesses
abseil abseiled abseiling
absence
absent absently
absentee absenteeism
absolute absolutely
absoluteness
absorb absorbed absorbing
absorption
absorbable absorbability
absorbent absorbency
abstain abstained abstainer
abstaining
abstemious abstemiously
abstemiousness
abstention
abstinence abstinent
abstract abstracted abstracting
abstraction
abstruse abstrusely
abstruseness
absurd absurdities absurdity
absurdly
abundance
abundant abundantly
abuse abuser abusing
abysmal abysmally
abyss abysses
academy academic academically
academies
accelerate accelerating
acceleration
accent accented accenting
accept accepted accepting

acceptable	acceptability
	acceptably
acceptance	
access	accessed accesses
	accession
accessible	accessibility accessibly
accessory	accessories
accident	accidental accidentally
acclaim	acclaimed acclaiming
acclamation	
acclimatise	acclimatising
	acclimatisation
accommodate	accommodating
	accommodation
accompanist	accompaniment
accompany	accompanied
	accompanies
	accompanying
accomplice	
accomplish	accomplished
	accomplishes
	accomplishing
accomplishment	
accord	accorded according
	accordingly
accordance	
accordion	
accost	accosted accosting
account	accounted accounting
accountable	accountability
	accountably
accountant	accountancy
accumulate	accumulating
	accumulation
	accumulator
accuracy	accuracies
accurate	accurately
accursed	
accuse	accusation accuser
	accusing
accustom	accustomed
	accustoming
ace	
ache	aching
achieve	achiever achieving
achievement	
acid	acidic acidity acidly

acknowledge	acknowledging
acknowledgement/acknowledgment	
acne	
acorn	
acoustic	acoustically
acoustics	
acquaint	acquainted
	acquainting
acquaintance	acquaintanceship
acquire	acquiring
acquisition	
acquit	acquitted acquitting
acquittal	
acre	acreage
acrid	acridity acridly
acrimonious	acrimoniously
acrimony	
acrobat	acrobatic acrobatically
acronym	
act	acted acting
action	actionable
active	actively
activity	activities
actor	
actress	actresses
actual	actuality actually
acumen	
acupuncture	acupuncturist
acute	acutely acuteness
	acuter acutest
adage	
adamant	adamantly
adapt	adaptation adapted
	adapting
adaptable	adaptability adaptably
adaptor/adapter	
add	added adding
adder	
addict	addicted addicting
	addiction
addictive	addictively
addition	additional additionally
additive	
address	addressed addresses
	addressing
addressee	addresser
adept	adeptly adeptness

6

adequacy   adequacies
adequate   adequately
adhere   adhering
adherence   adherent
adhesion
adhesive   adhesively
                    adhesiveness
adjacent   adjacently
adjective   adjectival adjectivally
adjoin   adjoined adjoining
adjourn   adjourned adjourning
adjournment
adjudicate   adjudicating
                    adjudication
adjudicator
adjust   adjusted adjusting
adjustment
administer   administered
                    administering
administrate
administration   administrative
                    administratively
administrator
admirable   admirably
admiral   admiralty
admiration
admire   admiring admiringly
admission
admit   admitted admittedly
                    admitting
admonish   admonished
                    admonishes
                    admonishing
admonishment
ado
adolescence
adolescent   adolescently
adopt   adopted adopting
                    adoption
adoptive
adore   adoring adoration
adorn   adorned adorning
adornment
adrenalin
adrift
adroit   adroitly adroitness
adulation   adulatory

adult   adulthood
adulterous   adulterously
adultery   adulteries
advance   advancing
advancement
advantage   advantageous
                    advantageously
advent (arrival)
Advent (season before Christmas)
adventure   adventurer
adventuresome
adventurous   adventurously
                    adventurousness
adverb   adverbial adverbially
adversary   adversaries
adverse   adversely
adversity   adversities
advertise   advertiser advertising
advertisement
advice (what you get)
advisable   advisability advisably
advise (to give advice)
                    advising
                    adviser/advisor
advocate   advocating
aeon/eon
aerate   aerating aeration
aerial   aerially
aerobatics   aerobatically
aerobics
aerodynamic   aerodynamically
aeroplane
aerosol
aesthetic/esthetic aesthetically/esthetically
affable   affability affably
affair
affect   affected affecting
affectation
affection   affectionate
                    affectionately
affiliate   affiliating affiliation
affirm   affirmed affirming
affirmative   affirmatively
affix   affixed affixes
                    affixing
afflict   afflicted afflicting
                    affliction

affluence	
affluent	affluently
afford	affordable afforded affording
affray	
affront	affronted affronting
afoot	
afraid	
aft	
after	
aftermath	
afternoon	
afterthought	
afterwards	
again	
against	
agate	
age	ageing/aging
agency	agencies
agenda	
agent	
aggravate	aggravating aggravatingly aggravation
aggression	aggressive aggressively
aggressor	
aggrieved	
aghast	
agile	agilely agility
agitate	agitating agitation
agitator	
ago	
agog	
agonise	agonising agonisingly
agony	agonies
agree	agreeing
agreeable	agreeably
agreement	
agriculture	agricultural agriculturally agriculturalist
aground	
ahead	
aid	aided aiding
aileron	
ailing	

ailment	
aim	aimed aiming
aimless	aimlessly aimlessness
air	aired airily airing
aircraft	
airfield	
airport	
airy	airier airiest airily airiness
aisle	
ajar	
akimbo	
akin	
alabaster	
alacrity	
alarm	alarmed alarming alarmingly
alarmist	
alas	
albatross	albatrosses
albino	
album	
alcohol	alcoholism
alcoholic	alcoholically
alcove	
ale	
alert	alerted alerting alertly alertness
algae	
algebra	algebraic algebraically
alias	aliases
alibi	
alien	
alienate	alienating alienation
alight	alighted alighting
align	aligned aligning
alignment	
alike	
alimony	alimonies
alive	
alkali	alkaline
all	
allay	allayed allaying
allegation	
allege	allegedly alleging
allegiance	
allergy	allergic allergies

alleviate | alleviating alleviation
alley
alliance
alligator
alliterate | alliterating alliteration
alliterative | alliteratively
allocate | allocating allocation
allot | allotted allotting
allotment
allow | allowed allowing
allowable | allowably
allowance
alloy
allude (to refer to) | alluding allusion
allure | alluring alluringly
allurement
ally | allied allies allying
almanac
almighty
almond
almost
alms
aloft
alone
aloof | aloofly aloofness
aloud
alphabet | alphabetic
alphabetical | alphabetically
already
alright | all right
Alsatian
also
altar (in Church)
alter (to change) | altered altering
alteration
alternate | alternately alternating
alternative | alternatively
although
altimeter
altitude
alto
altogether
altruism | altruist
altruistic | altruistically
aluminium
always
amalgam

amalgamate | amalgamating
 | amalgamation
amateur | amateurish
 | amateurishly
 | amateurishness
amateurism
amaze | amazing amazingly
amazement
ambassador | ambassadorial
ambassadress | ambassadresses
amber
ambidextrous | ambidextrously
 | ambidextrousness
ambiguity | ambiguities
ambiguous | ambiguously
ambition
ambitious | ambitiously
amble | ambling
ambulance
ambush | ambushed ambushes
 | ambushing
amen
amenable | amenability amenably
amend | amended amending
amendment
amethyst
amiable | amiability amiably
amicable | amicability amicably
amid/amidst
amiss
ammonia
ammunition
amnesia | amnesiac
amnesty | amnesties
amoeba/ameba
amok/amuck
among/amongst
amorous | amorously
 | amorousness
amount | amounted amounting
amp/ampere
amphibian | amphibious
 | amphibiously
amphitheatre
ample | ampleness amply
amplification

amplify   amplified amplifier
             amplifies amplifying
amputate   amputating
             amputation
amuck/amok
amulet
amuse   amusing amusingly
amusement
anachronism   anachronistic
             anachronistically
anaconda
anaemia/anemia   anaemic/anemic
anaesthesia/anesthesia
anaesthetic/anesthetic
anaesthetise/anesthetise
anaesthetist/anesthetist
anagram
analyse   analysing
analysis   analyses
analyst
analytical   analytically
anarchic   anarchically
anarchy   anarchism anarchist
anatomy   anatomical
             anatomically
ancestor   ancestral
ancestress   ancestresses
ancestry
anchor   anchored anchoring
anchovy   anchovies
ancient   anciently ancientness
ancillary   ancillaries
andante
anecdote   anecdotal anecdotally
anemone
angel   angelic angelically
angelus
anger   angered angering
angina
angle   angler angling
angora
angry   angrier angriest
             angrily
anguish   anguished
angular   angularity angularly
animal
animated   animating animation

animosity   animosities
aniseed
ankle
annals
annex (to add on)   annexed annexes
             annexing
annexation
annexe (part of a building)
annihilate   annihilating
             annihilation
anniversary   anniversaries
announce   announcer
             announcing
announcement
annoy   annoyed annoying
annoyance
annual   annually
annul   annulled annulling
annulment
annunciate (to proclaim)
             annunciating
             annunciation
anoint   anointed anointing
anomaly   anomalies anomalous
anonymity
anonymous   anonymously
anorak
anorexia (nervosa)   anorexic
answer   answered answering
answerable
antacid
antagonise   antagonising
antagonist   antagonism
antagonistic   antagonistically
Antarctic
antecedent   antecedently
antelope
antenatal
antenna   antennae (on insects,
             etc.) antennas (aerials)
anteroom
anthem
anthology   anthologies
anthropology   anthropological
             anthropologist
antibiotic

anticipate | anticipating
| anticipation
anticlimactic
anticlimax | anticlimaxes
anticlockwise
antics
anticyclone
antidote
antifreeze
antipathy | antipathetic
| antipathetically
| antipathies
antipodes/Antipodes
antiquated
antique
antiquity | antiquities
antiseptic | antiseptically
antisocial | antisocially
antler
anvil
anxiety | anxieties
anxious | anxiously
any
anybody
anyone
anything
anyway
anywhere
apart
apartheid
apartment
apathy | apathetic apathetically
ape | aping
aperture
apex | apexes
aphid
apiary | apiaries
aplomb
apologetic | apologetically
apologise | apologising
apology | apologies
apoplexy | apoplectic
| apoplectically
apostle
apostrophe
appal | appalled appalling
| appallingly

apparatus | apparatuses/apparatus
apparel
apparent | apparently
apparition
appeal | appealed appealing
appear | appeared appearing
appearance
appease | appeaser appeasing
appeasement
append | appended
appendicitis
appendix | appendices/appendixes
appetiser
appetising | appetisingly
appetite
applaud | applauded applauding
applause
apple
appliance
applicable | applicability applicably
applicant
application
appliqué
apply | applied applies
| applying
appoint | appointed appointing
appointment
appreciate | appreciating
| appreciation
appreciative | appreciatively
| appreciativeness
apprehend | apprehended
| apprehending
apprehension
apprehensive | apprehensively
| apprehensiveness
apprentice | apprenticeship
approach | approached
| approaches
| approaching
approachable | approachability
approbation
appropriate | appropriately
| appropriateness
approve | approval approving
approximate | approximately
| approximation

apricot
April
apron
apse
apt   aptly aptness
aptitude
aqualung
aquarium   aquariums/aquaria
Aquarius
aquatic
aqueduct
aquiline
arable
arbitrary   arbitrarily arbitrariness
arbitrate   arbitrating arbitration
arbitrator
arc (part of circle)
arcade
arch   arched arches arching
archaeological/archeological
archaeologist/archeologist
archaeology/archeology
archaic   archaically
archangel
archbishop
archer   archery
archipelago   archipelagos/
                             archipelagoes
architect   architectural
                             architecturally
archives
Arctic
ardent   ardently
ardour
arduous   arduously arduousness
area
arena
arguable   arguably
argue   arguing
argument   argumentation
argumentative   argumentatively
                             argumentativeness
aria
arid   aridity aridly
Aries
arise   arisen arising arose
aristocracy   aristocracies

aristocrat   aristocratic
                             aristocratically
arithmetic   arithmetical
                             arithmetically
ark (Noah's Ark)
arm   armed arming
armada
armadillo
armament
armchair
armour   armoured
armoury   armouries
army   armies
aroma   aromatic aromatically
arose
arouse   arousal arousing
arrange   arranger arranging
arrangement
array
arrears
arrest   arrested arresting
arrive   arrival arriving
arrogance
arrogant   arrogantly
arrow   arrowed arrowing
arsenal
arsenic
arson   arsonist
artefact/artifact
artery   arterial arteries
artful   artfully artfulness
artichoke
article
articulacy
articulate   articulating
                             articulation
artifact/artefact
artificial   artificiality artificially
artillery   artilleries
artist   artistic artistically
                             artistry
artless   artlessly artlessness
asbestos
ascend   ascended ascending
ascendancy/ascendency
Ascension
ascent (a climb)

ascertain	ascertained ascertaining	assist	assisted assisting
ash	ashen ashes	assistance	assistant
ashamed	ashamedly	**associate**	associating association
ashore		assorted	assortment
ashram		**assume**	assuming
aside		assumption	
asinine		assurance	
ask	asked asking	assure	assuring
askance		**aster**	
askew		asterisk	
asleep		**asthma**	asthmatic
asp			asthmatically
asparagus		**astonish**	astonished astonishes
aspect			astonishing
aspen			astonishingly
asphalt		astonishment	
asphyxiate	asphyxiating	astound	astounded astounding
	asphyxiation		astoundingly
aspic		**astray**	
aspidistra		astrology	astrologer astrological
aspire	aspiration aspiring	astronaut	
aspirin		astronomy	astronomical
ass	asses		astronomically
assail	assailed assailer	**astute**	
	assailing	**asunder**	
assailable		**asylum**	
assailant		**atheist**	atheism
assassin		atheistic	atheistically
assassinate	assassinating	**athlete**	
	assassination	athletic	athletically athleticism
assault	assaulted assaulting	**atlas**	atlases
assemble	assembling	**atmosphere**	atmospheric
assembly	assemblies		atmospherically
assent (to agree)	assented assenting	**atoll**	
assert	asserted asserting	**atom**	atomic
	assertion	**atrocious**	atrociously
assertive	assertively		atrociousness
	assertiveness	atrocity	atrocities
assess	assessed assesses	**attach**	attached attaches
	assessing assessor		attaching
assessment		attachment	
asset		attack	attacked attacker
assiduous	assiduously		attacking
	assiduousness	attain	attained attaining
assign	assigned assigning	attainable	attainability attainably
assignment		attainment	
		attempt	attempted attempting

attend | attended attending
attendance | attendant
attention
attentive | attentively
 | attentiveness
attic
attire | attiring
attitude
attorney
attract | attracted attracting
 | attraction
attractive | attractively
 | attractiveness
attribute | attributing attribution
attributive | attributively
aubergine
auburn
auction | auctioned auctioning
auctioneer
audacious | audaciously audacity
audible | audibility audibly
audience
audiovisual | audiovisually
audit | audited auditing
audition
auditorium | auditoriums/auditoria
augment | augmented
 | augmenting
August
aunt | auntie/aunty
au pair
aura
aural | aurally
aurora borealis
auspicious | auspiciously
 | auspiciousness
austere | austerely austerities
 | austerity
authentic | authentically
 | authenticity
author
authoress | authoresses
authorise | authorisation
 | authorising
authoritative | authoritatively
authority | authorities
autobiographical | autobiographically

autobiography | autobiographies
autocracy | autocracies
autocrat | autocratic
 | autocratically
Autocue
autograph | autographed
 | autographing
automatic | automatically
automation
automaton
automobile
autonomy | autonomies
 | autonomous
 | autonomously
autopsy | autopsies
autumn | autumnal
auxiliary | auxiliaries
available | availability
avalanche
avarice
avaricious | avariciously
 | avariciousness
avenge | avenger avenging
avenue
average | averaging
averse | aversion
avert | averted averting
aviary | aviaries
aviation
avid | avidity avidly
avocado
avoid | avoided avoiding
avoidable | avoidably
avoidance
await | awaited awaiting
awake
awaken | awakened awakening
 | awoke
award | awarded awarding
aware | awareness
awe
awesome | awesomely
 | awesomeness
awestruck
awful | awfully awfulness
awkward | awkwardly
 | awkwardness

awl
awning
awoke
awry
axe   axing
axis   axes axial
axle
azure

Bb

babble   babbling
baboon
baby   babies
babyhood
babysit   babysat babysitter
                    babysitting
bachelor   bachelorhood
bacillus   bacilli
back   backed backing
backache
backbite   backbiting
backbone
backfire   backfiring
background
backstroke
backwards
bacon
bacteriology   bacteriological
                    bacteriologically
                    bacteriologist
bacterium   bacteria bacterial
badge
badger   badgered badgering
badminton
baffle   baffling
bafflement
bag   bagged bagging
baggage
baggy   baggily bagginess
bagpipes
baguette
bail   bailed bailer bailing
bailiff
bait   baited baiting
baize

bake   baking
baker
bakery   bakeries
balance   balancing
balcony   balconies
bald   balder baldest baldly
                baldness
balderdash
bale   baling
baleful   balefully balefulness
balk/baulk balked/baulked
                balking/baulking
ball   balled balling
ballad   balladeer
ballast
ballerina
ballet   balletic balletically
ballet-dancer
ballistic   ballistics
balloon   ballooned ballooning
ballot   balloted balloting
balm
balmy   balmier balmiest
balsa-wood
balustrade
bamboo
bamboozle   bamboozling
bamboozlement
ban   banned banning
banal
banality   banalities
banana
bandage
bandit   banditry
bang   banged banger
                banging
bangle
banish   banished banishes
                banishing
banishment
banister
banjo   banjos/banjoes
bank   banked banker
                banking
bankrupt   bankrupted
                bankrupting
bankruptcy   bankruptcies

banner
banns (notice of wedding)
banquet   banqueted banqueting
bantam
banter   bantered bantering
baptise   baptising
baptism   baptismal
Baptist
bar   barred barring
barb   barbed
barbarian   barbaric
barbarity   barbarities
barbarous   barbarously
                barbarousness
barbecue   barbecuing
barber
bard
bare (empty; naked) barely bareness
                baring
bargain   bargained bargaining
barge   barging
baritone
bark   barked barker barking
barley
bar mitzvah
barn
barnacle
barometer
baron
baroness   baronesses
baronet   baronetcies baronetcy
barracks
barrage   barraging
barrel   barrelled barrelling
barren   barrenness
barricade   barricading
barrier
barrister
barrow
barter   bartered bartering
basalt
base   basing
baseball
basement
bashful   bashfully bashfulness
basic   basically
basil

basin	
basis	bases
bask	basked basking
basket	
basketball	
bass	basses
bassoon	
baste	basting
bastion	
bat	batted batting
batch	batches
bath (to wash someone)	
	bathed bathing
bathe (to wash self)	bather bathing
batman	batmen
baton	
batsman	batsmen
battalion	
batter	battered battering
battery	batteries
battle	battling
battlefield	
battlements	
battleship	
baulk/balk	baulked/balked
	baulking/balking
bawl	bawled bawling
bay	bayed baying
bayonet	bayoneted bayoneting
bazaar (market)	
beach (at the seaside)	
	beached beaches
	beaching
beachcomber	
beacon	
bead	beaded beading
beady	beadier beadiest
beagle	
beak	beaked
beaker	
beam	beamed beaming
bean	
bear (animal; to carry)	
	bearing bore borne
bearable	bearably
beard	bearded
bearer	

beast	beastliness beastly
beat	beating
beatable	
beaten	
beautician	
beautiful	beautifully
beautify	beautified beautifies
	beautifying
beauty	beauties beauteous
beaver	beavered beavering
because	
beckon	beckoned beckoning
bed	bedded bedding
bedlam	
bedraggled	
bedridden	
bee	
beech (tree)	beeches
beef	beefier beefiest
	beefiness beefy
beehive	
beer	
beetle	beetling
beetroot	
befall	befallen befalling
	befell
befell	
before	
befriend	befriended befriending
befuddle	befuddling
befuddlement	
beg	begged begging
began	
beggar	beggarliness beggarly
begin	began beginner
	beginning begun
begrudge	
beguile	beguiling
begun	
behave	behaving
behaviour	
behead	beheaded beheading
behest	
behind	
behold	beheld beholden
beige	
being	

belated | belatedly
belch | belched belches
 | belching

belfry | belfries
belief |
believe | believer believing
belittle | belittling
bell | belled belling
belligerence |
belligerent | belligerently
bellow | bellowed bellowing
bellows |
belly | bellied bellies bellying
belong | belonged belonging
belongings |
beloved |
below |
belt | belted belting
bench | benches
bend | bended/bent bending
beneath |
benediction |
benefactor |
beneficial | beneficially
beneficiary | beneficiaries
benefit | benefited benefiting
benevolence |
benevolent | benevolently
benign |
bent |
bequeath | bequeathed
 | bequeathing
bequest |
bereaved |
bereavement |
beret |
berry | berries
berserk |
berth | berthed berthing
beseech | beseeched beseeches
 | beseeching besought
beside |
besides |
besiege | besieging
besotted |
besought |
best |

bestial |
bestow | bestowed bestowing
bet | betting
betray | betrayed betrayer
 | betraying
betrothal |
betrothed |
better | bettered bettering
between |
bevel | bevelled bevelling
beverage |
beware |
bewilder | bewildered
 | bewildering
 | bewilderingly
bewilderment |
bewitch | bewitched bewitches
 | bewitching
beyond |
bias | biased
bib |
Bible | biblical
bicentenary | bicentenaries
 | bicentennial
biceps |
bicker | bickered bickering
bicycle | bicycler bicycling
 | bicyclist
bid | bidden bidding
biennial | biennially
bifocal |
bigamy | bigamies bigamist
 | bigamous bigamously
bigger |
bigot | bigoted bigotedly
bigotry | bigotries
bike | biker biking
bikini |
bilateral | bilaterally
bile |
bilingual |
bilious | biliousness
bill | billed billing
billet | billeted billeting
billiards |
billion |

billow   billowed billowing
                          billowy
bin
binary
bind   binder binding bound
bingo
binoculars
biochemist   biochemical
                          biochemistry
biodegradable
biographer
biographical   biographically
biography   biographies
biology   biologist biological
                          biologically
bionic
bionics
biped
biplane
birch   birched birches
                          birching
bird
birth
birthday
biscuit
bisect   bisected bisecting
                          bisection
bishop   bishopric
bison
bitch   bitches bitching
bite (with teeth)   bit biter biting
                          bitingly
bitten
bitter   bitterest bitterly
                          bitterness
bittern
bitty   bittier bittiest bittily
                          bittiness
bivouac   bivouacked
                          bivouacking
bizarre (strange)
blab   blabbed blabbing
black   blacked blacker
                          blackest blacking
blackberry   blackberries
blackbird
blackboard

blacken   blackened blackening
blackmail   blackmailed
                          blackmailer
                          blackmailing
blacksmith
bladder
blade
blame   blaming
blameless   blamelessly
                          blamelessness
blancmange
bland   blander blandest
                          blandly blandness
blank   blanked blanking
blanket   blanketed blanketing
blare   blaring
blaspheme   blasphemer
                          blaspheming
blasphemous   blasphemously
blasphemy
blast   blasted blaster
                          blasting
blatant   blatantly
blaze   blazing
blazer
bleach   bleached bleaches
                          bleaching
bleak   bleaker bleakest
                          bleakly bleakness
bleat   bleated bleating
bled
bleed   bled bleeding
bleep   bleeped bleeper
                          bleeping
blemish   blemished blemishes
blend   blended blending
                          blender
bless   blessed blesses
                          blessing
blew
blight   blighted blighting
blind   blinded blinding
                          blindly blindness
blindfold   blindfolded
                          blindfolding
blink   blinked blinking

blinker	blinkered blinkering
blip	blipped blipping
bliss	blissful blissfully
blister	blistered blistering
blithe	blithely blitheness
blitz	blitzed blitzes blitzing
blizzard	
bloated	
blob	
block	blocked blocking
blockade	blockading
blockage	
blond (male)	
blonde (female)	
blood	blooded
bloodhound	
bloodshed	
bloody	bloodier bloodiest
	bloodily bloodiness
bloom	bloomed bloomer
	blooming
bloomers	
blossom	blossomed blossoming
blot	blotted blotter
	blotting
blotch	blotched blotches
	blotching
blotchy	blotchier blotchiest
blouse	
blow	blew blowing blown
blubber	blubbered blubbering
bludgeon	bludgeoned
	bludgeoning
blue	bluer bluest
bluebell	
blueprint	
bluff	bluffed bluffer
	bluffing
blunder	blundered blunderer
	blundering
	blunderingly
blunt	blunted blunting
blur	blurred blurring
blurt	blurted blurting
blush	blushed blusher
	blushes blushing
boa constrictor	

boar (wild pig)	
board	boarded boarder
	boarding
boast	boasted boaster
	boasting
boastful	
boat	boated boater
	boating
boatswain/bo'sun	
bob	bobbed bobbing
bobbin	
bobsleigh	bobsleighed
	bobsleighing
bodice	
body	bodies bodily
bodyguard	
bog	bogged
boggle	boggling
boggy	boggier boggiest
	bogginess
bogus	
boil	boiled boiling
boiler	
boisterous	boisterously
	boisterousness
bold	bolder boldest boldly
	boldness
bollard	
bolster	bolstered bolstering
bolt	bolted bolter bolting
bomb	bombed bomber
	bombing
bombard	bombarded
	bombarding
bombardment	
bondage	
bone	boning
boneless	
bonfire	
bonnet	
bonny (pretty)	bonnier bonniest
	bonnily
bonsai	
bonus	bonuses
bony (like bone)	bonier boniest
	boniness
boo	booed booing

book	booked booking	bounteous	bounteously
book-keeper	book-keeping		bounteousness
boom	boomed booming	bountiful	bountifully
boomerang		bounty	bounties
boon		**bouquet**	
boorish	boorishly boorishness	**bourgeois**	bourgeoisie
boost	boosted booster	**bout**	
	boosting	boutique	
boot	booted booting	**bovine**	
bootee (child's shoe)		**bow**	bowed bowing
booth		**bowel**	
booty (plunder)		**bowl**	bowled bowler
border	bordered bordering		bowling
bore (to annoy)	boring boringly	bowls	
boredom		**box**	boxed boxer boxes
born (birth)	borne (carried)		boxing
borough/burgh		**boy**	boyish
borrow	borrowed borrower	**boycott**	boycotted boycotting
	borrowing	**bra/brassière**	
borzoi		**brace**	bracing
bosom		bracelet	
boss	bossed bosses	braces	
	bossing	bracken	
bossy	bossier bossiest	bracket	bracketed bracketing
	bossily bossiness	**brag**	bragged bragging
bo'sun/boatswain		braggart	
botany	botanical botanically	**braid**	braided braiding
	botanist	Braille	
botch	botched botcher	brain	brained braining
	botches botching	brainless	
both		brainy	brainier brainiest
bother	bothered bothering	braise	braising
bottle	bottling	**brake** (to stop)	braking
bottleneck		**bramble**	
bottom	bottomed bottoming	**branch**	branched branches
bottomless			branching
bough (a branch)		brand	branded branding
bought		brandish	brandished brandishes
boulder			brandishing
boulevard		brandy	brandies
bounce	bouncing	**brash**	brashly brashness
bouncy	bouncier bounciest	brass	brasses
	bouncily bounciness	brassière/bra	
bound	bounded bounding	**bravado**	
boundary	boundaries	brave	bravely braver bravery
boundless	boundlessly		bravest braving
	boundlessness	bravo	

brawl — brawled brawler brawling

brawny — brawnier brawniest brawniness

bray — brayed braying

brazen — brazenly brazenness

brazier

breach — breached breaches breaching

bread (food) — breaded

breadcrumbs

breadth

break (to damage) — breakable breaking broke broken

breakdown

breakfast — breakfasted breakfasting

breakwater

breast — breasted breasting

breath (air)

breathalyse — Breathalyser breathalysing

breathe (to draw breath) — breathing

breathless — breathlessly breathlessness

breathtaking — breathtakingly

bred (born from)

breech

breed — bred breeder breeding

breeze — breezier breeziest breezily breeziness breezy

brethren

brevity

brew — brewed brewer brewing

brewery — breweries

briar

bribe — briberies bribery bribing

bric-a-brac

brick — bricked bricking

bricklayer

bride — bridal

bridegroom

bridesmaid

bridge — bridging

bridle

brief — briefed briefer briefest briefing briefly

briefs

brigade

brigadier

brigand

bright — brighter brightest brightly brightness

brighten — brightened brightening

brilliance

brilliant — brilliantly

brim — brimmed brimming

brimful

brimstone

brine — briny

bring — bringing brought

brink

brisk — brisker briskest briskly briskness

bristle — bristling bristly

bristles

brittle — brittleness

broach (to burst open) — broached broaches broaching

broad — broader broadest broadly

broadcast — broadcaster broadcasting

broaden — broadened broadening

brocade

broccoli

brochure

broil — broiled broiler broiling

broke — broken

broker

bronchitis

brontosaurus — brontosauruses

bronze

brooch (ornament) — brooches

brood — brooded brooder brooding

brook — brooked brooking

broom	
broomstick	
broth	
brother	brotherliness brotherly
brotherhood	
brother-in-law	brothers-in-law
brought	
brow	
browbeat	browbeaten
	browbeating
brown	browner brownest
	brownness
Brownie	
browse	browsing
bruise	bruiser bruising
brunette	
brunt	
brush	brushed brushes
	brushing
brusque	brusquely brusqueness
Brussels sprouts	
brutalise	brutalising
brutality	brutalities
brute	brutal brutally
bubble	bubbling
buccaneer	buccaneering
buck	bucked bucking
bucket	bucketed bucketing
buckle	buckling
bud	budded budding
Buddhism	Buddhist
budge	budging
budgerigar/budgie	
budget	budgeted budgeting
buff	buffed buffing
buffalo	buffaloes
buffer	buffered buffering
buffet	buffeted buffeting
buffoon	buffooneries
	buffoonery
bug	bugged bugging
bugle	bugler bugling
build	builder building built
bulb	bulbous bulbously
	bulbousness
bulge	bulging
bulimia (nervosa)	

bulk	bulked bulking
bulky	bulkier bulkiest bulkily
	bulkiness
bull	
bulldog	
bulldoze	bulldozed bulldozer
	bulldozing
bullet	
bulletin	
bullion	
bullock	
bully	bullied bullies
	bullying
bulrush	bulrushes
bumblebee	
bump	bumped bumper
	bumping
bumptious	bumptiously
	bumptiousness
bumpy	bumpier bumpiest
	bumpily bumpiness
bunch	bunched bunches
	bunching
bundle	bundling
bungalow	
bungle	bungler bungling
bunion	
bunk	bunked bunking
bunk-bed	
bunker	
bunny	bunnies
bunting	
buoy	buoyed buoying
buoyancy	
buoyant	buoyantly
burden	burdened burdening
bureau	bureaux/bureaus
bureaucracy	bureaucracies
bureaucrat	bureaucratic
	bureaucratically
burger	
burgh/borough	
burglar	
burglary	burglaries
burgle	burgling
burial	

burly   burlier burliest
                burliness
burn   burned burning burnt
burner
burnish   burnished burnishes
                burnishing
burnt
burrow   burrowed burrowing
bury   buried buries burying
bus   buses
bush   bushes
bushy   bushier bushiest
                bushily bushiness
business (commerce) businesses
busk   busked busker
                busking
bust   busted busting
bustle   bustling
busy   busier busiest busily
                busyness (being busy)
butcher   butchered butchering
butler
butt   butted butting
butter   buttered buttering
buttercup
butterfly   butterflies
butterscotch
buttery   butteriness
buttocks
button   buttoned buttoning
buttress   buttressed buttresses
                buttressing
buxom   buxomly buxomness
buy   bought buyer buying
buzz   buzzed buzzer buzzes
                buzzing
buzzard
bye-law/by-law
by-election
bygone
by-law/bye-law
bypass   bypassed bypassing
by-product
bystander
byte (computing)

Cc

cabbage
cabin
cabinet
cable   cabling
cackle   cackling
cactus   cacti/cactuses
cadaver   cadaverous
caddie (in golf)
caddy (container for tea)
                caddies
cadenza
cadet
café
cafeteria
caffeine
caftan/kaftan
cage   caging
cagey/cagy   cagier cagiest cagily
                caginess/cageyness
cagoule
cajole   cajoling
cake   caking
calamine
calamitous   calamitously
calamity   calamities
calcium
calculate   calculating calculation
calculator
calculus
calendar
calf   calves calving
calibre
call   called caller calling
calligraphy   calligrapher
                calligraphic

callipers	
callous	callously callousness
callow	callowly callowness
calm	calmed calmer
	calmest calming
calmly	calmness
calorie	calorific
calves	
calypso	
camber	
camel	
camellia	
cameo	
camera	
camouflage	camouflaging
camp	camped camper
	camping
campaign	campaigned
	campaigner
	campaigning
campanology	campanologist
can (put in a tin; is able to)	
	canned canning could
canal	
canapé	
canary	canaries
cancel	cancellation cancelled
	cancelling
cancer	cancerous
Cancer	
candid	candidly
	candidness/candour
candidate	candidacies candidacy
candle	
candlestick	
candlewick	
candour	
candy	candied candies
cane	caning
canine	
canister	
cannabis	
cannibal	cannibalism
	cannibalistic
cannon	cannoned cannoning
cannot	
canoe	canoeing

canoeist	
canon	
canonise	canonisation
	canonising
canopy	canopies
cant (hypocrisy)	
can't (cannot)	
cantankerous	cantankerously
	cantankerousness
cantata	
canteen	
canter	cantered cantering
cantilever	
canvas (cloth)	canvases
canvass (to seek votes)	
	canvassed canvasser
	canvasses canvassing
canyon	
cap	capped capping
capability	capabilities
capable	capably
capacious	capaciously
	capaciousness
capacity	capacities
cape	
caper	capered capering
capillary	capillaries
capital	capitalism capitalist
capitalise	capitalising
	capitalisation
capitulate	capitulating
	capitulation
caprice	
capricious	capriciously
	capriciousness
Capricorn	
capsize	capsizing
capsule	
captain	captained captaining
caption	
captious	captiously
	captiousness
captivate	captivating
captive	captivities captivity
captor	
capture	capturing
carafe	

caramel
carapace
carat (measure of purity/weight)
caravan   caravanned
    caravanning
carbohydrate
carbolic
carbon
carbonated
carbuncle
carburettor/carburetter
carcass   carcasses
card
cardboard
cardiac
cardigan
cardinal
care   carer caring
career   careered careering
careful   carefully carefulness
careless   carelessly carelessness
caress   caressed caresses
    caressing
caretaker
cargo   cargoes/cargos
caricature   caricaturing
caricaturist
carillon
carnage
carnation
carnival
carnivore   carnivorous
    carnivorously
    carnivorousness
carol   carolled carolling
carouse   carousal (drinking)
    carousing
carousel (at the fair)
carp   carped carping
carpenter   carpentry
carpet   carpeted carpeting
carriage
carrier
carrion
carrot (vegetable)   carroty
carry   carried carrier carries
    carrying

cart   carted carter carting
cartel
cartilage
cartography   cartographer
carton (box)
cartoon (drawing)   cartoonist
cartridge
cartwheel   cartwheeled
    cartwheeling
carve   carver carving
cascade   cascading
case   casing
casement
cash   cashed cashing
cashier
cashmere
casino
cask   casked casking
casket
casserole
cassette
cassock
cast (threw)   casting
castanets
castaway
caste (type, kind)
castigate   castigating castigation
castle   castling
castor/caster
castor oil
castrate   castrating castration
casual   casually casualness
casualty   casualties
catacomb
catalogue   cataloguer
    cataloguing
catalyst
catamaran
catapult   catapulted catapulting
cataract
catarrh   catarrhal
catastrophe   catastrophic
    catastrophically
catch   catcher catches
    catching caught
catchment
catechism   catechist

categorical | categorically
category | categories
cater | catered caterer
 | catering
caterpillar
cathedral
Catherine wheel
catholic/Catholic | catholicism/Catholicism
catkin
cattle
catty | cattily cattiness
caught (held fast)
cauldron
cauliflower
cause | causation causing
caution | cautioned cautioning
cautionary
cautious | cautiously
cavalcade
cavalier | cavalierly
cavalry | cavalries
cave | caving
cavern
cavernous | cavernously
 | cavernousness
caviare/caviar
cavity | cavities
cavort | cavorted cavorting
caw | cawed cawing
cayenne (pepper)
cease | ceasing
ceaseless | ceaselessly
cedar
cede | ceding
ceiling
celandine
celebrant
celebrate | celebrating celebration
celebrity | celebrities
celeriac
celery
celestial | celestially
celibate | celibacy
cell | cellular
cellar
cello | cellist
Cellophane

celluloid
Celsius
cement | cemented cementing
cemetery | cemeteries
cenotaph
censor (to cut out from writing)
 | censored censoring
censorship
censure (to scold, criticise)
 | censuring
census | censuses
cent
centaur
centenary | centenaries centennial
centigrade
centimetre
centipede
central | centrally
centralise | centralisation
 | centralising
centre | centring
century | centuries
ceramic
ceramics
cereal
ceremonial | ceremonially
ceremonious | ceremoniously
ceremony | ceremonies
cerise
certain | certainly
certainty | certainties
certifiable | certifiably
certificate | certificating
 | certification
certify | certified certifies
 | certifying
chafe (to rub) | chafing
chaff (to tease, joke) | chaffed chaffing
chaffinch | chaffinches
chagrin
chain | chained chaining
chair | chaired chairing
chairman | chairmen
chairperson
chairwoman | chairwomen
chalet
chalice

chalk   chalked chalking chalky

challenge   challenger challenging

chamber   chambered

chamberlain

chameleon

champ   champed champing

champagne

champion   championed championing

chance   chancer chancing

chancel

Chancellor   Chancellor of the Exchequer

chandelier

change   changing

changeable   changeably changeableness

changeless   changelessly changelessness

changeling

channel   channelled channelling

chant   chanted chanter chanting

chaos   chaotic chaotically

chap   chapped chapping

chapatti/chapati/chupatty   chapattis

chapel

chaperon

chaplain

chapter

char   charred charring

character   characteristic characteristically

characterise   characterisation characterising

charade

charcoal

charge   charging

chariot   charioteer

charisma   charismatic

charitable   charitableness charitably

charity   charities

charlatan

charm   charmed charming charmingly

chart   charted charting

charter   chartered chartering

chary   charier chariest charily chariness

chase   chasing

chasm

chassis

chaste   chastely chastity

chasten   chastened chastening

chastise   chastisement chastising

chat   chatted chatting chatty

chateau   chateaux

chatter   chattered chatterer chattering

chauffeur

chauffeuse

chauvinist   chauvinism chauvinistic

cheap (inexpensive)   cheaply cheapness

cheapen   cheapened cheapening

cheat   cheated cheating

check   checked checking

checkmate

checkout

cheek   cheeked cheeking

cheeky   cheekier cheekiest cheekily cheekiness

cheep (bird noise)   cheeped cheeping

cheer   cheered cheering

cheerful   cheerfully cheerfulness

cheerio

cheerless   cheerlessly cheerlessness

cheery   cheerier cheeriest cheerily cheeriness

cheese

cheeseparing

cheetah

chef (cook)

chemical   chemically

chemist   chemistry

chemotherapy

cheque

chequered
cherish   cherished cherishes
                     cherishing
cheroot
cherry   cherries
cherub   ·   cherubs/cherubim
                     cherubic
chess
chest   chested chesting
chestnut
chew   chewed chewing
                     chewy
chic
chicanery   chicaneries
chicken   chickened chickening
chickenpox
chickpea
chicory   chicories
chide   chided chiding
chief (leader; main) chiefly
chieftain
chiffon
chihuahua
chilblain
child   children
childhood
childish   childishly childishness
childlike
chill   chilled chilling
chilli/chili (hot peppers)
                     chillies/chilies
chilly (cold)   chillier chilliest
                     chilliness
chime   chiming
chimney
chimpanzee
chin   chinned chinning
china
chinchilla
chink
chinos
chintz   chintzy
chip   chipped chipping
chipmunk
chipolata
chiropodist   chiropody
chirp   chirped chirping

chirpy   chirpier chirpiest
                     chirpily chirpiness
chirrup   chirruped chirruping
chisel   chiselled chiselling
chit-chat
chivalrous   chivalrously
                     chivalrousness
chivalry   chivalric
chives
chlorine
chloroform
chlorophyll
chock-a-block
chocolate
choice
choir   choirboy
choke   choking
cholera
choleric
cholesterol
choose   choosing chose
chop   chopped chopping
chopper
chopsticks
chopsuey
choral
chord (in music)
chore
choreography   choreographer
chorister
chortle   chortling
chorus   choruses
chose   chosen
chow mein
christen   christened christening
Christian   Christianity
Christmas   Christmases
                     Christmassy
chrome
chromium
chromosome
chronic   chronically
chronicle   chronicling
chronological   chronologically
                     chronologies
                     chronology
chronometer

chrysalis chrysalises
chrysanthemum
chubby chubbier chubbiest
chubbily chubbiness
chuckle chuckling
chug chugged chugging
chum chummed chumming
chummy chummier chummiest
chummily
chumminess

chunk
chunky chunkier chunkiest
chunkiness
church churches
churlish churlishly churlishness
churn churned churning
chute
chutney
cider
cigar
cigarette
cinder
Cinderella
cinema
cinnamon
cipher
circle circling
circuit circuitous circuitously
circuitousness
circuitry
circular circularities circularity
circulate circulating circulation
circumcise circumcising
circumcision
circumference
circumscribe circumscribing
circumspect circumspection
circumspectly
circumstance
circumstantial circumstantially
circumvent circumvented
circumventing
circus circuses
cistern
citadel
citation
citizen citizenry citizenship

citrus citric
city cities
civic
civil civilities civility civilly
civilian
civilise civilisation civilising
clack clacked clacking
clad cladding
claim claimed claimer
claiming
claimant
clam
clamber clambered clambering
clammy clammier clammiest
clammily clamminess
clamorous clamorously
clamorousness
clamour clamoured clamouring
clamp clamped clamping
clan clannish clannishness
clandestine
clang clanged clanger
clanging
clank clanked clanking
clap clapped clapper
clapping
claret
clarify clarification clarified
clarifies clarifying
clarinet clarinettist
clarity
clash clashed clashes
clashing
clasp clasped clasping
class classes
classic classical classically
classification
classify classified classifies
classifying
clatter clattered clattering
clause
claustrophobia claustrophobic
claw clawed clawing
clay clayey
claymore
clean cleaned cleaner
cleanest cleaning

cleanly	cleanliness	**close (–s)** (near)	closely closeness
cleanse	cleanser cleansing		closer closest
clear	cleared clearer	close **(–z)** (to shut)	closing
	clearest clearing	closet	closeted closeting
	clearly clearness	closure	
		clot	clotted clotting
clearance		cloth (material)	
cleat		clothe (to put on clothes)	
cleaver			clothing
clef		clothes	
cleft		**cloud**	cloudier cloudiest
clement			cloudiness cloudy
clementine		**clove**	
clench	clenched clenches	clover	
	clenching	**clown**	clowned clowning
clergy	clergies	**cloy**	cloyed cloying
clergyman	clergymen	**club**	clubbed clubbing
cleric		**cluck**	clucked clucking
clerk	clerical	**clue**	
clever	cleverer cleverest	**clump**	clumped clumping
	cleverly cleverness	clumsy	clumsier clumsiest
			clumsily clumsiness
cliché		**clung**	
click	clicked clicking	clunk	clunked clunking
client		**cluster**	clustered clustering
clientele		**clutch**	clutched clutches
cliff			clutching
climate	climatic climatically	clutter	cluttered cluttering
climax	climactic climactically	**coach**	coached coaches
	climaxes		coaching
climb	climbed climber	**coagulate**	coagulating
	climbing		coagulation
clinch	clinched clinches	**coal**	
	clinching	coalfield	
cling	clinging clung	coalition	
clinic	clinical clinically	coalmine	
clink	clinked clinking	**coarse**	coarsely coarseness
clip	clipped clipping	coarsen	coarsened coarsening
clipper		**coast**	coastal
clique		coastguard	
cloak	cloaked cloaking	**coat**	coated coating
clock	clocked clocking	**coax**	coaxed coaxes
clockwise			coaxing
clockwork		**cob**	
clod		cobalt	
clog	clogged clogging	**cobble**	cobbling
cloister		cobbler	
clone	cloning		

cobra	
cobweb	
cocaine	
cock	cocked cocking
cockade	
cock-a-hoop	
cockatoo	
cockerel	
cockle	
cockleshell	
cockney	
cockpit	
cockroach	cockroaches
cocktail	
cocky	cockier cockiest
	cockily cockiness
cocoa/coco	
coconut	
cocoon	cocooned cocooning
coddle	coddling
code	coding
codeine	
coerce	coercing coercion
coexist	coexisted coexisting
coexistence	
coffee	
coffin	coffined coffining
cogent	cogently
coherence	
coherent	coherently
cohesion	
cohesive	cohesively
	cohesiveness
cohort	
coiffure	
coil	coiled coiling
coin	coined coining
coinage	
coincide	coinciding
coincidence	coincidental
	coincidentally
coke	
colander	
cold	colder coldest coldly
	coldness
collaborate	collaborating
	collaboration

collaborator	
collage (form of art)	
collapse	collapsing
collapsible	collapsibility
collar	collared collaring
colleague	
collect	collected collecting
collection	collector
collective	collectively
college (place of education)	
collide	colliding
collie	
colliery	collieries
collision	
colon	
colonel	
colonial	colonialism colonialist
colonise	colonisation colonising
colonnade	
colony	colonies colonist
colossal	colossally
colossus	colossuses/colossi
colour	coloured colouring
colourful	colourfully
	colourfulness
colourless	colourlessly
	colourlessness
colt	
columbine	
column	columnal columnar
columnist	
coma (sickness)	comatose
comb	combed combing
combat	combated combating
combatant	
combination	
combine	combining
combustible	combustibility
	combustibly
combustion	
come	coming
comedian (male)	
comedienne (female)	
comedy	comedies
comely	comelier comeliest
	comeliness
comet	

comfort — comforted comforter comforting
comfortable — comfortably
comic — comical comicality comically
comma (punctuation mark)
command — commanded commanding
commandeer (to take over) — commandeered commandeering
commander (officer)
commandment
commando — commandos
commemorate — commemorating commemoration
commence — commencing
commencement
commend — commended commending
commendable — commendably
commendation — commendatory
commensurate — commensurately
comment — commented commenting
commentary — commentaries
commentate — commentator
commerce — commercial commercially
commiserate — commiserating commiseration
commission — commissioned commissioner (member of a commission) commissioning
commissionaire (doorkeeper)
commit — committed committing
commitment
committal
committee
commodious — commodiously commodiousness
commodity — commodities
common — commoner commonest commonly commonness

commonplace
commonwealth
commotion
communal — communally
commune
communicate — communicating communication
communion
communist/Communist — communism/Communism Communistic
community — communities
commute — commuter commuting
compact — compacted compacting
compact disc
companion
companionable — companionableness companionably
company — companies
comparable — comparability comparably
comparative — comparatively
compare — comparing
comparison
compartment
compass — compasses
compassion
compassionate — compassionately
compatible — compatibility compatibly
compatriot
compel — compelled compelling
compendium
compensate — compensating
compensation — compensatory
compère — compèring
compete — competing
competence
competent — competently
competition
competitive — competitively competitiveness
competitor
compile — compiler compiling compilation
complacency

complacent | complacently
complain | complained
 | complainer
 | complaining
complaint
complement (something that completes)
 | complementary
complete | completely completing
 | completion
complex | complexities
 | complexity
complexion
compliance
compliant | compliantly
complicate | complicating
 | complication
complicity
compliment (praise) | complimentary
comply | complied complies
 | complying
component
compose | composing
composer
composite
composition
compost
composure
compound | compounded
 | compounding
comprehend | comprehended
 | comprehending
comprehension
comprehensive | comprehensively
 | comprehensiveness
compress | compressed
 | compresses
 | compressing
 | compression
compressor
comprise | comprising
compromise | compromising
 | compromisingly
compulsion
compulsive | compulsively
 | compulsiveness
compulsory | compulsorily
 | compulsoriness

compunction
computation
compute | computing
computer
comrade | comradely
 | comradeship
con | conned conning
concave
conceal | concealed concealing
concealment
concede | conceding
conceit | conceited conceitedly
conceivable | conceivably
conceive | conceiving conception
concentrate | concentrating
 | concentration
concentric | concentrically
concept | conceptual
conception
conceptualise | conceptualisation
 | conceptualising
concern | concerned concerning
concert | concerted
concertina
concerto
concession
conch | conches
conciliate | conciliating
 | conciliation
 | conciliatory
concise | concisely
 | conciseness/concision
conclude | concluding
conclusion
conclusive | conclusively
concoct | concocted concocting
 | concoction
concomitant | concomitantly
concord
concourse
concrete | concreting
concur | concurred concurring
concurrence
concurrent | concurrently
concuss | concussed concusses
 | concussing
concussion

condemn — condemned
condemning
condemnatory
condense — condenser condensing
condescend — condescended
condescending
condescendingly
condescension
condiment
condition — conditional
condolence
condone — condoning
conduce — conducing conducive
conduct — conducted conducting
conductor
conduit
cone
confectioner — confectioneries
confectionery
confer — conferred conferring
conference
confess — confessed confesses
confessing
confession
confessor
confetti
confide — confiding
confidence
confident — confidently
confidential — confidentiality
confidentially
confine — confinement confining
confirm — confirmed confirming
confirmation — confirmatory
confiscate — confiscating
confiscation
conflagration
conflict — conflicted conflicting
conform — conformed
conforming
conformity — conformities
confound — confounded
confounding
confront — confronted
confronting
confrontation — confrontational
confuse — confusing confusion

congeal — congealed congealing
congenial — congenially
congested — congestion
conglomeration
congratulate — congratulating
congratulation — congratulatory
congregate — congregating
congregation
congregational/Congregational
congress/Congress — congresses
congressional
congruent — congruence
conical — conically
conifer
conjecture — conjecturing
conjugate
conjunction
conjunctivitis
conjure — conjuring
conjuror/conjurer
connect — connected connecting
connection/connexion
connive — conniver conniving
connoisseur
connotation
conquer — conquered conquering
conqueror
conquest
conscience
conscientious — conscientiously
conscientiousness
conscious — consciously
consciousness
conscript — conscripted
conscripting
conscription
consecrate — consecrating
consecration
consecutive — consecutively
consensus — consensual
consent — consented consenting
consequence
consequent — consequently
conservation — conservationist
conservative — conservatively
conservatism

conservatory — conservatories
conserve — conserving
consider — considered considering
considerable — considerably
considerate — considerately
considerateness
consideration
consign — consigned consigning
consignment
consist — consisted consisting
consistency — consistencies
consistent — consistently
consolation
console — consoling
consolidate — consolidating
consolidation
consommé
consonant
consort — consorted consorting
conspicuous — conspicuously
conspicuousness
conspiracy — conspiracies
conspirator — conspiratorial
conspiratorially
conspire — conspiring
constable
constabulary — constabularies
constancy
constant — constantly
constellation
consternation
constipate — constipating
constipation
constituency — constituencies
constituent
constitution — constitutional
constitutionally
constrain — constrained
constraining
constraint
constrict — constricted
constricting
construct — constructed
constructing
construction
constructive — constructively
construe — construing

consul — consulate
consult — consultation consulted
consulting
consultancy — consultancies
consultant
consumable
consume — consumer consuming
consummate — consummating
consummation
consumption
contact — contacted contacting
contagion
contagious — contagiously
contain — contained container
containing
contaminate — contaminating
contamination
contemplate — contemplating
contemplation
contemporaneous — contemporaneously
contemporaneousness/
contemporaneity
contemporary — contemporaries
contempt
contemptible — contemptibly
contemptuous — contemptuously
contend — contended contender
contending
content — contented contentedly
contenting
contentious — contentiously
contentiousness
contentment
contents
contest — contestant contested
contesting
context — contextual
contextually
continent/Continent
continental/Continental
contingency — contingencies
continual — continually
continuation
continue — continuing
continuities continuity
continuous — continuously
contort — contorted contorting

contour	contoured
contraband	
contraception	contraceptive
contract	contracted contracting
	contraction
contractor	
contradict	contradicted
	contradicting
	contradiction
contradictory	
contraflow	
contralto	
contraption	
contrary	contrarily contrariness
contrast	contrasted contrasting
	contrastingly
contravene	contravening
	contravention
contretemps	
contribute	contributing
	contribution
contributor	contributory
contrite	contrition
contrivance	
contrive	contriving
control	controlled controlling
controller	
controversial	controversially
controversy	controversies
conundrum	
conurbation	
convalesce	convalescence
	convalescent
	convalescing
convect	convected convecting
	convection
convector	
convene	convening
	convenor/convener
convenience	
convenient	conveniently
convent	
convention	
conventional	conventionally
converge	converging
convergence	
convergent	convergently

conversant	
conversation	conversationally
converse	conversing
conversion	
convert	converted converting
convertible	
convex	
convey	conveyed conveying
conveyance	conveyancing
conveyor	
convict	convicted convicting
	conviction
convince	convincing
	convincingly
convivial	conviviality convivially
convoluted	convolution
convolvulus	
convoy	convoyed convoying
convulse	convulsing convulsion
	convulsive
coo	cooed coos cooing
	cooingly
cook	cooked cooking
cooker	
cookery	cookeries
cool	cooler coolest coolly
	coolness
coop	cooped cooping
cooped up	
cooper	
cooperate	cooperating
	cooperation
cooperative	cooperatively
	cooperativeness
coordinate	coordinating
	coordination
coot	
cope	coping
copious	copiously copiousness
copper	coppery
copperplate	
copse/coppice	
copy	copied copier copies
	copying
copyright (legal right)	
copywriter (someone who writes copy)	

coquette	coquettish		corroborate	corroborating
	coquettishly			corroboration
	coquettishness		corrode	corroding
coracle			corrosion	
coral (rock)			corrosive	corrosively
cord	corded cording			corrosiveness
cordial	cordiality cordially		corrugated	
cordon	cordoned cordoning		corrupt	corrupted corrupting
cordon bleu				corruption corruptive
corduroy			corruptible	corruptibility
core	corer coring			corruptibly
corgi				
coriander			**corset**	
cork	corked corking		**cosmetic**	cosmetically
corkscrew			cosmic	cosmically
cormorant			cosmonaut	
corn			cosmopolitan	
cornea			cosmos	cosmology
corner	cornered cornering		**cosset**	cosseted cosseting
cornet			**cost**	costed costing
cornflower			costly	costlier costliest
cornice			costume	
corolla			**cosy**	cosier cosiest cosily
corollary				cosiness
corona				
coronary	coronaries		**cottage**	cottager
coronation			cotton	
coroner			cotton wool	
coronet			**couch**	couches couched
corporal			**cougar**	
corporate			cough	coughed coughing
corporation			**could**	couldn't
corporeal			**council** (assembly)	
corps (part of army)			councillor (public official)	
corpse (dead body)			counsel (advice; to advise)	
corpulence				counselled counselling
corpulent	corpulently		counsellor (adviser)	
corpuscle			count	counted counting
corral (enclosure; to fence in)			countenance	countenancing
	corralled corralling		counter	countered countering
correct	corrected correcting		counteract	counteracted
	correction corrective			counteracting
correlate	correlating correlation			counteraction
correspond	corresponded		counterfeit	counterfeited
	corresponding			counterfeiter
correspondence	correspondent			counterfeiting
corridor			counterfoil	

countermand	countermanded countermanding	**cowl**	cowled cowling
		cowslip	
counterpart		**coy**	coyer coyest coyly
counterpoint			coyness
countess	countesses		
countless		**coyote**	
country	countries	**crab**	crabbed
countryman	countrymen	**crack**	cracked cracking
countryside		cracker	
county	counties	crackle	crackling
coup		**cradle**	cradling
couple	coupling	**craft**	crafted crafting
couplet		craftsman	craftsmen
coupon		crafty	craftier craftiest
			craftily craftiness
courage	courageous courageously	**crag**	craggier craggiest craggily craggy
courgette		**cram**	crammed cramming
courier		cramp	cramped cramping
course	courser coursing	crampon	
court	courted courting	**cranberry**	cranberries
courteous	courteously	crane	craning
courtesy	courtesies	cranium	craniums/crania
courtier		crank	cranked cranking
courtly	courtlier courtliest courtliness	cranny	crannies
		crash	crashed crashes crashing
court martial	court martialled courts martial	**crate**	crating
courtship		crater	
courtyard		**cravat**	
couscous		crave	craving
cousin		craven	cravenly cravenness
cove	coving	**craw**	
coven		crawl	crawled crawling ·
covenant	covenanted covenanter covenanting	**crayfish**	
		crayon	
cover	covered covering	**craze**	crazed
coverage		crazy	crazier craziest crazily craziness
coverlet		**creak**	creaked creaking
covert	covertly	creaky	creakier creakiest creakiness
covet	coveted coveting		
covetous	covetously covetousness	cream	creamed creamer creaming
cow	cowed	creamy	creamier creamiest creamily creaminess
coward	cowardice cowardly		
cowboy		crease	creasing
cower	cowered cowering	create	creating creation

creative | creatively creativeness
creator
creature
crèche
credentials
credible | credibility credibly
credit | credited crediting
creditable | creditably
creditor
credulity | credulities
credulous | credulously
| credulousness

creed
creek
creep | creeper creeping
| crept
creepy | creepier creepiest
| creepily creepiness
cremate | cremating cremation
crematorium | crematoria/
| crematoriums

crêpe
crept
crescendo
crescent
cress
crest | crested cresting
crestfallen
crevasse (in ice)
crevice (split in rock)
crew | crewed crewing
crib . | cribbed cribbing
cribbage
crick | cricked cricking
cricket | cricketer cricketing
crime
criminal | criminality criminally
crimson
cringe | cringing
crinkle | crinkled
crinkly . | crinklier crinkliest
| crinkliness
crinoline
cripple | crippling
crisis | crises
crisp | crisper crispest

crispy | crispier crispiest
| crispily crispiness
crisscross | crisscrossed
| crisscrosses
| crisscrossing
criterion | criteria criterial
critic | critical critically
criticise | criticising
criticism
croak | croaked croaker
| croaking
croaky | croakier croakiest
| croakily croakiness
crochet (handicraft) | crocheted crocheting
crock | crocked
crockery
crocodile
crocus | crocuses
croft | crofted crofter
| crofting
croissant
crone
crony | cronies
crook | crooked crookedly
| crookedness
croon | crooned crooner
| crooning
crop | cropped cropping
croquet (game)
croquette (fried potato)
cross | crossed crosses
| crossing crossly
| crossness
cross-examination
cross-examine | cross-examining
crossroads
cross-section
crossword
crotchet (musical note)
| crotchety
crouch | crouched crouches
| crouching
croupier
crow | crowed crowing
crowbar
crowd | crowded crowding
crown | crowned crowning

crucial crucially
crucible
crucifix crucifixes crucifixion
crucify crucified crucifies
crucifying
crude crudely crudeness
crudities crudity
cruel cruelly cruelties
cruelty
cruise cruising
cruiser
crumb crumbier crumbiest
crumbiness crumby
crumble crumbling crumbly
crumpet
crumple crumpling
crunch crunched crunches
crunching
crunchy crunchier crunchiest
crusade crusader crusading
crush crushed crusher
crushes crushing
crust
crustacean
crusty crustier crustiest
crustiness
crutch crutches
crux cruxes/cruces
cry cried cries crying
crypt
cryptic cryptically
crystal crystalline
crystallise crystallisation
crystallising
cube cubic
cubicle
cuckoo
cucumber
cuddle cuddling
cudgel cudgelled cudgelling
cue cueing/cuing
cuff cuffed cuffing
cuisine
cul-de-sac culs-de-sac
culinary
cull culled culling

culminate culminating
culmination
culottes
culpable culpability culpably
culprit
cult
cultivate cultivating cultivation
culture cultural
cumbersome cumbersomely
cumbersomeness
cumulative cumulatively
cumulus cumuli
cunning cunningly
cupboard
cupful
cupidity
cur (a dog)
curable curably
curate
curative
curator
curb curbed curbing
curd
curdle curdling
cure (to heal) curing
curfew
curio
curiosity curiosities
curious curiously
curl curled curling
curler
curlew
curling
curly curlier curliest
curliness
currant (fruit)
currency currencies
current (present time; electricity)
currently
curriculum curriculums/curricula
curry curried curries
currying
curse cursing
cursory cursorily
curt curtly curtness
curtail curtailed curtailing
curtain curtained curtaining

curtsy	curtsies curtsied curtsying
curvaceous	
curvature	
curve	curving
cushion	cushioned cushioning
custard	
custodian	
custody	custodial
custom	customarily customary
customer	
cut	cutting
cutlass	cutlasses
cutlery	
cutlet	
cyanide	
cycle	cycling cyclist
cyclic	cyclical cyclically
cyclone	cyclonic
cygnet	
cylinder	cylindrical cylindrically
cymbal	
cynic	cynical cynically
cynicism	
cypress	cypresses
cyst	
cystitis	
czar/tsar	

Dd

dab	dabbed dabbing
dabble	dabbler dabbling
dachshund	
daffodil	
daft	dafter daftest daftly daftness
dagger	
dahlia	
daily	dailies
dainty	daintier daintiest daintily daintiness
dairy	dairies
dais	
daisy	daisies
dale	
dally	dallied dallies dallying
Dalmatian	
dam	dammed damming
damage	damaging
damask	
dame	
damn	damnation damned damning
damnable	damnably
damp	damper dampest damply dampness
dampen	dampened dampening
damsel	
damson	
dance	dancer dancing
dandelion	
dandle	dandling
dandruff	
dandy	dandies
danger	

dangerous	dangerously	dearth	
dangle	dangling	**death**	deathlier deathliest
dank	danker dankest		deathly
	dankly dankness	**débâcle**	
dapper		debar	debarred debarring
dappled		debase	debasing
dare	daring daringly	debasement	
daredevil		debatable	debatably
dark	darker darkest darkly	debate	debating
	darkness	**debit**	debited debiting
darken	darkened darkening	**debonair**	
darling		**debris**	
darn	darned darning	**debt**	
dart	darted darting	debtor	
dartboard		**debunk**	debunked debunking
dash	dashed dashes	début	
	dashing	débutante	
data	*singular* datum	**decade**	
database		decadence	
date	dating	decadent	decadently
daub	daubed daubing	decaffeinated	
daughter		decant	decanted decanting
daughter-in-law	daughters-in-law	decanter	
daunting	dauntingly	decapitate	decapitating
dauntless	dauntlessly		decapitation
	dauntlessness	decathlon	decathlete
dawdle	dawdling	decay	decayed decaying
dawn	dawned dawning	**deceased**	
day		deceit	
daydream	daydreamer	deceitful	deceitfully
	daydreaming		deceitfulness
daylight		deceive	deceiver deceiving
daze	dazing	decelerate	decelerating
dazzle	dazzling dazzlingly		deceleration
deacon		December	
deaconess	deaconesses	decency	decencies
dead		decent	decently
deaden	deadened deadening	deception	
deadline		deceptive	deceptively
deadly	deadlier deadliest		deceptiveness
	deadliness	**decibel**	
deaf	deafer deafest	decide	decidedly deciding
	deafness	deciduous	
deafen	deafened deafening	decimal	
	deafeningly	decimalise	decimalisation
deal	dealer dealing dealt		decimalising
dear	dearer dearest dearly	decimate	decimating decimation

decipher | deciphered
 | deciphering
decision |
decisive | decisively decisiveness
deck | decked decking
declaim | declaimed declaiming
declamatory |
declare | declaration declaring
decline | declining
decode | decoding
decompose | decomposing
decomposition |
decompression |
décor |
decorate | decorating decoration
 | decorator
decorative | decoratively
 | decorativeness
decorous | decorously
 | decorousness
decorum |
decoy | decoyed decoying
decrease | decreasing
 | decreasingly
decree | decreeing
decrepit |
decry | decried decries
 | decrying
dedicate | dedicating dedication
deduce | deducing
deduct | deducted deducting
 | deduction
deed |
deem | deemed deeming
deep | deeply deepness
deepen | deepened deepening
deer | *plural* deer
deface | defacing
defame | defamation
 | defamatory defaming
default | defaulted defaulter
 | defaulting
defeat | defeated defeating
defect | defected defecting
 | defection
defective | defectively
 | defectiveness

defence | defenceless
 | defencelessness
defend | defended defender
 | defending
defendant |
defensible |
defensive | defensively
 | defensiveness
defer | deferral deferred
 | deferring
deference | deferential
 | deferentially
deferment |
defiance | defiant defiantly
deficiency | deficient
deficit |
defile | defiling
defilement |
define | defining definition
definite | definitely definiteness
definitive | definitively
deflate | deflating deflation
deflationary |
deflect | deflected deflecting
 | deflection
defoliate | defoliating defoliation
deform | deformed deforming
deformity | deformities
defraud | defrauded defrauding
defray | defrayed defraying
defrost | defrosted defrosting
deft | defter deftest deftly
 | deftness
defunct |
defuse | defusing
defy | defied defies defying
degenerate | degenerating
 | degeneration
 | degenerative
degrade | degrading degradation
degree |
dehumanise | dehumanising
dehumidify | dehumidifier
dehydrate | dehydrating
 | dehydration
deign | deigned deigning
deity | deities

déjà vu
dejected   dejectedly dejection
delay   delayed delaying
delectable   delectability delectably
delegate   delegating delegation
delete   deleting deletion
deleterious   deleteriously
deliberate   deliberately
   deliberating
   deliberation

delicacy   delicacies
delicate   delicately
delicatessen   *plural* delicatessen
delicious   deliciously
   deliciousness
delight   delighted delighting
delightful   delightfully
delineate   delineating delineation
delinquent   delinquency
delirious   deliriously
delirium
deliver   delivered delivering
deliverance
delivery   deliveries
dell
delta
delude   deluding
deluge   deluging
delusion
de luxe
delve   delving
demagogue   demagoguery
demand   demanded demanding
demean   demeaned demeaning
demeanour
demented   dementedly
dementia
demerara (sugar)
demise
demob   demobbed demobbing
demobilise   demobilisation
   demobilising
democracy   democracies
democrat   democratic
   democratically

demolish   demolished
   demolishes
   demolishing
demolition
demon   demoniacal
   demoniacally demonic
demonstrable   demonstrably
demonstrate   demonstrating
   demonstration
   demonstrator
demonstrative   demonstratively
demoralise   demoralisation
   demoralising
demote   demoting demotion
demur (to object)   demurred demurring
demure (modest)   demurely demureness
denial
denigrate   denigrating
   denigration
denim
denomination   denominational
   denominationally
denominator
denote   denoting
denounce   denouncing
dense   densely denseness
density   densities
dent   dented denting
dental
dentist   dentistry
dentures
denunciation   denunciatory
deny   denied denies
   denying
deodorant
depart   departed departing
department   departmental
departure
depend   depended depending
dependable   dependability
   dependably
dependant (someone who depends on you)
dependent (needing help)
   dependence
   dependency
depict   depicted depicting
   depiction

deplorable	deplorably
deplore	deploring
deploy	deployed deploying
depopulate	depopulating
	depopulation
deport	deportation deported
	deporting
deportment	
depose	deposing deposition
deposit	deposited depositing
	deposition
depot	
deprave	depraving depravity
deprecate (to speak against)	
	deprecating
	deprecation
depreciate (to fall in value)	
	depreciating
	depreciation
depress	depressed depresses
	depressing depression
depressive	
depressurise	depressurising
deprive	deprivation depriving
depth	
deputation	
deputy	deputies
derail	derailed derailing
derailment	
derange	deranging
derangement	
derelict	dereliction
deride	deriding
derision	
derivative	derivatively
	derivativeness
derive	derivation deriving
derogatory	derogatorily
derrick	
dervish	dervishes
descant	
descend	descended
	descendent (adjective)
	descending
descendant (noun)	
descent	
describe	describing

description	descriptive
	descriptively
desecrate	desecrating
	desecration
desert (to leave; barren place)	
	deserted deserting
	desertion
deserter	
deserve	deservedly deserving
desiccated	
design	designed designer
	designing
designate	designating
	designation
desirable	desirability desirably
desire	desiring desirous
	desirously
desist	desisted desisting
desk	
desolate	desolately desolation
despair	despaired despairing
	despairingly
despatch/dispatch	despatched/dispatched
	despatches/dispatches
	despatching/dispatching
desperado	desperadoes
desperate	desperately
	desperation
despicable	despicably
despise	despising
despite	
despondency	despondencies
despondent	despondently
despot	despotic despotically
	despotism
dessert (pudding)	
dessertspoon	dessertspoonful
destination	
destined	
destiny	destinies
destitute	destitution
destroy	destroyed destroyer
	destroying
destruction	
destructive	destructively
	destructiveness

detach	detached detaches detaching
detachable	detachability
detachment	
detail	detailed detailing
detain	detained detaining
detainee	
detect	detected detecting detection
detective	
detector	
détente	
detention	
deter	deterred deterring
detergent	
deteriorate	deteriorating deterioration
determination	
determine	determining
deterrent	deterrence
detest	detested detesting
detestable	detestably
detestation	
detonate	detonating detonation
detonator	
detour	
detract	detracted detracting detraction detractor
detriment	detrimental detrimentally
deuce	
devastate	devastating devastation
develop	developed developing
developer	
development	developmental developmentally
deviate	deviating deviation
device (a trick, an implement)	
devil	devilish devilishly
devilry	devilment
devious	deviously deviousness
devise (to make)	devising
devoid	
devolution	
devolve	devolving

devote	devotedly devoting devotion
devotee	
devour	devoured devouring
devout	devoutly devoutness
dew	dewy
dexterity	
dexterous/dextrous	dexterously/dextrously
diabetes	diabetic
diabolical	diabolically
diagnose	diagnosing
diagnosis	diagnoses
diagnostic	diagnostically
diagonal	diagonally
diagram	diagrammatic diagrammatically
dial	dialled dialling
dialect	dialectal
dialogue	
dialysis	
diameter	diametric diametrical diametrically
diamond	
diaphragm	
diarrhoea	
diary	diaries
dice	dicing
dictate	dictating dictation
dictator	dictatorial dictatorially dictatorship
diction	
dictionary	dictionaries
die (to stop living)	dying
diesel	
diet	dietary dieted dietetics dietician
differ	differed differing
difference	
different	differently
differentiate	differentiating differentiation
difficult	difficulties difficulty
diffidence	
diffident	diffidently
dig	digger digging
digest	digested digesting digestible digestion

digestive
digit   digital digitally
dignify   dignified dignifies
                             dignifying
dignitary   dignitaries
dignity   dignities
digress   digressed digresses
                             digressing digression
dike/dyke
dilapidated   dilapidation
dilate   dilating dilation
dilatory
dilemma
dilettante
diligence
diligent   diligently
dilly-dally   dilly-dallied dilly-
                             dallies dilly-dallying
dilute   diluting dilution
dim   dimly dimmed
                             dimmer dimmest
                             dimming
dimension
diminish   diminished diminishes
                             diminishing
diminution
diminutive   diminutively
                             diminutiveness
dimple
din (noise; to sound)   dinned dinning
dine (to eat)   diner dining
dinghy (boat)   dinghies
dingy (dirty)   dingier dingiest
                             dingily dinginess
dinner
dinosaur
dint
diocese   diocesan
dip   dipper dipped dipping
diphtheria
diploma
diplomacy   diplomacies
diplomat   diplomatic
                             diplomatically
dire
direct   directed directing
                             direction directly

director
directory   directories
dirge
dirt
dirty   dirtied dirtier dirties
                             dirtiest dirtily
                             dirtiness dirtying
disability   disabilities
disable   disabling
disablement
disadvantage   disadvantaging
disadvantageous   disadvantageously
disaffected
disagree   disagreeing
disagreeable   disagreeableness
                             disagreeably
disagreement
disallow   disallowed
disappear   disappeared
                             disappearing
disappearance
disappoint   disappointed
                             disappointing
                             disappointingly
disappointment
disapprobation
disapprove   disapproval
                             disapproving
disarm   disarmed disarming
                             disarmingly
disarmament
disarray
disaster   disastrous disastrously
disband   disbanded disbanding
disbelief
disbelieve   disbelieving
disc/disk
discard   discarded discarding
discern   discerned discerning
discernment
discharge   discharging
disciple
discipline   disciplinary
disclose   disclosing disclosure
disco
discoloration/discolouration

discolour	discoloured	disentangle	disentangling
	discolouring	disentanglement	
discomfort		**disfavour**	
disconcert	disconcerted	disfigure	disfiguring
	disconcerting	disfigurement	
	disconcertingly	**disgrace**	disgracing
disconnect	disconnected	disgraceful	disgracefully
	disconnecting	disgruntled	
	disconnection	disguise	disguising
disconsolate	disconsolately	disgust	disgusted disgusting
discontent	discontented		disgustingly
	discontentedly	**dish**	dished dishes dishing
discontentment		dishearten	disheartened
discontinue	discontinuation		disheartening
	discontinuing		dishearteningly
discord	discordant	dishevel	dishevelled
	discordantly		dishevelling
discothèque		dishevelment	
discount	discounted	dishonest	dishonestly dishonesty
	discounting	dishonour	dishonoured
discourage	discouraging		dishonouring
	discouragingly	dishonourable	dishonourably
discouragement		dishwasher	
discourteous	discourteously	**disillusion**	disillusioned
discourtesy	discourtesies		disillusioning
discover	discovered discoverer	disillusionment	
	discovering	disinclined	disinclination
discovery	discoveries		disinclining
discredit	discredited	disinfect	disinfected
	discrediting		disinfecting
discreditable	discreditably	disinfectant	
discreet (tactful)	discreetly	disinherit	disinherited
	discreetness/discretion		disinheriting
discrepancy	discrepancies	disinheritance	
discrete (distinct)	discretely discreteness	disintegrate	disintegrating
discretion			disintegration
discriminate	discriminating	disinterested	disinterestedly
	discrimination		disinterestedness
discus (sport)	discuses	**disjointed**	disjointedly
discuss (to talk)	discussed discusses	**disk/disc**	
	discussing discussion	**dislikable/dislikeable**	
disdain	disdained disdaining	dislike	disliking
disdainful	disdainfully	dislocate	dislocating dislocation
	disdainfulness	dislodge	dislodging
disease		dislodgement	
disengage	disengaging	disloyal	disloyally disloyalty
disengagement			

dismal   dismally
dismantle   dismantling
dismay   dismayed dismaying
dismember   dismembered
                     dismembering
dismemberment
dismiss   dismissed dismisses
                     dismissing
dismissal
dismount   dismounted
                     dismounting

disobedience
disobedient   disobediently
disobey   disobeyed disobeying
disoblige   disobliging
disorder   disordered
                     disorderliness
                     disorderly
disorientate   disorientating
                     disorientation
disown   disowned disowning
disparage   disparaging
disparagement
disparate   disparately
disparity   disparities
dispassionate   dispassionately
dispatch/despatch   dispatched/despatched
                     dispatches/despatches
                     dispatching/despatching
dispel   dispelled dispelling
dispensable   dispensability
                     dispensably
dispensary   dispensaries
dispensation
dispense   dispenser dispensing
disperse   dispersal dispersing
displace   displacing
displacement
display   displayed displaying
displease   displeasing
displeasure
disposable
dispose   disposal disposing
                     disposition

dispossess   dispossessed
                     dispossesses
                     dispossessing
                     dispossession
disproportionate   disproportionately
disprove   disproving
disputable   disputably
disputatious   disputatiously
                     disputatiousness
dispute   disputing
disqualification
disqualify   disqualified
                     disqualifies
                     disqualifying
disquiet   disquieted disquieting
disregard   disregarded
                     disregarding
disreputable   disreputableness
                     disreputably
disrepute
disrespect   disrespected
                     disrespecting
disrespectful   disrespectfully
disrobe   disrobing
disrupt   disrupted disrupting
                     disruption
disruptive   disruptively
                     disruptiveness

dissatisfaction
dissatisfy   dissatisfied dissatisfies
                     dissatisfying
dissect   dissected dissecting
                     dissection
disseminate   disseminating
                     dissemination
dissension
dissent   dissented dissenter
                     dissenting
dissertation
disservice
dissident
dissimilar   dissimilarities
                     dissimilarity
dissipate   dissipating dissipation
dissociate   dissociating
dissolve   dissolution dissolving
dissuade   dissuading

distance   distancing
distant   distantly
distaste   distasteful
     distastefully

distemper
distend   distended distending
distil   distilled distilling
distillery   distilleries
distinct   distinction
distinctive   distinctively
distinctly
distinguish   distinguished
     distinguishes
     distinguishing

distort   distorted distorting
     distortion
distract   distracted distracting
     distraction
distraught
distress   distressed distresses
     distressing distressingly
distribute   distributing
     distribution
distributor
district
distrust   distrusted distrusting
distrustful   distrustfully
disturb   disturbed disturbing
disturbance
disused
ditch   ditched ditches
     ditching
dither   dithered dithering
ditto
diurnal   diurnally
divan
dive   diver diving
diverge   diverging
divergence   divergent divergently
diverse
diversification
diversify   diversified diversifies
     diversifying
diversion
diversity   diversities
divert   diverted diverting
divest   divested divesting

divide   dividing
dividend
divine   divinely
divinity   divinities
divisible   divisibility divisibly
division   divisional divisionally
divisive   divisively divisiveness
divorce   divorcing
divorcee
divot
divulge   divulging
dizzy   dizzier dizziest dizzily
     dizziness
do (perform)   does doing done
docile   docilely docility
dock   docked docker
     docking
docket
doctor   doctored doctoring
doctrinaire
doctrine   doctrinal doctrinally
document   documented
     documenting
documentary   documentaries
documentation
doddery   dodderiness doddering
dodge   dodging dodgy
dodgems
dodo   dodos/dodoes
doe (female animal)
doff   doffed doffing
dog   dogged doggedly
     doggedness dogging
doggerel
dogma   dogmatic dogmatically
doldrums
dole   doling
doleful   dolefully dolefulness
doll   dolled dolling
dollar
dollop
dolly   dollies
dolorous   dolorously
     dolorousness
dolphin
dolt
domain

dome
domestic   domestically
domesticate   domesticating
                    domestication
domesticity
domicile   domiciling
dominant   dominance
dominate   dominating
                    domination
domineer   domineered
                    domineering
dominion
domino   dominoes
don   donned donning
donate   donating donation
done
donkey
donor
don't
doodle   doodling
doom   doomed
door   doorway
doorknob
doorman   doormen
doormat
dope   doped doping
dormant   dormantly
dormer (window)
dormice
dormitory   dormitories
dormouse   dormice
dorsal   dorsally
dose   dosage dosing
dossier
dot   dotted dotting
dotage
dote   doting
double   doubling doubly
doublet
doubt   doubted doubting
doubtful   doubtfully
doubtless   doubtlessly
douche
dough   doughball doughnut
doughy   doughier doughiest
                    doughiness
douse   dousing

dove
dovecote/dovecot
dovetail   dovetailed dovetailing
dowager
dowdy   dowdier dowdiest
                    dowdily dowdiness

dowel
down
downfall
downstairs
downtrodden
downy
dowry   dowries
doze   dozing
dozen
drab   drabber drabbest
                    drably drabness
draft   drafted drafting
drag   dragged dragging
dragnet
dragon (creature)
dragonfly   dragonflies
dragoon (to force) dragooned dragooning
drain   drainage drained
                    draining
drake
dram
drama   dramatic dramatically
dramatise   dramatising
                    dramatisation
                    dramatist
drank
drape   draper draperies
                    drapery draping
drastic   drastically
draught   draughted draughting
draughts
draughtsman   draughtsmen
draughty   draughtier draughtiest
                    draughtily draughtiness
draw   drawing drawn drew
drawer
drawl   drawled drawling
drawn
dread   dreaded dreading
dreadful   dreadfully
                    dreadfulness

dream	dreamed/dreamt
dreamer	dreaming
dreamy	dreamier dreamiest
	dreamily dreaminess
dreary	drearier dreariest
	drearily dreariness
dredge	dredger dredging
dregs	
drench	drenched drenches
	drenching
dress	dressed dresses
	dressing
dressage	
dresser	
drew	
dribble	dribbler dribbling
drift	drifted drifter drifting
driftwood	
drill	drilled driller drilling
drink	drank drinker drinking
	drunk
drip	dripped dripping
drip-dry	drip-dried drip-dries
	drip-drying
drive	driven driver driving
	drove
drivel	drivelled drivelling
drizzle	drizzling drizzly
droll	drollery
dromedary	dromedaries
drone	droning
drool	drooled drooling
droop (to hang down)	drooped drooping
drop (to fall down)	dropped dropping
droplet	
droppings	
dross	
drought	
drove	
drown	drowned drowning
drowsy	drowsier drowsiest
	drowsily drowsiness
drudgery	
drug	drugged drugging
druggist	
druid	

drum	drummed drummer
	drumming
drumstick	
drunk	drunkard drunken
	drunkenly
	drunkenness
dry	dried dries driest
	drying dryly/drily
	dryness
dry–clean	dry-cleaned
	dry-cleaner
	dry-cleaning
dual (two)	duality
dub	dubbed dubbing
dubiety	dubieties
dubious	dubiously dubiousness
ducat	
duchess	duchesses
duchy	duchies
duck	ducked ducking
duckling	
duct	ducted ducting
due	
duel (a fight)	duelled duelling
duellist	dueller
duet	
duffle/duffel	duffle-bag/duffel-bag
	duffle-coat/duffel-coat
duke	dukedom
dulcet	
dull	dulled duller dullest
	dulling
dully (somewhat dull) dullness	
duly (at the proper time)	
dumb	dumbly dumbness
dumbfound	dumbfounded
	dumbfounding
dummy	dummies
dump	dumped dumping
dumpling	
dumpy	dumpier dumpiest
	dumpily dumpiness
dunce	
dunderhead	
dune	
dung	
dungarees	

dungeon
dunk   dunked dunking
dupe   duping
duplicate   duplicating
      duplication
duplicitous   duplicitously
      duplicitousness
duplicity
durable   durability durably
duration
duress
during
dusk
dusky   duskier duskiest
      duskiness
dust   dusted duster dusting
dusty   dustiness
dutiful   dutifully dutifulness
duty   duties
duvet
dwarf   dwarfed dwarfing
      dwarfs/dwarves
dwell   dwelled/dwelt dwelling
dwelt
dwindle   dwindling
dye (in colour)   dyer dyeing
dyke/dike
dynamic   dynamically
dynamism
dynamite   dynamiting
dynamo
dynastic   dynastically
dynasty   dynasties
dysentery
dyslexia   dyslectic/dyslexic
dyspepsia   dyspeptic dyspeptically

Ee

each
eager   eagerly eagerness
eagle
eaglet
ear
earache
eardrum
earl   earldom
early   earlier earliest
earn   earned earner earning
earnest   earnestly earnestness
earnings
earring
earth   earthly
earthenware
earthquake
earthworm
earthy   earthier earthiest
      earthily earthiness
earwig
ease   easing
easel
easement
east   easterlies easterly
      eastern
Easter
easy   easier easiest easily
      easiness
eat   eaten eating
eaves
eavesdrop   eavesdropped
      eavesdropper
      eavesdropping
ebb   ebbed ebbing
ebony

ebullience
ebullient   ebulliently
eccentric   eccentrically
    eccentricities
    eccentricity
echelon
echo   echoed echoes
    echoing
éclair
eclipse   eclipsing
ecology   ecological ecologically
    ecologist
economic   economical
    economically
economics
economise   economising
economy   economies
ecosystem
ecstasy   ecstasies
ecstatic   ecstatically
ECU (European currency unit)
ecumenical   ecumenically
    ecumenism
eczema
eddy   eddied eddies
    eddying
edelweiss
edge   edger edging
edgy   edgily edginess
edible   edibility edibly
edict
edifice
edit   edited editing editor
edition
editorial
educate   educating education
    educational educator
eel
eerie   eerier eeriest eerily
    eeriness
efface   effacing
effect (to bring about)
    effected effecting
effective   effectively
    effectiveness
effects

effectual   effectually
    effectualness
effeminacy
effeminate   effeminately
effervesce   effervescing
effervescent   effervescence
    effervescently
efficiency   efficiencies
efficient   efficiently
effigy   effigies
effluent   effluence
effort   effortless effortlessly
effrontery   effronteries
effulgence
effulgent   effulgently
effusive   effusively effusiveness
e.g. (for example)
egalitarian
egg   egged egging
ego
egoism (extreme selfishness)
    egoist egoistic
egotism (talking about oneself)
    egotist egotistical
    egotistically
egregious   egregiously
egress
egret
eiderdown
eight   eighteen eighteenth
    eighth
eighty   eightieth
either
ejaculate   ejaculating ejaculation
eject   ejected ejecting
    ejection ejector
eke   eking
elaborate   elaborating
    elaboration
élan
eland
elapse   elapsing
elastic   elasticity
elasticated
elated   elation
elbow   elbowed elbowing
elder   elderliness elderly

elderberry	elderberries
eldest	
elect	elected electing
	election elector
electoral	electorally
electorate	
electric	electrical electrically
electrician	
electricity	
electrification	
electrify	electrified electrifies
	electrifying
electrocute	electrocuting
	electrocution
electrode	
electron	
electronic	electronically
	electronics
elegance	
elegant	elegantly
elegy	elegiac elegies
element	elemental elementally
elementary	
elephant	elephantine
elevate	elevating elevation
elevator	
eleven	eleventh
elevenses	
elf	elfin elfish elves
elicit (to draw out)	elicited eliciting
eligible (suitable)	eligibility eligibly
eliminate	eliminating
	elimination
élite	élitism élitist
elixir	
elk	
ellipse	
elliptical	elliptically
elm	
elocution	
elongate	elongating elongation
elope	eloping
elopement	
eloquent	eloquence eloquently
else	elsewhere
elucidate	elucidating elucidation
elude (to escape)	eluding

elusive	elusively elusiveness
elver	
elves	
emaciated	emaciation
emanate	emanating emanation
emancipate	emancipating
	emancipation
emasculate	emasculating
	emasculation
embalm	embalmed embalming
embankment	
embargo	embargoed embargoes
	embargoing
embark	embarked embarking
	embarkation
embarrass	embarrassed
	embarrasses
	embarrassing
	embarrassingly
embarrassment	
embassy	embassies
embattled	
embellish	embellished
	embellishes
	embellishing
embellishment	
ember	
embezzle	embezzler embezzling
embezzlement	
embitter	embittered
	embittering
emblazon	emblazoned
	emblazoning
emblem	emblematic
	emblematically
embodiment	
embody	embodied embodies
	embodying
emboss	embossed embosses
	embossing
embrace	embracing
embrocation	
embroider	embroidered
	embroiderer
	embroidering
embroidery	embroideries
embroil	embroiled embroiling

embryo	embryonic
	embryonically
embryology	embryologist
emend	emendation emended
	emending
emerald	
emerge	emerging
emergence	
emergency	emergencies
emergent	emergently
emetic	
emigrant	
emigrate	emigrating emigration
eminence	
eminent (distinguished)	
	eminently
emir	
emissary	emissaries
emission	
emit	emitted emitting
emotion	emotional emotionally
emotive	emotively
empathy	empathetic
	empathetically
emperor	
emphasis	emphases
emphasise	emphasising
emphatic	emphatically
empire	
empirical	empirically
emplacement	
employ	employed employing
employee	employer
employment	
emporium	emporiums/emporia
empress	empresses
emptiness	
empty	emptied empties
	emptily emptying
emu	
emulate	emulating emulation
emulsion	
enable	enabling
enablement	
enact	enacted enacting
enactment	
enamel	enamelled enamelling

enamoured	
encampment	
encapsulate	encapsulating
enchant	enchanted enchanter
	enchanting
enchantment	
enchantress	enchantresses
encircle	encircling
enclave	
enclose	enclosing
enclosure	
encompass	encompassed
	encompasses
	encompassing
encore	encoring
encounter	encountered
	encountering
encourage	encouraging
	encouragingly
encouragement	
encroach	encroached
	encroaches
	encroaching
encroachment	
encrust	encrusted encrusting
encumber	encumbered
	encumbering
encumbrance	
encyclopaedia/encyclopedia	
encyclopaedic/encyclopedic	
end	ended ending
endanger	endangered
	endangering
endear	endeared endearing
	endearingly
endearment	
endeavour	endeavoured
	endeavouring
endemic	
ending	
endless	endlessly
endorse	endorsing
endorsement	
endow	endowed endowing
endowment	
endurance	
endure	enduring enduringly

enema
enemy   enemies
energetic   energetically
energise   energising
energy   energies
enfeeble   enfeebling
enfeeblement
enfold   enfolded enfolding
enforce   enforcing
enforcement
engage   engaging
engagement
engender   engendered
                               engendering
engine
engineer   engineered
                               engineering
engrave   engraver engraving
engross   engrossed engrosses
                               engrossing
engulf   engulfed engulfing
enhance   enhancing
enhancement
enigma   enigmatic
                               enigmatically
enjoy   enjoyed enjoying
enjoyable   enjoyably
enjoyment
enlarge   enlarging
enlargement
enlighten   enlightened
                               enlightening
enlightenment
enlist   enlisted enlisting
enmity   enmities
ennui
enormity   enormities
enormous   enormously
enough
enquire/inquire   enquiring/inquiring
                               enquiringly/inquiringly
enquiry/inquiry   enquiries/inquiries
enrage   enraging
enrich   enriched enriches
enrichment
enrol   enrolled enrolling
enrolment

ensemble
ensign
enslave   enslaving
enslavement
ensue   ensuing
ensure   ensuring
entail   entailed entailing
entangle   entangling
entanglement
enter   entered entering
enterprise   enterprising
                               enterprisingly
entertain   entertained entertainer
                               entertaining
                               entertainingly
entertainment
enthral   enthralled enthralling
                               enthrallingly
enthuse   enthusing
enthusiasm   enthusiast enthusiastic
                               enthusiastically
entice   enticing enticingly
enticement
entire   entirely entirety
entitle   entitling
entitlement
entity   entities
entomb   entombed entombing
entomologist (study of insects)
                               entomological
                               entomology
entourage
entrance (way in; put into trance)
                               entrancing
entrant
entreat   entreated entreating
entreaty   entreaties
entrée
entrench   entrenched entrenches
                               entrenching
entrenchment
entrepreneur   entrepreneurial
entrust   entrusted entrusting
entry   entries
entwine   entwining

enumerate (to count)		equator	equatorial
	enumerating	**equerry**	equerries
	enumeration	equestrian	equestrianism
enunciate (to pronounce clearly)		**equilateral**	
	enunciating	equilibrium	
	enunciation	equine	
envelope	enveloped enveloping	equinox	equinoctial
envelopment		equip	equipped equipping
enviable	enviably	equipment	
envious	enviously	equitable	equitably
environment	environmental	equity	equities
	environmentally	equivalence	
environmentalist		equivalent	equivalently
envisage	envisaging	equivocal	equivocally
envoy		**era**	
envy	envied envies envying	**eradicate**	eradicating eradication
enzyme		**erase**	eraser erasing
eon/aeon		**erect**	erected erecting
epaulette/epaulet			erection
ephemera	ephemeral	**ermine**	
	ephemerally	**erode**	eroding
epic		**erosion**	
epicentre		**erotic**	erotically eroticism
epicure	epicurean	**err**	erred erring
epidemic	epidemically	**errand**	
epidural		erratic	erratically
epigram	epigrammatic	**erroneous**	erroneously
	epigrammatically	error	
epilepsy	epileptic	**ersatz**	
epilogue		**erudite**	eruditely erudition
Epiphany		**erupt**	erupted erupting
episcopacy	episcopacies		eruption
episcopal	episcopalian	**escalate**	escalating escalation
episode	episodic episodically	escalator	
Epistle/epistle		escapade	
epitaph		escape	escapee escaping
epithet		escapism	escapist
epitome		escarpment	
epitomise	epitomising	**eschew**	eschewed eschewing
epoch		**escort**	escorted escorting
equable	equability equably	**escutcheon**	
equal	equalled equalling	**Eskimo**	
	equally	**esoteric**	esoterically
equalise	equaliser equalising	**esparto**	
equality	equalities	**especial**	especially
equanimity		**espionage**	
equate	equating equation	**esplanade**	

espouse	espousal espousing
espresso	
essay	essayist
essence	
essential	essentially
establish	established establishes establishing
establishment	
estate	
esteem	esteemed
estimable	estimableness estimably
estimate	estimating estimation
estrange	
estrangement	
estuary	estuaries
etc. (et cetera)	
etch	etched etcher etches etching
eternal	eternally
eternity	eternities
ether	ethereal ethereally
ethic	ethical ethically
ethics	
ethnic	ethnically
ethos	
etiquette	
etymology (origins of words)	
	etymological
	etymologies
	etymologist
eucalyptus	eucalyptuses/eucalypti
eulogise	eulogising
eulogy	eulogies
euphemism	euphemistic
	euphemistical
	euphemistically
euphoria	euphoric euphorically
euthanasia	
evacuate	evacuating evacuation
evacuee	
evade	evading
evaluate	evaluating evaluation
evangelical	evangelically
evangelise	evangelising
	evangelism evangelist
evaporate	evaporating evaporation

evasion	evasive evasively
eve	
even	evenly evenness
evening	
event	
eventful	eventfully
eventing	
eventual	eventually
eventuality	eventualities
ever	
evergreen	
everlasting	everlastingly
evermore	
every	
everybody	
everyday	
everyone	
everything	
everywhere	
evict	evicted evicting eviction
evidence	evidential evidentially
evident	evidently
evil	evilly evilness
evil-doer	
evince	evincing
evocative	evocatively evocativeness
evoke	evoking
evolution	evolutionary
evolve	evolving
ewe	
ewer	
exacerbate	exacerbating
exact	exacted exacting
exactly	exactness
exaggerate	exaggerating exaggeration
exalt	exalted exalting
exaltation	
examine	examiner examining examination
example	
exasperate	exasperating exasperatingly exasperation

excavate	excavating excavation
	excavator
exceed	exceeded exceeding
	exceedingly
excel	excelled excelling
excellence	
excellent	excellently
except	excepted excepting
exception	exceptional
	exceptionally
exceptionable	
excerpt	excerpted excerpting
excess	excesses
excessive	excessively
exchange	exchanging
exchangeable	exchangeability
	exchangeably
exchequer	
excise	excising excision
excitable	excitability excitably
excite	exciting excitingly
excitement	
exclaim	exclaimed exclaiming
exclamation	exclamatory
exclude	excluding
exclusion	
exclusive	exclusively
excommunicate	excommunicating
	excommunication
excrement	
excreta	
excrete	excreting excretion
excruciating	excruciatingly
excursion	
excusable	excusably
excuse	excusing
execrable	execrably
execrate	execrating execration
execute	executing execution
	executioner
executive	
executor	
exemplar	exemplary
exemplify	exemplified exemplifies
	exemplifying
exempt	exempted exempting
	exemption

exercise	exercising
exert	exerted exerting
	exertion
exfoliate	exfoliation
exhalation	
exhale	exhaling
exhaust	exhausted exhausting
	exhaustion
exhaustible	exhaustibly
exhaustive	exhaustively
exhibit	exhibited exhibiting
	exhibition
exhibitionist	exhibitionism
exhibitor	
exhilarate	exhilarating exhilaration
exhort	exhorted exhorting
exhortation	
exhumation	
exhume	exhuming
exile	exiling
exist	existed existing
existence	existent
exit	exited exiting
exodus	
exonerate	exonerating
	exoneration
exorbitant	exorbitantly
exorcise	exorcising
exorcist	exorcism
exotic	exotically
expand	expanded expander
	expanding
expandable	expandability
	expandably
expanse	
expansion	
expansive	expansively
expect	expected expecting
expectancy	
expectant	expectantly
expectation	
expectorate	expectorant
	expectorating
expedience	
expedient	expediently
expedition	

expeditious	expeditiously	extend	extended extending
	expeditiousness	extendable/extendible	
expel	expelled expelling		extendability/
expend	expended expending		extendibility
expendable		extension	
expenditure		extensive	extensively
expense			extensiveness
expensive	expensively	extent	
experience	experiencing	extenuate	extenuating
experiment	experimental		extenuation
	experimentally	exterior	
experimentation		exterminate	exterminating
expert	expertly expertness		extermination
expertise			exterminator
expire	expiring expiry	external	externally
explain	explained explaining	**extinct**	extinction
explanation	explanatory	extinguish	extinguished
expletive			extinguishes
explicable	explicability explicably		extinguishing
explicit	explicitly explicitness	extinguishable	
explode	exploding	extinguisher	
exploit	exploited exploiting	**extol**	extolled extolling
exploitation		extort	extorted extorting
exploratory			extortion
explore	exploration exploring	extortionate	extortionately
explorer		**extra**	
explosion	explosive explosively	extract	extracted extracting
exponent			extraction
export	exported exporting	extracurricular	
exportable	exportability	extradite	extradition
	exportation	extraneous	extraneously
expose	exposing	extraordinary	extraordinarily
exposure		extrapolate	extrapolating
expound	expounded expounding	extrasensory	
express	expressed expresses	extraterrestrial	
	expressing expression	extravagance	
expressionless		extravagant	extravagantly
expressive	expressively	extravaganza	
	expressiveness	extreme	extremely
		extremist	extremism
expulsion		extremity	extremities
exquisite	exquisitely	extricate	extricating
	exquisiteness	extrovert/extravert	extroverted/extraverted
			extroversion/extraversion
extant		extrovertly/extravertly	
extemporaneous	extemporaneously	**exuberance**	
	extemporaneousness	exuberant	exuberantly
extemporary	extemporarily		
extempore			

exude   exuding
exult   exulted exulting
exultant   exultantly
exultation
eye   eyeing
eyeball
eyebrow
eyeful
eyelash
eyelet
eyelid
eyeshadow
eyesight
eyesore
eyrie

fable
fabric
fabricate   fabricating fabrication
fabulous   fabulously
                   fabulousness
façade
face   facing
faceless
face-saving
facet   faceted
facetious   facetiously
                   facetiousness
facial (of the face)   facially
facile (easy)   facilely
facilitate   facilitating
facility   facilities
facsimile
fact
faction   factious factiously
                   factiousness
factor
factory   factories
factotum
factual   factually factualness
faculty   faculties
fad
faddish   faddishly faddishness
faddy   faddier faddiest
fade   fading
faeces
fag   fagged fagging
faggot
Fahrenheit
fail   failed failing
failure

faint (weak; to pass out)

	fainted fainter
	faintest fainting
	faintly faintness
fair	fairer fairest fairly
	fairness
fairy	fairies
faith	
faithful	faithfully faithfulness
faithless	faithlessly
	faithlessness
fake	faking
fakir	
falcon	falconer falconry
fall	fallen falling fell
fallacious	fallaciously
	fallaciousness
fallacy	fallacies
fallible	fallibility fallibly
fallow	
false	falsely falsehood
falsetto	
falsification	
falsify	falsified falsifies
	falsifying
falsity	
falter	faltered faltering
	falteringly
fame	
familiar	familiarity familiarly
familiarise	familiarisation
	familiarising
family	families
famine	
famished	famishing
famous	famously
fan	fanned fanning
fanatic	fanatical fanatically
	fanaticism
fanciful	fancifully
fancy	fancied fancies
	fancying
fanfare	
fang	fanged
fanlight	
fantasise	fantasising
fantastic	fantastically

fantasy	fantasies
far (in distance)	
farce	farcical farcically
fare (to do; payments for journey)	
	faring
farewell	
far-fetched	
farm	farmed farmer
	farming
farmhouse	
farmyard	
farrier	
farrow	farrowed farrowing
farther	farthest
fascinate	fascinating
	fascinatingly
	fascination
Fascist	Fascism
fashion	fashioned fashioning
fashionable	fashionableness
	fashionably
fast	fasted faster fastest
	fasting
fasten	fastened fastener
	fastening
fastidious	fastidiously
	fastidiousness
fat (not thin)	fatted fatter fattest
fatal	fatalities fatality
	fatally
fatalist	fatalism
fate (destiny)	
fateful	fatefully fatefulness
father	fathered fathering
	fatherly
father-in-law	fathers-in-law
fathom	fathomable fathomed
	fathoming
fathomless	
fatigue	fatiguing
fatten	fattened fattening
fatty	fattier fattiest
fatuous	fatuously fatuousness
fault	faulty
faultless	faultlessly
	faultlessness
faun (mythical creature)	

fauna — faunae/faunas
favour — favoured favouring
favourable — favourableness favourably
favourite — favouritism
fawn (colour; deer; to cringe) — fawned fawning
fax — faxed faxes faxing
fear — feared fearing
fearful — fearfully fearfulness
fearless — fearlessly fearlessness
fearsome — fearsomely fearsomeness
feasible — feasibility feasibly
feast — feasted feasting
feat
feather — feathered featheriness feathery
feature — featuring
featureless
February
feckless — fecklessly fecklessness
fecund — fecundity
fed
federal — federally
federated — federation
fee
feeble — feebleness feebler feeblest feebly
feed — fed feeding
feel — feeling felt
feeler
feelings
feet
feign — feigned feigning
feint (to pretend) — feinted feinting
feisty — feistier feistiest feistily feistiness
felicitous — felicitously felicitousness
felicity — felicities
feline
fell — felled felling
fellow
fellowship
felon — felonious feloniously feloniousness

felony — felonies
felt
female
feminine — femininity
feminism — feminist
femur
fen
fence — fencer fencing
fend — fended fending
fender
fennel
feral
ferment (to brew; to agitate) — fermented fermenting
fermentation
fern
ferocious — ferociously ferociousness
ferocity
ferret — ferreted ferreting
ferrule
ferry — ferried ferries ferrying
ferryman — ferrymen
fertile — fertility
fertilisation
fertilise — fertiliser fertilising
fervent — fervently
fervour
fester — festered festering
festival
festive — festively festiveness
festivity — festivities
festoon — festooned festooning
fetch — fetched fetches fetching
fête — fêting
fetid — fetidness
fetish — fetishes fetishist
fetlock
fetter — fettered fettering
fettle
feud — feuded feuding
feudal — feudalism
fever — fevered feverish feverishly
few — fewer fewest
fez — fezzes

fiancé (male)
fiancée (female)
fiasco
fib   fibbed fibber fibbing
fibre   fibroid fibrous
fibreglass
fickle   fickleness
fiction   fictional
fictitious   fictitiously
                                     fictitiousness
fiddle   fiddler fiddling
fiddly   fiddlier fiddliest
                                     fiddliness
fidelity   fidelities
fidget   fidgeted fidgeting
field   fielded fielder fielding
Field Marshal
field mouse   field mice
fiend   fiendish fiendishly
                                     fiendishness
fierce   fiercely fierceness
                                     fiercer fiercest
fiery   fierier fieriest fierily
                                     fieriness
fife
fifteen   fifteenth
fifth
fifty   fifties fiftieth
fig
fight   fighter fighting
                                     fought
figment
figurative   figuratively
figure   figuring
figurehead
filament
filch   filched filches filching
file   filing
filial
filigree
filings
fill   filled filler filling
fillet   filleted filleting
filly   fillies
film   filmed filming
filmic

filmy   filmier filmiest
                                     filminess
Filofax
filter   filtered filtering
filth
filthy   filthier filthiest filthily
                                     filthiness
fin   finned finny
final (last)   finally
finale (end of performance)
finalise   finalisation finalising
finalist
finality   finalities
finance   financing
financial   financially
financier
finch   finches
find   finder finding found
fine   finely finer finest
                                     fining
finery   fineries
finesse
finger   fingered fingering
fingerprint
finicky   finickiness
finish   finished finisher
                                     finishes finishing
finite   finitely finitude
fiord/fjord
fir (tree)
fire (flames; to shoot)
                                     firing
firearm
firebrand
fire extinguisher
fire-fighter
fireman   firemen
fireproof
firework
firm   firmed firmer firmest
                                     firming
firmament
firmly   firmness
first   firstly
fiscal
fish   fished fisher fishes
                                     fishing

fisherman | fishermen
fishery | fisheries
fishmonger
fishy | fishier fishiest fishily
 | fishiness
fission
fissure | fissuring
fist | fisted fisting
fisticuffs
fit | fitted fitter fittest
 | fitting fittingly
fitful | fitfully
fitment
five | fivefold
fix | fixed fixes fixing
fixable
fixated | fixation
fixative
fixity | fixities
fixture
fizz | fizzed fizzes fizzing
fizzle | fizzling
fizzy | fizzier fizziest fizzily
 | fizziness
fjord/fiord
flabbergasted
flabby | flabbier flabbiest
 | flabbily flabbiness
flaccid | flaccidly flaccidity
flag | flagged flagging
flagellate | flagellating
 | flagellation
flagon
flagrant | flagrancy flagrantly
flagstone
flail | flailed flailing
flair
flak (anti-aircraft fire; criticism)
flake (to peel off) | flaking flakiness
flaky | flakier flakiest
flamboyance
flamboyant | flamboyantly
flame | flaming
flamingo | flamingos/flamingoes
flammable
flan
flank | flanked flanking

flannel | flannelled flannelling
flannelette
flap | flapped flapping
flare | flaring
flash | flashed flashes
 | flashing
flashback
flashlight
flashy | flashier flashiest
 | flashily flashiness
flask
flat | flatter flattest flatly
 | flatness
flatfish
flatfooted
flatten | flattened flattening
flatter | flattered flatterer
 | flattering
flattery | flatteries
flatulence
flatulent | flatulently
flaunt | flaunted flaunting
flautist
flavour | flavoured flavouring
flavourful
flavourless
flavoursome
flaw | flawed
flawless | flawlessly flawlessness
flax | flaxen
flay | flayed flaying
flea
fleabite | fleabitten
fleck | flecked flecking
fled
fledged
fledgling/fledgeling
flee | fled fleeing
fleece | fleecing
fleecy | fleecier fleeciest
 | fleecily fleeciness
fleet | fleeting fleetingly
 | fleetness
flesh | fleshed fleshes
 | fleshing
flew (did fly)
flex | flexed flexes flexing

flexible	flexibility flexibly
flick	flicked flicking
flicker	flickered flickering
flight	flighted flighting
flighty	flightier flightiest
	flightily flightiness
flimsy	flimsier flimsiest
	flimsily flimsiness
flinch	flinched flinching
fling	flinging
flint	
flinty	flintier flintiest flintily
	flintiness
flip	flipped flipping
flippancy	
flippant	flippantly
flipper	
flirt	flirted flirting
flirtation	flirtatious flirtatiously
	flirtatiousness
flit	flitted flitting
	flittingly
float	floated floater
	floating
flock	flocked flocking
floe (floating ice)	
flog	flogged flogger
	flogging
flood	flooded flooding
floodlight	floodlit floodlighting
floodlit	
floor	floored flooring
floorboard	
flop	flopped flopping
floppy	floppier floppiest
	floppily floppiness
flora	floras/florae
floral	florally
floret	
florid	floridly floridness
florist	floristry
floss	flossy
flotilla	
flotsam	
flounce	flouncing
flounder	floundered
	floundering

flour	floured flouring
flourish	flourished flourishes
	flourishing
floury	flourier flouriest
	flourily flouriness
flout	flouted flouting
flow (moving liquid)	flowed flowing
	flowingly
flower	flowered flowering
flowery	flowerier floweriest
	flowerily floweriness
flown	
flu (illness)	
fluctuate	fluctuating fluctuation
flue (chimney)	
fluency	
fluent	fluently
fluff	fluffed fluffing
fluffy	fluffier fluffiest
	fluffily fluffiness
fluid	fluidity fluidly
fluke	fluky
flung	
flunk	flunked flunking
fluorescent	fluorescence
fluoridate	fluoridating
	fluoridation
fluoride	
flurry	flurried flurries
	flurrying
flush	flushed flushes
	flushing
fluster	flustered flustering
flute	fluting
flutter	fluttered fluttering
flux	fluxes
fly	flew flies flown
	flying
flyover	
flywheel	
foal	foaled foaling
foam	foamed foaming
foamy	foamier foamiest
	foamily foaminess
fob	fobbed fobbing
focal	
fo'c's'le/forecastle	

focus	focused focuses/foci
	focusing
fodder	
foe	
foetus/fetus	foetal/fetal
	foetuses/fetuses
fog	fogged fogging
fogbound	
foggy	foggier foggiest
	foggily fogginess
foghorn	
foible	
foil	foiled foiling
foist	foisted foisting
fold	folded folder folding
foliage	
folio	
folk	
folklore	
folksong	
follicle	
follow	followed follower
	following
folly	follies
foment (to stir up trouble)	
	fomented fomenting
fond	fondly fondness
fondant	
fondle	fondling
fondue	
font	
food	
foodstuff	
fool	fooled fooling
foolery	fooleries
foolhardy	foolhardily
	foolhardiness
foolish	foolishly foolishness
foolproof	
foolscap	
foot	footed footing
footage	
football	footballer footballing
footbridge	
foothold	
footing	
footlights	

footloose	
footnote	
footplate	
footprint	
footstep	
footstool	
footwear	
footwork	
fop	foppish foppishly
	foppishness
for	
forage	foraging
foray	
forbade	
forbear	forbearance forbearing
	forbore
forbid	forbade forbidden
	forbidding
forbore	
force	forcing
forceful	forcefully forcefulness
forceps	
forcible	forcibly
	forcibleness/forcibility
ford	forded fording
fore (in front)	
forearm	forearmed forearming
foreboding	
forecast	forecasted forecaster
	forecasting
forecastle/fo'c's'le	
forefather	
forefinger	
forefront	
forego/forgo	foregoes/forgoes
	foregoing/forgoing
foregone/forgone	
foreground	
forehand	
forehead	
foreign	foreigner foreignness
foreknowledge	
forelock	
foreman	foremen
foremost	
forensic	
forerunner	

foresaw	
foresee	foresaw foreseen foreseeing
foreseeable	
foreshadow	foreshadowed foreshadowing
foreshore	
foresight	
forest	forested forester forestry
forestall	forestalled forestalling
foretaste	
foretell	foretelling foretold
forethought	
foretold	
forever (always happening)	
	for ever (for all time)
forewarn	forewarned forewarning
foreword	
forfeit	forfeited forfeiting
forfeiture	
forgave	
forge	forged forging
forger	forgeries forgery
forget	forgetting forgot forgotten
forgetful	forgetfully forgetfulness
forgive	forgave forgiven forgiveness forgiving
forgo/forego	forgoes/foregoes forgoing/foregoing
forgone/foregone	
forgot	forgotten
fork	forked forking
forlorn	forlornly
form	formed forming
formal	formality formally
format	formatted formatting
formation	
formative	
former	formerly
formidable	formidableness formidably
formless	formlessly formlessness

formula	formulas/formulae
formulate	formulating formulation
fornicate	fornicating fornication
forsake	forsaken forsaking forsook
fort (defended place)	
forte (ability)	
forth (forward)	
forthcoming	
forthright	forthrightly forthrightness
forthwith	
fortification	
fortify	fortified fortifies fortifying
fortissimo	
fortitude	
fortnight	fortnightly
fortress	fortresses
fortuitous	fortuitously fortuitousness
fortunate	fortunately
fortune	
fortune-teller	
forty	forties fortieth
forum	
forward	forwarded forwarding forwardness forwards
fossil	
fossilised	fossilisation
foster	fostered fostering
fought	
foul	fouled fouler foulest fouling foully foulness
foul-mouthed	
found	founded founding
foundation	
founder	foundered foundering
foundling	
foundry	foundries
fount	
fountain	
fountain-head	
four (number)	fourth fourthly
fourfold	

foursome	
four-square	
fourteen	fourteenth
fowl	fowled fowler fowling
fox	foxed foxes foxing
foxglove	
foxhound	
foxhunter	foxhunting
foxtrot	
foyer	
fracas	*plural* fracas
fraction	fractionally
fractious	fractiously
	fractiousness
fracture	fracturing
fragile	fragilely fragility
fragment	fragmented
	fragmenting
	fragmentation
fragmentary	
fragrance	
fragrant	fragrantly
frail	frailer frailest frailly
	frailness
frailty	frailties
frame	framing
framework	
franc (money)	
franchise	franchising
frank (to stamp; outspoken)	
	franked franking
	franker frankest
	frankly frankness
frankfurter	
frankincense	
frantic	frantically franticness
fraternal	fraternally
fraternise	fraternising
	fraternisation
fraternity	fraternities
fraud	
fraudulence	
fraudulent	fraudulently
fraught	
fray	frayed fraying
frazzle	frazzling

freak	freakish freakishly
	freakishness
freckle	freckling freckly
free	freeing freely freer
	freest
freedom	
free-for-all	
freelance	freelancer freelancing
Freemason	Freemasonry
freesia	
freestyle	
freewheel	freewheeled
	freewheeling
freezable	freezability
freeze	freezing
freeze-dried	
freight	freighted freighter
	freighting
frenetic	frenetically
frenzy	frenzied frenziedly
	frenzies
frequency	frequencies
frequent	frequently
fresco	frescoes/frescos
fresh	fresher freshest
	freshly freshness
freshen	freshened freshener
	freshening
freshwater	
fret	fretted fretting
fretful	fretfully fretfulness
fretwork	
friar	
friary	friaries
friction	
frictionless	
Friday	
fridge/refrigerator	
fried	
friend	
friendly	friendlier friendliest
	friendlily friendliness
friendship	
frieze	
frigate	
fright	

frighten	frightened frightening	fructose	
	frighteningly	frugal	frugality frugally
frightful	frightfully	fruit	fruited fruiterer
	frightfulness	fruitful	fruitfully fruitfulness
frigid	frigidity frigidly	fruition	
frill	frilled	fruitless	fruitlessly fruitlessness
frilly	frillier frilliest	fruity	fruitier fruitiest
fringe	fringing		fruitily fruitiness
Frisbee		frump	frumpish frumpishly
frisk	frisked frisking	frumpy	frumpier frumpiest
frisky	friskier friskiest		frumpily frumpiness
	friskily friskiness	frustrate	frustrating frustration
fritter	frittered frittering	fry	fried fries frying
frivolity	frivolities	fuchsia	
frivolous	frivolously	fudge	fudging
	frivolousness	fuel	fuelled fuelling
frizz	frizzed frizzes	fugitive	
frizzle	frizzling	fugue	
frizzy	frizzier frizziest	fulcrum	
	frizzily frizziness	fulfil	fulfilled fulfilling
			fulfilment
frock		full	fuller fullest fully
frog	froggy		fullness
frogman	frogmen		
frogmarch	frogmarched	fullback	
	frogmarches	full-blooded	
	frogmarching	full-blown	
		full-length	
frogspawn		full time	
frolic	frolicked frolicking	fulsome	fulsomely fulsomeness
frolicsome		fumble	fumbling
from		fume	fuming
frond		fumigate	fumigating fumigation
front	fronted fronting	function	functioned
frontage			functioning
frontal	frontally	functional	functionally
frontier		functionary	
frontiersman	frontiersmen	fund	funded funding
frontispiece		fundamental	fundamentally
frontrunner		funeral	funereal funereally
frost	frosted frosting	funfair	
frostbite	frostbitten	fungus	funguses/fungi
frosty	frostier frostiest	funnel	funnelled funnelling
	frostily frostiness	funny	funnier funniest
froth	frothed frothing		funnily funniness
frothy	frothier frothiest	fur	furred furring
	frothily frothiness	furbish	furbished furbishes
frown	frowned frowning		furbishing
froze	frozen		

furious	furiously
furl	furled furling
furlong	
furnace	
furnish	furnished furnishes furnishing
furniture	
furore	
furrier	
furrow	furrowed furrowing
furry (with fur)	furrier furriest
further	furthered furthering
furtherance	
furthermore	furthermost
furthest	
furtive	furtively furtiveness
fury (anger)	furies
fuse	fusing
fuselage	
fusilier	
fusillade	
fusion	
fuss	fussed fusses fussing
fussy	fussier fussiest fussily fussiness
fusty	fustier fustiest fustily fustiness
futile	futilely futility
futon	
future	futuristic futuristically
fuzz	fuzzed fuzzes fuzzing
fuzzy	fuzzier fuzziest fuzzily fuzziness

Gg

gabardine/gaberdine	
gabble (to talk fast)	gabbling
gable (part of house)	
gad	gadded gadding
gadfly	gadflies
gadget	gadgetry
Gaelic (language of Scots, Irish)	
gaff (to catch fish)	gaffed gaffing
gaffe (a mistake)	
gaffer	
gag	gagged gagging
gaggle	
gaiety	gaieties
gaily	
gain	gained gainer gaining
gainful	gainfully
gait	
gaiters	
gala	
galactic	galactically
galaxy	galaxies
gale	
gall	galled galling
gallant	gallantly
gallantry	gallantries
galleon	
gallery	galleried galleries
galley	
Gallic (French)	
gallivant	gallivanted gallivanting
gallon	
gallop	galloped galloping
gallows	
gallstone	

galore	
galoshes	
galvanise	galvanising
gambit	
gamble (to bet)	gambler gambling
gambol (to jump)	gambolled gambolling
game	gamely gameness
gamekeeper	
gamesmanship	
gammon	
gamut	
gander	
gang	ganged ganger
	ganging
gangling	
gangrene	gangrenous
gangster	
gangway	
gannet	
gantry	gantries
gaol/jail	gaoled/jailed
	gaoling/jailing
gaoler/jailer	
gap (opening)	
gape (to stare at)	gaping
garage	
garb	garbed
garbage	
garble	garbling
garden	gardened gardener
	gardening
gardenia	
gargle	gargling
gargoyle	
garish	garishly garishness
garland	garlanded garlanding
garlic	garlicky
garment	
garnet	
garnish	garnished garnishes
	garnishing
garret (a room)	
garrison	garrisoned garrisoning
garrotte (to strangle)	garrotting
garrulity	
garrulous	garrulously
	garrulousness

garter	gartered gartering
gas	gases gassed gassing
gaseous	
gash	gashed gashes
	gashing
gasket	
gaslight	
gasp	gasped gasping
gassy	gassier gassiest
	gassiness
gastric	
gasworks	
gate	
gateau	gateaus/gateaux
gatecrash	gatecrashed
	gatecrasher
	gatecrashes
	gatecrashing
gather	gathered gathering
gauche	gauchely gaucheness
gaucherie	
gaucho	
gaudy	gaudier gaudiest
	gaudily gaudiness
gauge	gauging
gaunt	gauntly gauntness
gauntlet	
gauze	
gave	
gavel	
gawk	gawked gawking
gawky	gawkier gawkiest
	gawkily gawkiness
gay	gayer gayest gaily
	gaiety
gaze	gazing
gazebo	gazebos/gazeboes
gazelle	
gazette	
gazetteer	
gazump	gazumped gazumping
gear	geared gearing
geese	
Geiger counter	
geisha	
gel	gelled gelling

gelatine gelatinous
gelatinously
geld gelded gelding
gelignite
gem
geminate (to double, repeat)
geminating
Gemini
gender
gene
genealogical genealogically
genealogy genealogies
genealogist
general generality generalities
generally
generalise generalisation
generalising
generate generating generation
generator
generic generically
generosity generosities
generous generously
generousness
genesis
genetic genetically
genetics geneticist
genial geniality genially
genie
genital genitalia
genius geniuses/genii
genocide
genre
genteel genteelly
genteelness/gentility
gentian
gentile
gentility
gentle gentler gentlest
gently
gentleman gentlemanly
gentlemen
gentleness
gentry
genuflect genuflected
genuflecting
genuflection/genuflexion
genuine genuinely genuineness

genus genera
geography geographer
geographical
geographically
geology geological geologically
geologist
geometry geometric
geometrically
geothermal
geranium
gerbil/jerbil
geriatric geriatrically
germ
germinate (to sprout) germinating
germination
gerrymander gerrymandered
gerrymandering
gestalt
gestate gestating gestation
gesticulate gesticulating
gesticulation
gesture gesturing
get getting got
geyser
ghastly ghastlier ghastliest
ghastliness
ghee
gherkin
ghetto
ghillie/gillie
ghost ghostliness ghostly
ghostlike
ghoul ghoulish ghoulishly
ghoulishness
giant
giantess giantesses
gibber gibbered gibbering
gibberish
gibbet
gibbon
gibe/jibe giber/jiber
gibing/jibing
giblets
giddy giddier giddiest
giddily giddiness
gift gifted gifting

gift-wrap	gift-wrapped gift-wrapping	glass	glassed glasses glassing
gigantic	gigantically	glassy	glassily glassiness
giggle	giggling	**glaze** (to put glass in)	glazing
gigolo		glazier	
gild	gilded gilding	**gleam**	gleamed gleaming
gill		glean	gleaned gleaning
gillie/ghillie		**glee**	
gilt		gleeful	gleefully gleefulness
gimlet		**glen**	
gimmick	gimmickry gimmicky	**glib**	glibber glibbest glibly glibness
gin			
ginger	gingery	**glide**	gliding
gingerbread		glider	
gingerly		**glimmer**	glimmered glimmering
gingham		glimpse	glimpsing
ginseng		**glint**	glinted glinting
gipsy/gypsy	gipsies/gypsies	**glissando**	
giraffe		glisten	glistened glistening
gird	girded girding	**glitter**	glittered glittering glitteringly
girder			
girdle	girdling	**gloaming**	
girl	girlish girlishly girlishness	gloat	gloated gloating gloatingly
girlhood		**globe**	global globally
giro		globule	globular
girth		**gloom**	
gist		gloomy	gloomier gloomiest gloomily
give	gave given giving		
gizzard		**glorification**	
glacé (shining, like ice)		glorify	glorified glorifies glorifying
glacial	glacially	glorious	gloriously
glaciation	glaciated	glory	glories
glacier		**gloss**	glossed glosses glossing
glad (happy)	gladly	glossary	glossaries
gladden	gladdened gladdening	glossy	glossier glossiest glossily glossiness
glade (in a wood or forest)			
gladiator	gladiatorial	**glove**	
gladiolus	gladioli/gladioluses	**glow**	glowed glowing
gladsome		glower	glowered glowering
glamorous	glamorously	glow-worm	
glamour		**glucose**	
glance	glancing	**glue**	gluey gluing/glueing
gland		**glum**	glummer glummest
glandular		glumly	glumness
glare	glaring glaringly		
glasnost			

glut	glutted glutting
glutton	gluttonous
	gluttonously
	gluttonousness/gluttony
glycerine	
gnarled	
gnash	gnashed gnashes
	gnashing
gnat	
gnaw	gnawed gnawing
gnome	
gnomic	gnomically
gnu	
go	goes going gone
goad	goaded goading
goal	
goalkeeper	
goalless	
goalmouth	
goat	
goatskin	
gobble	gobbling
goblet	
goblin	
go-cart	go-carted go-carting
god/God	godliness godly
godchild	
god-daughter	
goddess	goddesses
godfather	
godless	godlessly godlessness
godlike	
godmother	
godsend	
godson	
goggle	goggling
going	
goitre	
gold	golden
goldfish	
golf	golfed golfer golfing
gondola	
gondolier	
gone	
gong	gonged gonging
good	goodly goodness
goodbye	

good-for-nothing	
good-humoured	good-humouredly
good-looking	
good-natured	good-naturedly
goods	
goodwill	
goose	geese
gooseberry	gooseberries
gopher	
gore	goring
gorge	gorging
gorgeous	gorgeously
	gorgeousness
gorgon	
Gorgonzola	
gorilla	
gorse	
gory	gorier goriest gorily
	goriness
goshawk	
gosling	
gospel/Gospel	gospeller
gossamer	
gossip	gossiped gossiping
	gossipy
got	
Gothic	
gouge	gouging
goulash	goulashes
gourd	
gourmand	
gourmet	
gout	
govern	governed governing
governable	governableness
	governably
government	
governess	governesses
governor	
gown	gowned
grab	grabbed grabbing
grace	gracing
graceful	gracefully gracefulness
graceless	gracelessly
	gracelessness
gracious	graciously graciousness
gradation	

grade	grading	gratify	gratified gratifies
gradient			gratifying gratifyingly
gradual	gradually gradualness	gratitude	
graduate	graduating graduation	gratuitous	gratuitously
graffiti	*singular* graffito		gratuitousness
graft	grafted grafting	gratuity	gratuities
grain	grained graining	**grave**	gravely graver gravest
grainy	grainier grainiest	gravel	gravelly
	grainily graininess	graven	
		graveyard	
gram/gramme		gravitate	gravitating gravitation
grammar		gravity	gravities
grammatical	grammatically	gravy	gravies
gramophone		**graze**	grazing
granary	granaries	**grease**	greasing
grand	grandly	greasy	greasier greasiest
grandchild	grandchildren		greasily greasiness
granddaughter		great	greater greatest
grandeur			greatly greatness
grandfather			
grandiose	grandiosely	**greed**	
	grandiosity	greedy	greedier greediest
grandmother/granny			greedily greediness
grandson		green	greenish greenness
grandstand		greenery	
grange		greengage	
granite	granitic	greengrocer	
granny/grandmother		greenhouse	
grant	granted granting	greet	greeted greeting
granulated		**gregarious**	gregariously
granule			gregariousness
grape			
grapefruit		**grenade**	
graph		grenadier	
graphic	graphically	**grew**	
graphics		**grey/gray**	greyer/grayer
graphite			greyest/grayest
grapple	grappling		greyly/grayly
grasp	grasped grasping		greyness/grayness
grass	grassed grasses	greyhound	
	grassing	**grid**	
grasshopper		griddle	
grassy	grassier grassiest	**grief**	
	grassiness	grievance	
grate	grating gratingly	grieve	grieving
grateful	gratefully gratefulness	grievous	grievously grievousness
grater		**griffin**	
gratification		**grill** (type of cooker; to cook on this)	
			grilled grilling

grille (a grating)
grim (stern)   grimmer grimmest
  grimly grimness
grimace
grime (dirt)   grimy
grin   grinned grinning
grind   ground grinder
  grinding
grip   gripped gripping
grisly (horrid)   grislier grisliest
  grisliness
gristle   gristly (tough to chew)
grit   gritted gritter gritting
grizzled
grizzly   grizzlier grizzliest
  grizzliness
groan   groaned groaning
grocer   groceries grocery
groggy   groggier groggiest
  groggily grogginess
groin
groom   groomed grooming
groove   grooving
grope   groping
gross   grossed grosses
  grossing grossly
  grossness
grotesque   grotesquely
  grotesqueness
grotto   grottoes/grottos
ground   grounded grounding
groundless   groundlessly
  groundlessness
group   grouped grouping
groupie
grouse   groused grousing
grove
grovel   grovelled grovelling
grow   grew grower growing
  grown
growl   growled growler
  growling
growth
grub   grubbed grubbing
grubby   grubbier grubbiest
  grubbily grubbiness
grudge   grudging

gruel
gruelling
gruesome   gruesomely
  gruesomeness
gruff   gruffer gruffest
  gruffly gruffness
grumble   grumbling grumblingly
grumpy   grumpier grumpiest
  grumpily grumpiness
grunt   grunted grunting
guarantee   guaranteeing
guarantor
guard   guarded guardedly
  guarding
guardian   guardianship
guerrilla
guess   guessed guesses
  guessing
guest   guested guesting
guffaw   guffawed guffawing
guidance
guide   guider guiding
guidebook
guild
guile
guileful   guilefully guilefulness
guileless   guilelessly
  guilelessness
guillemot
guillotine   guillotining
guilt
guilty   guiltier guiltiest
  guiltily guiltiness
guinea-pig
guise   guiser guising
guitar   guitarist
gulf
gull   gulled gulling
gullet
gullible   gullibility gullibly
gully   gullies
gulp   gulped gulping
gum   gummed gumming
gummy   gummily gumminess
gumption
gun   gunned gunner
  gunning

gunfire
gunpowder
gunwale/gunnel
gurgle   gurgling
guru
gush   gushed gusher
                  gushes gushing
gusset   gusseted
gust   gusted gusting
gusto
gusty   gustier gustiest
                  gustily
gut   gutted gutting
gutsy   gutsier gutsiest
                  gutsily gutsiness
gutter   guttering
guttersnipe
guttural   gutturally
guy
guyrope
guzzle   guzzler guzzling
gymkhana
gymnasium   gymnasiums/gymnasia
gymnast   gymnastics
                  gymnastically
gypsy/gipsy   gypsies/gipsies
gyrate   gyrating gyration
                  gyratory
gyroscope

haberdasher   haberdashery
habit
habitable   habitability habitably
habitat
habitation
habitual   habitually habitualness
hacienda
hack   hacked hacker
                  hacking
hackles
hackney   hackneyed
hacksaw
had
haddock
haemoglobin/hemoglobin
haemophilia/hemophilia
haemophiliac/hemophiliac
haemorrhage/hemorrhage
haemorrhaging/hemorrhaging
haemorrhoid/hemorrhoid
hag
haggard
haggis   haggises
haggle   haggling
haiku
hail   hailed hailer hailing
hailstone
hailstorm
hair
hairdresser
hair-raising
hairstyle   hairstyling hairstylist
hairy   hairier hairiest
                  hairiness

halcyon
hale
half   half-heartedly
half-hearted   half-heartedly
                       half-heartedness
half-hour   half-hourly
half-time
halfway
halfwit   halfwitted
halibut
halitosis
hall
hallelujah
hallmark
hallo/hello/hullo
hallowed
Halloween/Hallowe'en
hallucinate   hallucinating
                       hallucination
halo   haloes
halt   halted halting
                       haltingly
halter
halve   halving
ham   hammed hamming
hamburger
ham-fisted
hamlet
hammer   hammered hammering
hammock
hamper   hampered hampering
hamster
hamstring   hamstringing
                      hamstrung
hand   handed handing
handbag
handbrake
handcuff   handcuffed
                     handcuffing
handful
handicap   handicapped
                     handicapping
handicraft
handiwork
handkerchief   hanky/hankie
handle   handling
handlebars

handless   handlessly
                     handlessness
handsome   handsomely
                     handsomeness
handwriting   handwritten
handy   handier handiest
                     handily handiness
handyman   handymen
hang   hanged/hung hanging
hangar (for aircraft)
hanger (for clothes)
hang-glide   hang-glider
                     hang-gliding
hangover
hank
hanker   hankered hankering
hanky/hankie   hankies
haphazard   haphazardly
                     haphazardness
hapless   haplessly haplessness
happen   happened happening
happy   happier happiest
                     happily happiness
happy-go-lucky
hara-kiri
harangue   haranguing
harass   harassed harasses
                     harassing
harassment
harbour   harboured harbouring
hard   harder hardest
                     hardness
harden   hardened hardening
hard-hearted
hardly
hardship
hardware
hardy   hardier hardiest
                     hardily hardiness
hare   haring
harebell
harebrained
harem
hark   harked harking
harlequin
harm   harmed harming
harmful   harmfully harmfulness

harmless	harmlessly	haven	
	harmlessness	haven't	
harmonica		haver	havered havering
harmonious	harmoniously	haversack	
harmonise	harmonisation	**havoc**	
	harmonising	**hawk**	hawked hawking
harmonium		**hawthorn**	
harmony	harmonic harmonies	**hay**	
harness	harnessed harnesses	**hayfever**	
	harnessing	**haystack**	
harp	harped harping	**haywire**	
harpoon	harpooned	**hazard**	hazardous hazardously
	harpooning		hazardousness
harpsichord		**haze**	
harpy	harpies	hazel	
harrier		**hazy**	hazier haziest hazily
harrow	harrowed harrowing		haziness
harry	harried harries	**head**	headed header
	harrying		heading
harsh	harsher harshest	headache	
	harshly harshness	head-dress	head-dresses
hart (deer)		headland	
harvest	harvested harvesting	headlight	
harvester		headline	
hash	hashed hashes	headlong	
	hashing	headmaster	
hassle	hassling	headmistress	headmistresses
haste	hastily hastiness	headphones	
	hasty	headquarters	
hasten	hastened hastening	headscarf	headscarves
hat		headstrong	
hatch	hatched hatches	headway	
	hatching	heady	headier headiest
hatchback			headily headiness
hatchet		**heal**	healed healer healing
hatchway		health	
hate	hater hating	healthy	healthier healthiest
hateful	hatefully hatefulness		healthily healthiness
hatred		**heap**	heaped heaping
haughty	haughtier haughtiest	**hear**	hearing
	haughtily haughtiness	heard	
haul	hauled hauling	hearsay	
haulage		hearse	
haunch	haunches	heart (part of the body)	
haunt	haunted haunting	heartburn	
	hauntingly	**hearten**	heartened heartening
have	had has having		hearteningly

heartfelt	
hearth	
heartless	heartlessly
	heartlessness
hearty	heartier heartiest
	heartily heartiness
heat	heated heatedly
	heating
heater	
heath	
heathen	
heather	
heatwave	
heave	heaving
heaven	heavenly
heavy	heavier heaviest
	heavily heaviness
heckle	heckler heckling
hectare	hectarage
hectic	hectically
hedge	hedger hedging
hedgehog	
hedgerow	
heed	heeded heeding
heedless	heedlessly
	heedlessness
heel	heeled heeling
hefty	heftier heftiest heftily
	heftiness
heifer	
height	
heighten	heightened
	heightening
heinous	heinously heinousness
heir	
heiress	heiresses
heirloom	
held	
helicopter	
heliport	
helium	
hell	
hellish	hellishly hellishness
hello/hallo/hullo	
helm	
helmet	
help	helped helper helping

helpful	helpfully helpfulness
helpless	helplessly helplessness
helter-skelter	
hem	hemmed hemming
hemisphere	hemispherical
	hemispherically
hemlock	
hemp	hempen
hence	
henceforth	
henchman	henchmen
henna	
henpecked	
hepatitis	
her	
herald	heraldic heraldically
heraldry	heraldries
herb	
herbaceous	
herbal	herbalist
herbivore	herbivorous
herd	herded herding
here	
hereabouts	
hereafter	
hereby	
hereditary	
heredity	
heresy	heresies
heretic	heretical heretically
heritage	
hermit	
hero	heroes
heroic	heroically
heroin (drug)	
heroine (brave woman)	
heroism	
heron	heronry
herring	
herself	
hesitancy	hesitancies
hesitant	hesitantly
hesitate	hesitating hesitation
hessian	
hew	hewn hewed hewer
	hewing
hexagon	hexagonal

heyday	
hibernate	hibernating
	hibernation
hiccup/hiccough	hiccuped/hiccoughed
	hiccuping/hiccoughing
hid	hidden
hide	hid hidden hiding
hideous	hideously hideousness
hierarchy	hierarchical
	hierarchically
	hierarchies
hieroglyphics	
higgledy-piggledy	
high	higher highest highly
	highness
highbrow	
Highlands	
highway	
highwayman	highwaymen
hijack	hijacked hijacker
	hijacking
hike	hiker hiking
hilarious	hilariously
	hilariousness
hilarity	
hill	hilly
hillock	
hilt	
himself	
hind	
hinder	hindered hindering
hindrance	
hindsight	
Hindu	Hinduism
hinge	hinging
hint	hinted hinting
hinterland	
hip	
hippie/hippy	hippies
hippopotamus	hippopotamuses/
	hippopotami
hire	hiring
hirsute	hirsuteness
hiss	hissed hisses hissing
historian	
historic	historical historically
history	histories

hit	hitting
hitch	hitched hitches
	hitching
hitchhike	hitchhiker hitchhiking
hither	
hitherto	
hive	
hoar	hoarier hoariest
	hoarily hoariness
	hoary
hoard	hoarded hoarder
	hoarding
hoar-frost	
hoarse	hoarsely hoarseness
hoax	hoaxer hoaxes
hob	
hobble	hobbling
hobby	hobbies
hobby-horse	
hobgoblin	
hobnail	
hock	
hockey	
hocus-pocus	
hod	
hoe	hoeing
hog	hogged hogging
Hogmanay	
hoist	hoisted hoisting
hold	held holder holding
holdall	
hole	holing
holiday	
hollow	hollowed hollowing
holly	hollies
hollyhock	
holocaust	
hologram	
holster	
holy	holier holiest holily
	holiness
homage	
home	homing
homeless	homelessness
homely	homelier homeliest
	homeliness
home-made	

homesick	homesickness
homeward/homewards	
homework	
homicide	homicidal homicidally
homogeneous	homogeneously
	homogeneity/
	homogeneousness
homosexual	homosexuality
hone	honing
honest	honestly honesty
honey	
honeycomb	honeycombed
	honeycombing
honeymoon	
honeysuckle	
honk	honked honking
honorary	
honour	honoured honouring
honourable	honourably
hood	hooded hooding
hoodlum	
hoodwink	hoodwinked
	hoodwinking
hoof	hoofs/hooves
hook	hooked hooking
hooligan	hooliganism
hoop	hooped hooping
hooray	
hoot	hooted hooting
hoover	hoovered hoovering
hop	hopped hopping
hope	hoped hoping
hopeful	hopefully hopefulness
hopeless	hopelessly
	hopelessness
hopper	
hopscotch	
horde	
horizon	horizontal horizontally
hormone	hormonal
horn	horned horning
hornet	
hornpipe	
horny	hornier horniest
	horniness
horoscope	

horrendous	horrendously
	horrendousness
horrible	horribleness horribly
horrid	horridly horridness
horrific	horrifically
horrify	horrified horrifies
	horrifying
horror	
horse	horsing
horseback	
horseplay	
horsepower	
horseshoe	
horsy/horsey	horsier horsiest
	horsily horsiness
horticulture	horticultural
	horticulturally
horticulturist	
hosanna	
hose	hosed hosing
hose-pipe	
hosiery	hosieries
hospice	
hospitable	hospitableness
	hospitably
hospital	
hospitality	
host	hosted hosting
hostage	
hostel	
hostelry	hostelries
hostess	hostesses
hostile	hostilely
hostility	hostilities
hot	hotter hottest hotly
	hotness
hotchpotch	
hot-dog	
hotel	
hotfoot	hotfooted hotfooting
hothead	hotheaded
hothouse	
hotplate	
hotpot	
hound	hounded hounding
hour	hourly
house	housing

housebound	
household	householder
housekeeper	
housekeeping	
housewife	housewives
housework	
hovel	
hover	hovered hovering
hovercraft	
how	
howdah	
however	
howl	howled howler
	howling
hub	
hubbub	
huddle	huddling
hue	
hue and cry	
huff	huffed huffing
huffy	huffier huffiest
	huffily huffiness
hug (to embrace)	hugged hugging
huge (large)	hugely hugeness
hula hoop	
hulk	
hull	hulled hulling
hullabaloo	
hullo/hallo/hello	
hum	hummed humming
human (belonging to human race)	
	humanly humanness
humane (kind)	humanely
	humaneness
humanist	humanism
humanitarian	humanitarianism
humanities	
humanity	
humble	humbleness/humility
	humbly
humbug	
humdrum	
humid	humidity
humiliate	humiliating
	humiliatingly
	humiliation
humility	

hummock	hummocky
humorist	
humorous	humorously
	humorousness
humour	humoured humouring
humourless	humourlessness
hump	humped humping
humpback	humpbacked
humus	
hunch	hunched hunches
	hunching
hundred	hundredth
hundredweight	
hung	
hunger	hungered hungering
hungry	hungrier hungriest
	hungrily hungriness
hunk	
hunt	hunted hunter
	hunting
huntress	huntresses
huntsman	huntsmen
hurdle	hurdling
hurl	hurled hurling
hurly-burly	
hurrah	hurrahed hurrahing
hurricane	
hurry	hurried hurriedly
	hurries hurrying
hurt	hurting
hurtful	hurtfully hurtfulness
hurtle	hurtling
husband	husbanded
	husbanding
husbandry	husbandries
hush	hushed hushes
	hushing
hush-hush	
husk	
husky	huskier huskies
	huskiest huskily
	huskiness
hussar	
hussy	hussies
hustings	
hustle	hustler hustling
hut	

hutch   hutches
hyacinth
hybrid
hydrangea
hydrant
hydraulic   hydraulically
hydraulics
hydroelectric   hydroelectricity
hydrofoil
hydrogen
hyena
hygiene   hygienic hygienically
hymn   hymned hymning
hymnal
hymnary   hymnaries
hyperactive   hyperactively
        hyperactivity
hyperbole   hyperbolic
        hyperbolically
hypermarket
hyphen
hyphenate   hyphenating
        hyphenation
hypnosis   hypnotic hypnotically
hypnotise   hypnotism
hypnotist
hypochondria   hypochondriac
hypocrisy   hypocrisies
hypocrite   hypocritical
        hypocritically
hypodermic
hypotenuse
hypothesis   hypotheses
        hypothetical
        hypothetically
hysteria   hysterical hysterically
hysterics

Ii

ibex (wild goat)   ibexes
ibis (bird)   ibises
ice   icing
iceberg
ice-cream
icicle
icon/ikon
icy   icier iciest icily
        iciness

idea
ideal   ideally
idealise   idealising
idealism   idealist
identical   identically
identification
identify   identifiable identified
        identifier identifies
        identifying
Identikit
identity   identities
ideological   ideologically
ideology   ideologies
idiocy   idiocies
idiom   idiomatic idiomatically
idiosyncrasy   idiosyncrasies
idiosyncratic   idiosyncratically
idiot   idiotic idiotically
idle (not working)   idleness idler idlest
        idling idly
idol (statue)
idolatrous   idolatrously
        idolatrousness
idolatry   idolatries
idolise   idolising
idyll   idyllic idyllically

igloo	
igneous	
ignite	igniting ignition
ignoble	ignobly
ignominious	ignominiously
	ignominy
ignoramus	ignoramuses
ignorance	
ignorant	ignorantly
ignore	ignoring
iguana	
ikon/icon	
ill	iller illest
illegal	illegally
illegality	illegalities
illegible (unreadable)	illegibility illegibly
illegitimacy	illegitimacies
illegitimate	illegitimately
illicit (unlawful)	illicitly illicitness
illiteracy	illiteracies
illiterate	illiterately illiterateness
illness	illnesses
illogical	illogicality illogically
ill-treat	ill-treated ill-treating
ill-treatment	
illuminate	illuminating
	illumination
illumine	illumining
illusion	illusionist
illustrate	illustrating illustration
illustrative	illustratively
	illustrativeness
illustrator	
illustrious	illustriously
	illustriousness
image	imaging
imagery	imageries
imaginable	imaginably
imaginary	
imaginative	imaginatively
	imaginativeness
imagine	imagining imagination
imam	
imbecile	imbecilic
imbibe	imbiber imbibing
imbue	imbuing

imitate	imitating imitation
	imitator
immaculate	immaculately
	immaculateness
immaterial	immateriality
	immaterially
immature	immaturely
immaturity	immaturities
immeasurable	immeasurably
immediacy	
immediate	immediately
	immediateness
immemorial	immemorially
immense	immensely
	immenseness/
	immensity
immensity	immensities
immerse	immersing immersion
immigrant	
immigrate (coming into a country)	
	immigrating
	immigration
imminence	
imminent (about to happen)	
	imminently
immobile	immobility
immobilise	immobilising
	immobilisation
immoderate	immoderately
	immoderateness/
	immoderation
immodest	immodestly
immodesty	immodesties
immoral	immorally
immorality	immoralities
immortal	immortality
immortalise	immortalising
immovable/immoveable	
	immovableness/
	immoveableness
	immovably/immoveably
immune	immunities immunity
immunise	immunising
	immunisation
imp	impish impishly
	impishness

impact	impacted impacting	impertinence	
	impaction	impertinent	impertinently
impair	impaired impairing	imperturbable	imperturbability
impairment			imperturbably
impala		impervious	imperviously
impale	impaling		imperviousness
impalement		impetuosity	impetuosities
impalpable	impalpability	impetuous (hasty)	impetuously
	impalpably		impetuousness/
impart	imparted imparting		impetuosity
impartial	impartiality impartially	impetus (force)	
impassable	impassableness/	**impinge**	impinging
	impassability	impious	impiously impiousness
	impassably	**implacable**	implacability
impasse			implacably
impassioned		implant	implanted implanting
impassive	impassively	implausible	implausibility
	impassiveness		implausibly
impatience		implement	implemented
impatient	impatiently		implementing
impeach	impeaching		implementation
impeachment		implicate	implicating implication
impeccable	impeccably	implicit	implicitly implicitness
impecunious	impecuniously	implode	imploding
	impecuniousness	implore	imploring
impede	impeding	implosion	
impediment		imply	implied implies
impel	impelled impelling		implying
impending		**impolite**	impolitely impoliteness
impenetrable	impenetrability	imponderable	imponderability
	impenetrableness		imponderably
	impenetrably	import	imported importer
imperative	imperatively		importing
imperceptible	imperceptibility	importance	
	imperceptibly	important	importantly
imperfect	imperfectly	impose	imposing imposition
imperfection		impossible	impossibility
imperial	imperially		impossibly
imperialism	imperialist imperialistic	impostor/imposter	
	imperialistically	impotence	
imperil	imperilled imperilling	impotent	impotently
imperious	imperiously	impound	impounded
	imperiousness		impounding
impersonal	impersonally	impoverish	impoverished
impersonate	impersonating		impoverishes
	impersonation		impoverishing
impersonator		impoverishment	

impracticable	impracticability	**inaccessible**	inaccessibility
	impracticably		inaccessibly
impractical	impracticality	inaccuracy	inaccuracies
	impractically	inaccurate	inaccurately
impregnable	impregnability	inaction	
	impregnably	inactive	inactivity
impregnate	impregnating	**inadequacy**	inadequacies
	impregnation	inadequate	inadequately
impresario		inadmissible	inadmissibility
impress	impressed impresses		inadmissibly
	impressing	inadvertence	
impression		inadvertent	inadvertently
impressionable	impressionability	inadvisable	inadvisability
	impressionably		inadvisably
impressionism	impressionist	**inane**	inanely
	impressionistic	inanimate	inanimately
	impressionistically	inanity	inanities
impressive	impressively	**inapplicable**	inapplicability
	impressiveness		inapplicably
imprint	imprinted imprinting	inappropriate	inappropriately
imprison	imprisoned		inappropriateness
	imprisoning	inapt	inaptly inaptness
imprisonment		**inarticulacy**	inarticulacies
improbable	improbability	inarticulate	inarticulately
	improbably		inarticulateness
impromptu		**inasmuch**	
improper	improperly	**inattention**	
impropriety	improprieties	inattentive	inattentively
improvable	improvability		inattentiveness
	improvably	**inaudible**	inaudibility inaudibly
improve	improving	inaugural	
improvement		inaugurate	inaugurating
improvisation			inauguration
improvise	improviser improvising	inauspicious	inauspiciously
imprudence (rash, indiscreet)			inauspiciousness
imprudent	imprudently	**inborn**	
impudence		**inbred**	
impudent (disrespectful)		inbreeding	
	impudently	**inbuilt**	
impulse	impulsion	**incalculable**	incalculability
impulsive	impulsively		incalculably
	impulsiveness	incandescence	
impunity		incandescent	incandescently
impure	impurely	incantation	
	impureness/impurity	incapable	incapability incapably
impurity	impurities	incapacitate	incapacitating
inability	inabilities		incapacitation

incapacity | incapacities
incarcerate | incarcerating
| incarceration
incarnate | incarnating
| incarnation
incendiary | incendiaries
incense | incensing
incentive
inception
incessant | incessantly
| incessantness/
| incessancy
incest | incestuous
| incestuously
| incestuousness
inch | inched   inches   inching
incidence
incident
incidental | incidentally
incinerate | incinerating
| incineration
incinerator
incise | incising   incision
incisive | incisively   incisiveness
incisor
incite | inciting
incitement
inclemency | inclemencies
inclement | inclemently
inclination
incline | inclining
include | including
inclusion
inclusive | inclusively
| inclusiveness
incognito
incoherence
incoherent | incoherently
incombustible | incombustibility
| incombustibly
income
incomer
incoming
incommunicado
incomparable | incomparability
| incomparably

incompatible | incompatibility
| incompatibly
incompetence
incompetent | incompetently
incomplete | incompletely
| incompleteness
incomprehensible | incomprehensibility
| incomprehensibly
incomprehension
inconceivable | inconceivability
| inconceivably
inconclusive | inconclusively
| inconclusiveness
incongruity | incongruities
incongruous | incongruously
| incongruousness
inconsequential | inconsequentiality
| inconsequentially
inconsiderable | inconsiderableness
| inconsiderably
inconsiderate | inconsiderately
| inconsiderateness
inconsistency | inconsistencies
inconsistent | inconsistently
inconsolable | inconsolability
| inconsolably
inconspicuous | inconspicuously
| inconspicuousness
incontinent | incontinence
| incontinently
incontrovertible | incontrovertibility
| incontrovertibly
inconvenience
inconvenient | inconveniently
incorporate | incorporating
| incorporation
incorrect | incorrectly
| incorrectness
incorrigible | incorrigibility
| incorrigibly
incorruptible | incorruptibility
| incorruptibly
increase | increasing   increasingly
incredible | incredibility   incredibly
incredulity | incredulities
incredulous | incredulously
| incredulousness

increment	incremental	indict	indictable indicting
	incrementally	indictment	
incriminate	incriminating	indifference	
	incrimination	indifferent	indifferently
	incriminatory	indigenous	indigenously
incubate	incubating incubation	indigestible	indigestibility
incubator	incubatory		indigestibly
inculcate	inculcating inculcation	indigestion	
incumbent	incumbency	indignant	indignantly
incur	incurred incurring	indignation	
incurable	incurability incurably	indignity	indignities
incursion	incursive	indigo	
indebted	indebtedness	indirect	indirectly indirectness
indecency	indecencies	indiscreet	indiscreetly
indecent	indecently	indiscretion	
indecipherable		indiscriminate	indiscriminateness
indecision		indispensable	indispensability
indecisive	indecisively		indispensably
	indecisiveness	indisposed	
indeed		indisposition	
indefatigable	indefatigability	indisputable	indisputability
	indefatigably		indisputably
indefensible	indefensibility	indistinct	indistinctly
	indefensibly		indistinctness
indefinable	indefinability	individual	individuality
	indefinably		individually
indefinite	indefinitely	individualise	individualising
	indefiniteness		individualisation
indelible	indelibility indelibly	indivisible	indivisibility indivisibly
indelicacy	indelicacies	**indoctrinate**	indoctrinating
indelicate	indelicately		indoctrination
indent	indented indenting	indolence	
indentation		indolent	indolently
independence		indomitable	indomitability
independent	independently		indomitably
in-depth		indoor	indoors
indescribable	indescribability	**indubitable**	indubitably
	indescribably	induce	inducing
indestructible	indestructibility	inducement	
	indestructibly	induct	inducted inducting
indeterminate	indeterminately		induction
	indetermination	inductive	inductively
index	indexes/indices		inductiveness
indicate	indicating indication	indulge	indulging
indicative	indicatively	indulgence	
	indicativeness	indulgent	indulgently
indicator		industrial	industrially

industrialisation
industrialise   industrialising
industrious   industriously
                          industriousness
industry   industries
inebriated   inebriation
inedible   inedibility
ineffective   ineffectively
                          ineffectiveness
ineffectual   ineffectually
                          ineffectualness
ineligible   ineligibility ineligibly
inept   ineptly
                          ineptitude/ineptness

inequality   inequalities
inequitable   inequitably
inequity   inequities
inert   inertly inertness
inertia
inescapable   inescapability
                          inescapably

inessential
inestimable   inestimability
                          inestimably

inevitable   inevitability inevitably
inexact   inexactly inexactness
inexactitude
inexcusable   inexcusability
                          inexcusably
inexhaustible   inexhaustibility
                          inexhaustibly
inexorable   inexorability
                          inexorably
inexpensive   inexpensively
                          inexpensiveness
inexperience
inexpert   inexpertly inexpertness
inexplicable   inexplicability
                          inexplicably
inexpressible   inexpressibility
                          inexpressibly
inextinguishable   inextinguishably
infallible   infallibility infallibly
infamous   infamously
infamy   infamies
infancy
infant   infantile

infantry
infatuated   infatuation
infect   infected infecting
                          infection
infectious   infectiously
                          infectiousness
infer   inferred inferring
inference
inferior   inferiority
infernal   infernally
inferno
infertile   infertility
infest   infestation infested
                          infesting

infidel
infidelity   infidelities
infighting
infiltrate   infiltrating infiltration
infinite   infinitely
infinitesimal   infinitesimally
infinitive
infinity   infinities
infirm
infirmary
infirmity   infirmities
inflame   inflaming
inflammable   inflammability
inflammation
inflammatory
inflate   inflatable inflating
                          inflation
inflexible   inflexibility inflexibly
inflict   inflicted inflicting
                          infliction
influence   influencing
influential   influentially
influenza/flu
influx
inform   information informed
                          informer informing
informal   informality informally
informative
infrared
infrastructure
infrequency   infrequencies
infrequent   infrequently

infringe | infringement
| | infringing
infuriate | infuriating
| | infuriatingly
infuse | infusing   infusion
ingenious | ingeniously
| | ingeniousness
ingenuity | ingenuities
inglorious | ingloriously
ingot |
ingrain | ingrained   ingraining
ingratitude |
ingredient |
ingrowing |
inhabit | inhabited   inhabiting
inhabitable |
inhabitant |
inhalant |
inhalation |
inhale | inhaling
inherent | inherently
inherit | inherited   inheriting
inheritance |
inhibit | inhibited   inhibiting
| | inhibition
inhospitable | inhospitableness
| | inhospitably
inhuman | inhumanity   inhumanly
inimical | inimically
inimitable | inimitability   inimitably
iniquitous | iniquitously
| | iniquitousness
iniquity | iniquities
initial | initialled   initialling
| | initially
initiate | initiating   initiation
initiative |
inject | injected   injecting
| | injection
injure | injuring
injury | injuries
injustice |
ink | inked   inking
inkling |
inlaid |
inland |
in-law |

inlay | inlaid   inlaying
inlet |
inmate |
inmost |
inn |
innards |
inner | innermost   inmost
innings |
innocence |
innocent | innocently
innocuous | innocuously
| | innocuousness
innovate | innovating   innovation
| | innovative
innovator |
innuendo | innuendoes/innuendos
innumerable | innumerability
| | innumerably
innumerate (poor at arithmetic) |
| | innumeracy
inoculate | inoculating
| | inoculation
inoffensive | inoffensively
| | inoffensiveness
inoperable | inoperability
| | inoperably
inoperative |
inopportune | inopportunely
| | inopportuneness
inordinate | inordinately
| | inordinateness
inorganic | inorganically
input |
inquest |
inquire/enquire | inquiring/enquiring
| | inquiringly/enquiringly
inquiry/enquiry | inquiries/enquiries
inquisition |
inquisitive | inquisitively
| | inquisitiveness
inquisitor | inquisitorial
| | inquisitorially
inroads |
inrushing |
insalubrious | insalubriously
| | insalubriousness
insane | insanely   insanity

insanitary
insatiable   insatiability insatiably
inscribe   inscribing
inscription
inscrutable   inscrutability
                       inscrutably

insect
insecticide
insecure   insecurely insecurity
inseminate   inseminating
                       insemination
insensible   insensibility insensibly
insensitive   insensitively
                       insensitivity
inseparable   inseparability
                       inseparably
insert   inserted inserting
                       insertion
in-service
inset
inshore
inside   insider
insidious   insidiously
                       insidiousness
insight
insignia
insignificance
insignificant   insignificantly
insincere   insincerely insincerity
insinuate   insinuating
                       insinuatingly
                       insinuation
insipid   insipidly
                       insipidness/insipidity
insist   insisted insisting
insistence
insistent   insistently
insole
insolence
insoluble   insolubility insolubly
insolvent   insolvency
insomnia   insomniac
inspect   inspected inspecting
                       inspection
inspector   inspectorate

inspire   inspiration
                       inspirational inspiring
                       inspiringly
instability   instabilities
install/instal   installation installed
                       installing
instalment
instance
instant   instantly
instantaneous   instantaneously
                       instantaneousness
instead
instep
instigate   instigating instigation
instil   instilled instilling
instinct   instinctive instinctively
                       instinctiveness
institute   instituting institution
institutional   institutionally
institutionalise institutionalisation
instruct   instructed instructing
instruction   instructional
instructive   instructively
                       instructiveness
instructor
instructress   instructresses
instrument   instrumental
                       instrumentalist
                       instrumentally
instrumentation
insubordinate insubordinately
insubordination
insubstantial   insubstantiality
                       insubstantially
insufferable   insufferableness
                       insufferably
insufficiency
insufficient   insufficiently
insular   insularity
insulate   insulating insulation
                       insulator
insulin
insult   insulted insulting
                       insultingly
insuperable   insuperability
                       insuperably

insupportable   insupportability
                 insupportably
insurable   insurability
insurance
insure   insurer insuring
insurgent   insurgence insurgency
insurmountable   insurmountability
                 insurmountably
insurrection
inswinger
intact   intactness
intake
intangible   intangibility intangibly
integer
integral   integrally
integrate   integration
integrity   integrities
intellect   intellectual
                 intellectuality
                 intellectually
intelligence
intelligent   intelligently
intelligentsia
intelligible   intelligibility
                 intelligibly

intemperance
intemperate   intemperately
                 intemperateness
intend   intended intending
intense   intensely intenseness
intensify   intensified intensifies
                 intensifying
intensity   intensities
intensive   intensively
                 intensiveness
intent   intention intently
intentional   intentionally
inter   interment interred
                 interring
interact   interacted interacting
                 interaction
interactive
interbreed   interbred
                 interbreeding
intercede   interceding
                 intercession

intercept   intercepted intercepting
                 interception
intercession
interchange   interchanging
interchangeable interchangeability
                 interchangeably
intercom
interconnect   interconnected
                 interconnecting
                 interconnection
intercourse
interdependence
interdependent   interdependently
interest   interested interesting
                 interestingly
interface   interfacing
interfere   interfering
                 interferingly
interference
interim
interior
interject   interjected interjecting
interjection
interleave   interleaving
interlock   interlocked
                 interlocking
interloper
interlude
intermediacy
intermediary
intermediate   intermediately
intermezzo   intermezzi/intermezzos
interminable   interminableness
                 interminably
intermingle   intermingling
intermission
intermittent   intermittently
intermix   intermixed intermixing
intern   interned internee
                 interning internment
internal   internally
internalise   internalisation
                 internalising
international   internationally
interpersonal interpersonally
interplanetary
interplay

interpolate	interpolating
	interpolation
interpose	interposing
interpret	interpreted interpreter
	interpreting
interpretation	
interracial	
interregnum	interregnums/interregna
interrogate	interrogating
	interrogation
	interrogator
interrupt	interrupted interrupting
	interruption
intersect	intersected intersecting
	intersection
intersperse	interspersing
intertwine	intertwining
interval	
intervene	intervening
intervention	
interview	interviewed interviewee
	interviewer interviewing
interweave	interweaving interwove
	interwoven
intestate	
intestine	intestinal intestinally
intimacy	
intimate	intimating intimation
intimidate	intimidating
	intimidatingly
	intimidation
into	
intolerable	intolerableness
	intolerably
intolerance	
intolerant	intolerantly
intonation	
intone	intoning
intoxicate	intoxicating
	intoxication
intractable	intractability
	intractably
intransigence	
intransigent	intransigently
intransitive	
intravenous	intravenously
intrepid	intrepidity intrepidly

intricate	intricately intricacy
intrigue	intriguing intriguingly
intrinsic	intrinsically
introduce	introducing
introduction	
introductory	
introspective	introspectively
	introspection
introversion	
introvert	introverted
intrude	intruding intrusion
intrusive	intrusively
	intrusiveness
intuition	
intuitive	intuitively
	intuitiveness
inundate	inundating inundation
inured	
invade	invader invading
	invasion
invalid	invalidity
invalidate	invalidating
	invalidation
invaluable	invaluably
invariable	invariability invariably
invasion	
invective	
inveigh	inveighed inveighing
inveigle	inveigling
invent	invented inventing
	invention
inventive	inventively
	inventiveness
inventor	
inventory	inventories
inverse	inversely
invert	inverted inverting
	inversion
invertebrate	
invest	invested investing
	investor
investigate	investigating
	investigation
	investigative
investigator	investigatory
investment	
inveterate	inveterately inveteracy

invidious	invidiously	irrelevance	
	invidiousness	irrelevant	irrelevantly
invigilate	invigilating invigilation	irreligious	irreligiously
	invigilator		irreligiousness/irreligion
invigorate	invigorating	irremediable	irremediableness
	invigoration		irremediably
invincible	invincibility invincibly	irremovable	irremovability
inviolable	inviolability inviolably		irremovably
inviolate		irreparable	irreparability irreparably
invisible	invisibility invisibly	irreplaceable	irreplaceably
invitation		irrepressible	irrepressibility
invite	inviting invitingly		irrepressibly
invocation		irreproachable	irreproachability
invoice	invoicing		irreproachably
invoke	invoking	irresistible	irresistibility irresistibly
involuntary	involuntarily	irresolute	irresolutely
	involuntariness		irresoluteness/
involve	involvement involving		irresolution
invulnerable	invulnerability	irrespective	irrespectively
	invulnerably	irresponsible	irresponsibility
inward	inwardly		irresponsibly
iodine		irretrievable	irretrievability
ion			irretrievably
iota		irreverence	
irascible	irascibility irascibly	irreverent	irreverently
ire	irate	irreversible	irreversibility
iridescence			irreversibly
iridescent	iridescently	irrevocable	irrevocability
iris			irrevocably
irk	irked irking	**irrigate**	irrigating irrigation
irksome	irksomely irksomeness	irritable	irritability irritably
iron	ironed ironing	irritant	
irony	ironic ironically	irritate	irritating irritatingly
	ironies		irritation
irradiate	irradiating irradiation	**Islam**	Islamic
irrational	irrationality irrationally	island	
irreconcilable	irreconcilability	**isle**	
	irreconcilably	islet	
irrecoverable	irrecoverability	**isn't**	
	irrecoverably	**isobar**	
irredeemable	irredeemability	**isolate**	isolating isolation
	irredeemably	**isometrics**	
irreducible	irreducibility	**isosceles**	
	irreducibly	**isotope**	
irrefutable	irrefutability	**issue**	issuing
	irrefutably	**isthmus**	isthmuses/isthmi
irregular	irregularity irregularly	**italic**	

itch — itched itches itching
itchy — itchier itchiest itchily itchiness

item
itemise — itemisation itemising
itinerant
itinerary — itineraries
its (of it)
it's (it is/has)
itself
ivory — ivories
ivy — ivies

jab — jabbed jabbing
jabber — jabbered jabbering
jack — jacked jacking
jackal
jackass — jackasses
jackdaw
jacket — jacketed jacketing
jackknife
jackpot
Jacuzzi
jade
jaded
jag — jagged jagging
jaguar
jail/gaol — jailed/gaoled jailing/gaoling
jailer/gaoler
jam — jammed jamming
jamb
jamboree
jangle — jangling
January
jar — jarred jarring jarringly
jargon
jasmine
jaundice
jaunt
jaunty — jauntier jauntiest jauntily jauntiness
javelin
jaw
jay
jaywalk — jaywalked jaywalker jaywalking
jazz

jazzy	jazzier jazziest jazzily jazziness	joint	jointed jointly
jealous	jealously jealousy	**joist**	
jeans		**joke**	joker jokily joking
Jeep		**jolly**	jollied jollier jolliest jollily jollity/jolliness jollying
jeer	jeered jeering jeeringly		
Jehovah		**jolt**	jolted jolting
jelly	jellied jellies	**joss–stick**	
jeopardise	jeopardising jeopardy	**jostle**	jostling
jerbil/gerbil		**jot**	jotted jotter jotting
jerk	jerked jerking	**journal**	
jerky	jerkily jerkiness	journalism	journalist
jersey		journey	journeyed journeying
jester		**joust**	jousted jousting
Jesus		**jovial**	joviality jovially
jet	jetted jetting	**jowl**	
jetsam		**joy**	joyous joyously joyousness
jettison	jettisoned jettisoning		
jetty	jetties	**joyful**	joyfully joyfulness
Jew	Jewish Jewishness Jewry	**joyless**	joylessly joylessness
jewel	jewelled jeweller jewelling	**joystick**	
		jubilant	jubilantly
jewellery		jubilation	
Jewess	Jewesses	jubilee	
jib	jibbed jibbing	**Judas**	
jiffy	jiffies	**judge**	judging
jig	jigged jigging	judgement/judgment	
jigsaw		**judicial**	judicially
jilt	jilted jilting	judiciary	judiciaries
jingle	jingling	judicious	judiciously judiciousness
jink (to dodge)	jinked jinking		
jinx (to bring bad luck)		**judo**	
	jinxed jinxing	**jug**	jugged jugging
jitter	jittered jittering	**juggernaut**	
jittery	jitteriness	juggle	juggler juggling
jive	jived jiving	**jugular**	
job	jobbed jobbing	**juice**	
jobber		juicy	juicier juiciest juicily juiciness
jockey	jockeyed jockeying		
jocular	jocularity jocularly	**ju–jitsu**	
jodhpurs		**jukebox**	
joey		**July**	
jog	jogged jogger jogging	**jumble**	jumbling
join	joined joining	jumbo	
joiner	joinery	**jump**	jumped jumper jumping

jumpy　　　　　jumpier jumpiest
　　　　　　　　jumpily jumpiness

junction
June
jungle
junior
juniper
junk　　　　　junked junking
junket
junkie
junta
Jupiter
jurisdiction
jury　　　　　juries juror
just　　　　　justly justness
justice
justifiable　　　justifiableness
　　　　　　　　justifiably
justification
justify　　　　　justified justifies
　　　　　　　　justifying
jut　　　　　jutted jutting
jute
juvenile
juxtapose　　juxtaposing
　　　　　　　　juxtaposition

Kk

kaftan/caftan
kale/kail
kaleidoscope　　kaleidoscopic
kamikaze
kangaroo
karate
karma
kayak
kazoo
kebab
kedgeree
keel　　　　　keeled keeling
keen　　　　　keener keenest keenly
　　　　　　　　keenness
keep　　　　　keeper keeping kept
keepsake
keg
kelp
kendo
kennel　　　　kennelled kennelling
kept
kerb
kernel
kestrel
ketch
ketchup
kettle
kettledrum
key　　　　　keyed keying
keyboard
keyhole
khaki
kibbutz　　　kibbutzim
kick　　　　　kicked kicker kicking
kid　　　　　kidded kidding

kidnap	kidnapped kidnapper kidnapping	**knack**	
		knapsack	
kidney		**knave**	knavish knavishly knavishness
kill	killed killer killing		
killjoy		knavery	knaveries
kiln		**knead**	kneaded kneading
kilo	kilogram(me) kilometre kilowatt	**knee**	
		kneecap	
kilt	kilted	kneel	kneeler kneeling knelt
kimono		**knell**	
kin		knelt	
kind	kinder kindest kindness	**knew**	
		knickerbockers	
kindergarten		knickers	
kindle	kindling	knick-knack	
kindly	kindlier kindliest kindliness	**knife**	knifing knives
		knight	knighted knighthood knighting
kindred	kindredship	**knit**	knitted knitting
king	kingliness kingly	knitwear	
kingdom		**knives**	
kingfisher		**knob**	
king-size		**knock**	knocked knocker knocking
kink	kinkier kinkiest kinkily kinkiness kinky		
		knockout	
		knoll	
kinsfolk		**knot**	knotted knotting
kinship		knotty	
kinsman	kinsmen	**know**	knew knowing knowingly knowingness
kinswoman	kinswomen		
kiosk			
kipper	kippered kippering	knowledge	
kirk		knowledgeable	knowledgeability knowledgeably
kismet			
kiss	kissed kisser kissing	**knuckle**	knuckling
kissable		**koala**	
kit	kitted kitting	**kofta**	
kitbag		**kookaburra**	
kitchen		**Koran**	Koranic
kite		**korma**	
kitsch		**kosher**	
kitten	kittenish kittenishly kittenishness	**kowtow**	kowtowed kowtowing
kittiwake		**kraal**	
kitty	kitties	**kris**	
kiwi		**kumquat**	
klaxon		**kung fu**	
Kleenex	Kleenexes		
kleptomania	kleptomaniac		

label	labelled labelling
laboratory	laboratories
laborious	
labour	laboured labourer labouring
laburnum	
labyrinth	labyrinthine
lace	lacier laciest lacily lacing laciness lacy
lacerate	lacerating laceration
lack	lacked lacking
lackadaisical	lackadaisically
lackey	
lacklustre	
lacquer	lacquered lacquering
lacrosse	
lacy	lacier laciest laciness
ladder	laddered
ladle	ladling
lady	ladies ladyship
ladylike	
lag	lagged lagging
lager	
lagoon	
laid	
lair	
laird	
lake	
lama (Buddhist monk)	
lamb	lambed lambing
lame	lamer lamest lamely lameness laming
lament	lamented lamenting
lamentable	
lamp	

lampoon	lampooned lampooning
lance	lancing
lance-corporal	
lancer	
land	landed landing
landfill	
landlady	landladies
landlord	
landlubber	
landmark	
landscape	
landslide	
lane	
language	
languid	languidly languidness
languish	languished languishes languishing
languor	languorous languorously
lank	lankly lankness
lanky	lankier lankiest lankily lankiness
lanolin	
lantern	
lap	lapped lapping
lapel	
lapidary	lapidaries lapidarist
lapse	lapsing
laptop	
lapwing	
larceny	larcenies larcenous larcenously
larch	larches
lard	larded larding
larder	
large	largely largeness larger largest (biggest)
largesse/largess (generosity)	
largo	
lariat	
lark	larked larking
larva	larvae larval
laryngitis	
larynx	larynxes
lasagne	

lascivious	lasciviously
	lasciviousness
laser	
lash	lashed lashes lashing
lass	lasses
lasso	lassoed lassoes
	lassoing
last	lasted lasting
latch	latched latches
	latching
late	lately lateness
latency	latencies
latent	latently
lateral	laterally
latex	
lath (piece of wood)	
lathe (machinery)	
lather	lathered lathering
Latin	Latinate
latitude	latitudinal latitudinally
latter	latterly
lattice	
laud	lauded lauding
laudable	laudably
laugh	laughed laughing
	laughingly
laughable	laughably
laughing-stock	
laughter	
launch	launched launcher
	launches launching
launder	laundered laundering
launderette/laundrette	
laundress	laundresses
laundry	laundries
laurel	
lava (molten rock)	
lavatory	lavatories
lavender	
lavish	lavished lavishes
	lavishing lavishly
	lavishness
law	
lawful	lawfully lawfulness
lawless	lawlessly lawlessness
lawn	
lawnmower	

lawyer	
lax	
laxative	
lay	laid laying
layabout	
lay-by	
layer	layered
layout	
laze	lazing
lazy	lazier laziest lazily
	laziness
lea	
leach (to wash out)	leached leaches
	leaching
lead	leader leading led
leaden	
leader	leadership
leaf	leafed leafing leaves
leaflet	
leafy	leafier leafiest
	leafiness
league	
leak	leaked leaking
leakage	
leaky	leakier leakiest
	leakiness
lean	leaned leaner leanest
	leaning leant
leant	
leap	leaped leaping leapt
leapt	
learn	learned/learnt learner
	learning
lease	leasing
leash	leashed leashes
	leashing
least	
leather	leatheriness leathery
leave	leaving
lecherous	lecher lechery
lectern	
lecture	lecturer lecturing
led	
ledge	
ledger	
lee	
leech (creature)	leeches

leek

leer   leered leerer leering

left

leftovers

leg   legged legging

legacy   legacies

legal   legality legally

legalise   legalising legalisation

legalism

legalistic   legalistically

legato

legend   legendary

leggings

legible   legibility legibly

legion

legionnaire

legislate   legislating legislation
     legislative legislator

legitimacy   legitimacies

legitimate   legitimately

legitimise   legitimising

leisure   leisurely

lemming

lemon

lemonade

lemur

lend   lender lending lent

length

lengthen   lengthened
     lengthening

lengthy   lengthier lengthiest
     lengthily lengthiness

leniency

lenient   leniently

lens   lenses

Lent/lent   Lenten

lentil

lento

Leo

leopard   leopardess

leotard

leper

leprechaun

leprosy

less

lessen (make less)   lessened lessening

lesser

lesson (instruction)

let   letting

lethal   lethally

lethargy   lethargic lethargically

letter   lettered lettering

letter-box   letter-boxes

letterhead

lettuce

leukaemia

level   levelled leveller
     levelling

lever   levered levering

leverage

leveret

leviathan

levitate   levitating levitation

levity   levities

levy   levied levies levying

lewd   lewder lewdest lewdly
     lewdness

lexicon   lexical lexically

liability   liabilities

liable

liaise   liaising

liaison

liar

libel   libelled libelling
     libellous

liberal   liberality liberally

liberate   liberating liberation

liberty   liberties

Libra

library   librarian libraries

libretto   librettist

lice

licence (noun)

license (verb)   licensee licensing

lichen

lick   licked licking

lid   lidded

lido

lie (to tell untruths)   liar lied lies lying

lie (to rest in a horizontal position)
     lain lay lying

lieutenant

life   lifer lives

lifebelt

lifeboat
lifeless   lifelessly lifelessness
lifestyle
lift   lifted lifting
ligament
light   lighted/lit lighter
                              lightest lighting
                              lightly lightness
lighten   lightened lightening
                              (making lighter)
lightning (flash in the sky)
like   likelihood
likeable/likable
likely   likelier likeliest
liken   likened likening
lilac
Lilo
lilt   lilted lilting liltingly
lily   lilies
limb
limber   limbered limbering
limbless   limblessness
limbo
lime
limelight
limerick
limestone
limit   limited limiting
limitation
limitless   limitlessly limitlessness
limousine
limp   limped limping
limpet
linchpin
linctus
line   lining
lineage
linear   linearity linearly
linen
liner
linger   lingered lingering
                              lingeringly
lingerie
linguistics   linguist
link   linked linking
linnet
linoleum

linseed
lint
lintel
lion
lioness
lionise   lioniser lionising
lip   lipped lipping
lipstick
liquefaction
liquefy   liquefied liquefies
                              liquefying
liqueur
liquid   liquidity liquidly
liquidate   liquidating liquidation
liquidise   liquidising .
liquidiser
liquor
liquorice/licorice
lisp   lisped lisping
lissom/lissome   lissomly lissomness
list   listed listing
listen   listened listener
                              listening
listless   listlessly listlessness
litany   litanies
literacy
literal   literally literalness
literary
literate   literately literateness
literature
litigate   litigating litigation
                              litigator
litmus
litre
litter   littered littering
little   littleness
liturgy   liturgical liturgically
                              liturgies
live   living
liveable
livelihood
lively   livelier liveliest
                              liveliness
liver
liverish   liverishly liverishness
livery   liveries
lives

livid lividness
lizard
llama (animal)
load loaded loader loading
loaf loafed loafing loaves
loam loamy
loan
loath/loth (unwilling)
loathe (to detest) loathing
loathsome
loaves
lob lobbed lobbing
lobby lobbies
lobe
lobelia
lobster
local (nearby) locality locally
locale (place)
locate locating location
loch (Scottish lake)
lock locked locker locking
locket
locomotion locomotive
locust
lodge lodger lodging
loft lofted lofting
lofty loftier loftiest loftily
loftiness
log logged logging
logarithm logarithmic
logic logical logicality
logically
logistics
loin
loincloth
loiter loitered loiterer
loitering
loll · lolled lolling
lollipop
lone
lonely lonelier loneliest
loneliness
loner
lonesome lonesomely
lonesomeness
long longed longer longest
longing longingly

longevity
longitude longitudinal
longitudinally
loofah
look looked looker looking
loom loomed looming
loop looped looping
loose (not tight, untied)
loosely looseness
looser loosest loosing
loosen loosened loosening
loot looted looter looting
lop lopped lopping
lopsided lopsidedly
lopsidedness
loquacious loquaciously loquacity
lord lorded lording
lordly lordliness
lordship
lore
lorry lorries
lose (not to win; misplace)
loser losing lost
loss losses
lost
lotion
lottery lotteries
lotus lotuses
loud louder loudest loudly
loudness
loudspeaker
lounge lounging
louse lice
lousy lousier lousiest lousily
lousiness
lout loutish loutishly
loutishness
louvre
lovable/loveable lovability lovableness
lovably
love lover loving lovingly
lovely lovelier loveliest
loveliness
low lower lowest
lower lowered lowering
lowly lowlier lowliest
lowliness

loyal	loyally loyalty
lozenge	
lubricant	
lubricate	lubricating lubrication
lucid	lucidity lucidly
luck	
luckless	lucklessly lucklessness
lucky	luckier luckiest luckily
lucrative	
ludicrous	ludicrously
	ludicrousness
ludo	
lug	lugged lugging
luggage	
lugubrious	lugubriously
	lugubriousness
lukewarm	
lull	lulled lulling
lullaby	lullabies
lumbago	
lumber	lumbered lumbering
	lumberingly
luminous	luminosity luminously
	luminousness
lump	lumped lumping
	lumpy
lumpen	
lumpish	lumpishly lumpishness
lunar	
lunatic	lunacy
lunch	lunched lunches
	lunching
luncheon	
lung (part of body)	
lunge (to move forward)	
	lunging
lupin	
lurch	lurched lurches
	lurching
lure	luring
lurid	luridly luridness
lurk	lurked lurking
luscious	lusciously lusciousness
lush	lushly lushness
lustre	lustrous
luxuriance	
luxuriant	luxuriantly

luxuriate	
luxurious	luxuriously
	luxuriousness/luxury
luxury	luxuries
lychee	
Lycra	
lymph	
lynch	lynched lynches
	lynching
lynx	lynxes
lyre	
lyric	lyricist
lyrical	lyrically

Mm

macabre
macadam
macaroni
macaroon
macaw
mace
machete
machiavellian
machine · machining
machinery
machinist
machismo · macho
mackerel
mackintosh/macintosh
· mackintoshes/
macintoshes
macramé
mad · madder maddest
madly madness
madam
madden · maddened maddening
maddeningly
made
Madeira (cake; wine)
madonna/Madonna
madrigal
maestro
Mafia · Mafioso (member)
Mafiosi (plural)
magazine
magenta
maggot · maggoty
Magi
magic · magical magically
magician

magisterial · magisterially
magistrate
magma
magnanimity
magnanimous · magnanimously
magnate
magnesia
magnesium
magnet · magnetic magnetically
magnetism
magnification
magnificence
magnificent · magnificently
magnify · magnified magnifies
magnifying
magnitude
magnolia
magnum
magpie
maharaja/maharajah
maharanee/maharani
mahogany · mahoganies
maid
maiden · maidenly
maidenhood
mail · mailed mailing
maim · maimed maiming
main · mainly
mainframe
mainland
mainspring
mainstay
maintain · maintained
maintaining
maintenance
maisonette/maisonnette
maître (d'hôtel)
maize
majestic · majestically
majesty · majesties
major
majorette
majority · majorities
make · made maker making
makeshift
maladjusted · maladjustment

109

maladroit	maladroitly
	maladroitness
malady	maladies
malaise	
malapropism	
malaria	
male	maleness
malefactor	
malevolence	
malevolent	malevolently
malfunction	malfunctioned
	malfunctioning
malice	
malicious	maliciously
	maliciousness/malice
malign	malignities malignity
	malignly
malignancy	malignancies
malignant	malignantly
malinger	malingered malingerer
	malingering
mall	
mallard	
malleable	malleability
mallet	
malnutrition	
malpractice	
malt	malted malting
maltreat	maltreated
	maltreating
maltreatment	
mammal	mammalian
mammoth	
man	manned manning
manacle	
manage	manager managing
manageable	manageability
	manageably
management	
manatee	
mandarin	
mandate	mandating
mandatory	
mandible	
mandolin	
mane	
manfully	

manger	
mange-tout	
mangle	mangling
mango	mangoes/mangos
mangy	mangier mangiest
	mangily manginess
manhood	
mania	manic maniac
	maniacal maniacally
manicure	manicurist
manifest	manifested
	manifesting manifestly
manifestation	
manifesto	
manifold	
manikin (dwarf; model of body)	
manipulate	manipulating
	manipulation
	manipulator
manipulative	
mankind	
manly	manlier manliest
	manliness
manna (miracle food)	
mannequin (shop window dummy; fashion model)	
manner (way thing is done)	
	mannered mannerly
	mannerliness
mannerism	
manoeuvrable	manoeuvrability
manoeuvre	manoeuvrer
	manoeuvring
manor (large house)	
manse	
mansion	
manslaughter	
mantelpiece	
mantelshelf	
mantis	mantises
mantle (clothing)	
mantra	
manual	manually
manufacture	manufacturing
manure	
manuscript	
many	

map	mapped mapping
maple	
mar	marred marring
marathon	
maraud	marauder marauding
marble	marbling
March	
march	marched marcher
	marches marching
marchioness	marchionesses
mare	
margarine	
margin	
marginal	marginalise
	marginality marginally
marigold	
marijuana/marihuana	
marina	
marinade/marinate	marinading/marinating
marine	mariner
marionette	
marital	maritally
maritime	
marjoram	
mark	marked marker
	marking
market	marketable marketing
marksman	marksmen
marksmanship	
marmalade	
marmoset	
maroon	
marquee (tent)	
marquess (British nobleman)	
	marquesses
marquis (foreign nobleman)	
	marquises
marriage	
marriageable	marriageability
marrow	
marry	married marries
	marrying
Mars	
marsh	marshes
marshal (an official)	marshalled marshalling
marshmallow	
marsupial	

marten (animal)	
martial (to do with warfare)	
	martially
Martian	
martin (bird)	
martingale	
martyr	martyred martyring
martyrdom	
marvel	marvelled marvelling
marvellous	marvellously
	marvellousness
marzipan	
mascara	
mascot	
masculine	masculinity
mash	mashed masher
	mashes mashing
mask	masked masking
masochism	masochist
mason	masonry
Mason	Masonic
masque	
masquerade	
mass/Mass	massed massing
massacre	massacring
massage	massaging
masseur	
masseuse	
massive	massively massiveness
mast	masted
master	mastered mastering
masterful	masterfully
	masterfulness
masterly	masterliness
mastermind	
mastery	
mastic	
masticate	masticating
	mastication
mastiff	
mat (piece of fabric)	matted matting
matador	
match	matched matches
	matching
matchless	
mate	mating
material	materially

materialise	materialising	**mean**	meaner meanest
materialism	materialist materialistic		meaning meanly
maternal	maternally		meanness meant
maternity	maternities	meander	meandered
mathematical	mathematically		meandering
mathematics	mathematician		meanderingly
matinée		meaningful	
matins		meaningless	
matriarch	matriarchal	means	
	matriarchies	meanwhile	
	matriarchy	**measles**	
matricide		measurable	measurability
matriculate	matriculating		measurably
	matriculation	measure	measuring
matrimony	matrimonial	measurement	
	matrimonially	**meat**	
matrix	matrices/matrixes	meaty	meatier meatiest
matron	matronly		meatily meatiness
matt (paint finish)		**Mecca**	
matter	mattered mattering	Meccano	
matting		**mechanic**	mechanical
mattress	mattresses		mechanically
mature	maturely maturing	mechanise	mechanising
	maturity		mechanisation
matzo		mechanism	
maudlin		**medal** (award, prize)	medallist
maul	mauled mauling	medallion	
mausoleum		**meddle** (interfere)	meddling
mauve		**media**	
maverick		mediaeval/medieval	
mawkish	mawkishly	median	
	mawkishness	mediate	mediating mediation
		mediator	
maxim		medical	medically
maximise	maximisation	medicament	
maximum	maximums/maxima	medication	
may/May		medicinal	medicinally
maybe		medicine	
mayhem		medieval/mediaeval	
mayonnaise		mediocre	mediocrities
mayor	mayoral		mediocrity
mayoress	mayoresses	meditate	meditating meditation
maze			meditator
meadow		meditative	meditatively
meagre	meagrely meagreness		meditativeness
meal	mealy	Mediterranean	
		medium	media/mediums

medley
meek   meeker   meekest
                                  meekly   meekness
meet   meeting   met
megabyte
megaphone
megastar
melancholy   melancholia
                                  melancholic
                                  melancholically
                                  melancholies
melanoma
mêlée
mellifluence   mellifluent
mellifluous   mellifluously
                                  mellifluousness
mellow   mellowed   mellower
                                  mellowest   mellowing
melodic   melodically
melodious   melodiously
                                  melodiousness
melodrama   melodramatic
                                  melodramatically
melody   melodies
melon
melt   melted   melting
                                  meltingly
member   membership
membrane   membranous
memento   mementos/mementoes
memo
memoir
memorabilia
memorable   memorability
                                  memorably
memorandum   memoranda/
                                  memorandums
memorial   memorially
memory   memories
menace   menacing   menacingly
menagerie
mend   mended   mender
                                  mending
mendacious
mendicant
menial   menially
meningitis

menopause   menopausal
menstrual
menstruate   menstruating
                                  menstruation
mental   mentally
mentality   mentalities
menthol
mention   mentionable
                                  mentioned   mentioning
mentor
menu
mercantile
mercenary   mercenaries
merchandise
merchant
merciful   mercifully
                                  mercifulness
merciless   mercilessly
                                  mercilessness
mercurial   mercurially
mercury/Mercury
mercy   mercies
mere
merge   merging
merger
meridian
meringue
merit   merited   meriting
meritocracy   meritocracies
meritorious   meritoriously
                                  meritoriousness
merlin
mermaid
merriment
merry   merrier   merriest
                                  merrily   merriness
mesh   meshed   meshes
                                  meshing
mesmerise   mesmeric   mesmerising
mess   messed   messes
                                  messing
message
messenger
Messiah
messy   messier   messiest
                                  messily   messiness
metabolism

metal (steel, for example)
                        metallic
metamorphic
metamorphosis   metamorphoses
metaphor   metaphoric
                        metaphorical
                        metaphorically
metaphysical   metaphysically
                        metaphysics
meteor   meteoric meteorically
meteorite
meteorology   meteorological
                        meteorologically
meter (measuring device)
methane
method   methodical
                        methodically
Methodist
meticulous   meticulously
                        meticulousness
metre (measure of length)
metric   metrical metrically
metrication
metronome
metropolis   metropolitan
mettle (courage)
mew   mewed mewing
miaow
mice
microbe
microchip
microcomputer
microcosm
microfiche
microlight
microphone
microprocessor
microscope   microscopic
                        microscopically
microsurgery
microwave
midday
midden
middle   middling
midge
midget
midnight

midriff
midships
midst
midsummer
midwife   midwifery midwives
midwinter
miffed
might (could/possible/power)
mighty   mightier mightiest
                        mightily mightiness
migraine
migrant
migrate   migrating migration
                        migratory
mild   milder mildest mildly
                        mildness
mildew   mildewed
mile   miler
mileage/milage
milieu   milieus/milieux
militancy
militant   militantly
military   militarily
militate   militating
militia
milk   milked milker milking
milky   milkier milkiest
                        milkiness
mill   milled miller milling
millennium   millennia/millenniums
millet
milliner   millinery
million
millionaire
millionairess
millipede/millepede
milometer
mime   miming
mimic   mimicked mimicking
mimicry   mimicries
minaret
mince   mincer mincing
                        mincingly
mincemeat
mind   minded minder
                        minding
mindful   mindfully mindfulness

mindless	mindlessly	misapprehensive	
	mindlessness	misappropriate	misappropriation
mine	miner mining	**misbehave**	misbehaving
mineral		misbehaviour	
minestrone		**miscalculate**	miscalculating
mingle	mingling		miscalculation
miniature	miniaturisation	miscarriage	
	miniaturise	miscellaneous	miscellaneously
minibus	minibuses	miscellany	miscellanies
minicab		mischief	
minim		mischievous	mischievously
minimal	minimally		mischievousness
minimise	minimisation	misconduct	
	minimising	misconstrue	misconstruction
minimum	minimums/minima		misconstruing
minion			
miniskirt		**misdeed**	
minister	ministered ministering	misdemeanour	
	ministration	**miser**	miserliness miserly
ministry	ministries	miserable	miserably
mink		misery	miseries
minnow		**misfit**	
minor		misfortune	
minority	minorities	**misgiving**	
minster		misguided	
minstrel		**mishap**	
mint	minted minting	mishear	misheard
minuet		**misinform**	misinformed
minus			misinforming
minuscule		misinformation	
minute	minutely minuteness	misinterpret	misinterpreted
miracle			misinterpreting
miraculous	miraculously		misinterpretation
	miraculousness	**misjudge**	misjudging
mirage		misjudgement/misjudgment	
mire	miring	**mislead**	misleading misled
mirror	mirrored mirroring	**misplace**	misplacing
mirth		misplacement	
mirthful	mirthfully	misprint	
mirthless	mirthlessly	**miss**	missed misses
miry	miriness		missing
misadventure		missal	
misanthropist	misanthropic	misshapen	
	misanthropy	missile	
misapprehend	misapprehended	mission	
	misapprehending	missionary	missionaries
misapprehension		misspell	misspelt/misspelled
			misspelling

mist
mistake | mistaken mistakenly
mister
mistletoe
mistreat | mistreated mistreating
| mistreatment
mistress | mistresses
mistrust | mistrusted mistrusting
mistrustful | mistrustfully
| mistrustfulness/mistrust
misty | mistier mistiest
| mistiness
misunderstand | misunderstanding
| misunderstood
misuse | misusing
mite (small spider; small child)
mitre
mitten
mix | mixed mixes mixing
mixer
mixture
moan | moaned moaner
| moaning
moat | moated
mob | mobbed mobbing
mobile | mobility
mobilise | mobilisation
| mobilising
moccasin
mock | mocked mocker
| mocking mockingly
mockery | mockeries
mock-up
mode | modish modishly
| modishness
model | modelled modelling
modem
moderate | moderately moderating
| moderation
moderator
modern | modernity
modernise | modernisation
modest | modestly
modesty | modesties
modification
modify | modified modifies
| modifying

modulate | modulating
| modulation modulator
module | modular
mohair
moist | moistly moistness
moisten | moistened moistening
moisture
moisturise | moisturiser
| moisturising

molar
molasses
mole
molecule | molecular
molehill
moleskin
molest | molested molester
| molesting molestation
mollify | mollified mollifies
| mollifying

mollusc
molten
moment
momentary | momentarily
momentous | momentously
| momentousness
momentum
monarch | monarchical
| monarchically
| monarchist
monarchy | monarchies
monastery | monasteries
monastic | monastically
monasticism
Monday
monetary | monetarism
| monetarist
money | moneyed
mongoose | *plural* mongooses
mongrel
monitor | monitored monitoring
monk | monkish
monkey
monochrome
monocle
monogamy | monogamous
| monogamously
monologue

monopolise | monopolising
| monopolisation
monopoly | monopolies
monosyllable | monosyllabic
| monosyllabically
monotonous | monotonously
| monotonousness
monotony | monotonies
monsoon
monster
monstrosity | monstrosities
monstrous | monstrously
| monstrousness
montage
month | monthly
monument | monumental
| monumentally
mood | moody moodier
| moodiest moodiness
moon | mooned mooning
moor | moored mooring
moose
mop | mopped (wiped floor)
| mopping
mope | moping
moped (motor)
moral (right and wrong)
| morality morally
morale (confidence)
moralise | moralising
morass | morasses
morbid | morbidly
| morbidness/morbidity
morbidity
more
moreover
morgue
morning (time of day)
morocco
moron | moronic moronically
morose | morosely moroseness
morphine
Morse code
morsel
mortal | mortally
mortality | mortalities
mortar

mortgage | mortgaging
mortgagee
mortgager/mortgagor
mortify | mortification mortified
| mortifies mortifying
mortuary | mortuaries
mosaic
Moslem/Muslim | Moslemism/Muslimism
mosque
mosquito | mosquitoes
moss | mosses mossed
| mossing
mossy | mossier mossiest
| mossiness
most | mostly
mote
motel
moth
mother | mothered mothering
motherhood
mother-in-law | mothers-in-law
motif (idea)
motion | motioned motioning
motionless
motivate | motivating motivation
motive (reason, purpose)
motiveless | motivelessly
| motivelessness
motley
motor | motored motoring
motorist
motorway
mottle | mottling
motto | mottoes
mould | moulded moulding
mouldy | mouldier mouldiest
| mouldiness
moult | moulted moulting
mound
mount | mounted mounting
mountain | mountainous
mountaineer | mountaineered
| mountaineering
mourn | mourned mourner
| mourning (showing
| sorrow)

mournful	mournfully
	mournfulness
mouse	mice mouser
	mousing
moussaka/mousaka	
mousse	
moustache	
mousy	
mouth	mouthed mouthing
movable/moveable	movably/moveably
move	moving movingly
movement	
movie	
mow	mowed mower
	mowing
mozzarella	
much	muchness
muck	mucked mucking
mucus	
mud	
muddle	muddling
muddy	muddied muddies
	muddiness muddier
	muddiest muddily
	muddying
muesli	
muezzin	
muff	muffed muffing
muffin	
muffle	muffler muffling
mug	mugged mugger
	mugging
muggy	muggier muggiest
	mugginess
mulatto	mulattos/mulattoes
mulberry	mulberries
mulch	mulches
mule	mulish mulishly
	mulishness
mull	mulled mulling
mullah	
mullet	
mulligatawny	
mullion	
multicultural	multiculturally
multifaceted	

multifarious	multifariously
	multifariousness
multinational	
multiple	
multiply	multiplied multiplier
	multiplies multiplying
multiracial	
multistorey	
multitude	multitudinous
	multitudinously
mum	
mumble	mumbling mumblingly
mummify	mummification
	mummified
	mummifies
	mummifying
mummy	mummies
mumpish	mumpishly
	mumpishness
mumps	
munch	munched munches
	munching
mundane	mundanely
	mundaneness
municipal	municipalities
	municipality
	municipally
munitions	
mural	
murder	murdered murdering
murderer	
murderess	
murderous	murderously
	murderousness
murk	
murky	murkier murkiest
	murkily murkiness
murmur	murmured murmuring
muscle (part of body)	muscling
muscular	muscularity
muse	musing musingly
museum	
mush	
mushroom	mushroomed
	mushrooming
mushy	mushier mushiest
	mushily mushiness

music musician
musical musicality musically
musk
musket musketeer
Muslim/Moslem Muslimism/Moslemism
muslin
muss mussed mussing
mussel (sea creature)
must
mustang
mustard
muster mustered mustering
musty mustier mustiest
mustily mustiness

mutant
mutation
mute muted mutely
muteness
mutilate mutilating mutilation
mutiny mutineer mutinies
mutinous
mutter muttered muttering
mutton
mutual mutuality mutually
muzzle muzzling
myopia myopic myopically
myriad
myrrh
myrtle
myself
mysterious mysteriously
mysteriousness
mystery mysteries
mystic (holy person) mystical mystically
mysticism
mystify mystified mystifying
mystifyingly
mystique (power)
myth mythic mythical
mythically
mythological mythologically
mythology mythologies
myxomatosis

Nn

nab nabbed nabbing
nadir
nag nagged nagging
nail nailed nailing
naive naively naivety
naked nakedly nakedness
namby-pamby
name namely naming
nameless namelessly
namelessness
nanny nannies
nap (sleep) napped napping
napalm
nape (of neck)
napkin
nappy nappies
narcissism narcissist narcissistic
narcissistically
narcissus narcissi
narcotic
narcotics
narrate narrating narration
narrator
narrative
narrow narrowed narrower
narrowest narrowing
nasal nasally
nasturtium
nasty nastier nastiest
nastily nastiness
nation national nationally
nationalisation
nationalise nationalising

nationalism	nationalist
	nationalistic
	nationalistically
nationality	nationalities
native	
nativity	
natter	nattered nattering
natterjack (toad)	
natty	nattier nattiest nattily
	nattiness
natural	naturally naturalness
naturalise	naturalising
naturalist	naturalism naturalistic
	naturalistically
nature	
naturist	naturism
naught	
naughty	naughtier naughtiest
	naughtily naughtiness
nausea	nauseous nauseously
	nauseousness
nauseate	nauseating
	nauseatingly
nautical	nautically
naval (of a navy)	
nave (part of church)	
navel (centre of belly)	
navigable	navigability
navigate	navigating navigation
	navigator
navy	navies
Nazi	Nazism
Neanderthal	
neap tide	
near	neared nearer nearest
	nearing nearly
	nearness
neat	neater neatest neatly
	neatness
nebula	nebulae/nebulas
	nebular
nebulous	nebulosity nebulously
necessarily	
necessary	necessaries
necessitate	necessitating
necessitous	
necessity	necessities

neck	necked necking
necklace	
necklet	
necromancy	necromantic
nectar	
nectarine	
need	needed needing
needful	needfully needfulness
needle	needling
needless	needlessly
	needlessness
needy	needier neediest
nefarious	nefariously
	nefariousness
negate	negating negation
negative	negatively negativity
neglect	neglected neglecting
neglectful	neglectfully
	neglectfulness
negligée	
negligence	
negligent	negligently
negligible	negligibly
negotiable	negotiability
negotiate	negotiating
	negotiation
Negress	Negresses
Negro	Negroes Negroid
neigh	neighed neighing
neighbour	neighbourliness
	neighbourly
neighbourhood	
neither	
nemesis	nemeses
neoclassical	
neocolonial	neocolonialism
neolithic	
neologism	neologist
neon	
nephew	
nepotism	
Neptune	
nerve	
nerveless	nervelessly
	nervelessness

nervous	nervously nervousness
nervy	nervier nerviest
	nervily nerviness
nest	nested nesting
nestle	nestling
net	netted netting
netball	
nettle	
network	
neural	
neuralgia	
neurosis	neuroses neurotic
	neurotically
neuter	neutered neutering
neutral	neutrality neutrally
neutralise	neutralisation
	neutralising
neutrino	
neutron	
never	
nevermore	
nevertheless	
new	newer newest newly
	newness
newborn	
newcomer	
newel	
newfangled	
newsagent	
newsflash	
newspaper	
newsworthy	newsworthiness
newt	
next	
nexus	
nib	
nibble	nibbling
nice	nicely niceness nicer
	nicest
Nicene (Creed)	
nicety	niceties
niche	
nick	nicked nicking
nickel	
nickname	
nicotine	
niece	

nifty	niftier niftiest niftily
	niftiness
niggardly	niggardliness
niggle	niggling
nigh	
night	nightly
nightdress	
nightgown	
nightie	
nightingale	
nightlight	
nightmare	
nightshade	
nightshift	
nil	
nimble	nimbleness nimbler
	nimblest nimbly
nimbus	nimbi/nimbuses
nincompoop	
nine	
nineteen	nineteenth
ninety	nineties ninetieth
ninny	ninnies
ninth	ninthly
nip	nipped nipper nipping
nipple	
nippy	nippier nippiest
	nippily nippiness
nirvana	
nit	
nit-pick	nit-picked nit-picker
	nit-picking
nitrate	
nitric	
nitrogen	
nitroglycerine	
nitty-gritty	
nitwit	
nobble (to hamper)	nobbling
Nobel (prize)	
noble (splendid)	nobility nobler
	noblest nobly
noblesse	
nobody	nobodies
noctambulism	noctambulist
nocturnal	nocturnally
nocturne	

nod (bend head) nodded nodding
node (knot) nodal
nodule nodular
noggin
noise
noiseless noiselessly
noiselessness
noisome noisomely
noisomeness
noisy noisier noisiest noisily
noisiness
nomad nomadic nomadically
nom de plume
nomenclature
nominal nominally
nominate nominating
nomination
nominative
nominee
nonagenarian
nonchalance
nonchalant nonchalantly
noncommittal
nonconformist nonconformity
nondescript
none
nonentity nonentities
nonetheless
nonplussed
non-returnable
nonsense nonsensical
nonsensically
non-stop
noodles
nook
noon
no one
noose
nor
norm
normal normality normally
normative
north northerly northern
northernmost
nose nosing
nosey/nosy nosier nosiest nosily
nosiness

nostalgia nostalgic nostalgically
nostril
nosy/nosey nosier nosiest nosily
nosiness
notable notability notably
notary notaries
notation
notch notched notches
notching
note noting
notebook
notelet
noteworthy noteworthiness
nothing nothingness
notice noticing
noticeable noticeably
notifiable notifiably
notification
notify notified notifies
notifying
notion notional notionally
notoriety
notorious notoriously
notwithstanding
nougat
nought
noun
nourish nourished nourishes
nourishing
nourishment
nous
nova novae/novas
novel novelist
novelette novelettish
novella
novelty novelties
November
novena
novice noviciate
now
nowadays
nowhere
noxious noxiously noxiousness
nozzle
nuance
nub
nubile

nuclear
nucleus — nuclei
nude — nudism nudist nudity
nudge — nudging
nugget
nuisance
nullify — nullified nullifies nullifying
numb — number numbest numbly numbness
number — numbered numbering
numberless
numeral
numerate
numeration
numerator
numerical — numerically
numerology
numerous — numerously numerousness
numinous
numismatist — numismatic numismatics
numskull
nun
nunnery — nunneries
nuptial
nurse — nursing
nursery — nurseries
nurture — nurturing
nutcracker
nutmeg
nutrient
nutrition — nutritional nutritionally nutritionist
nutritious — nutritiously nutritiousness
nutshell
nutty — nuttier nuttiest
nuzzle — nuzzling
nylon
nymph — nymphet

Oo

oaf — oafish oafishly oafishness
oak
oakum
oar — oared oaring
oasis — oases
oat
oath
oatmeal
obbligato
obduracy — obduracies
obdurate — obdurately
obedience
obedient — obediently
obeisance
obelisk
obese — obesities obesity
obey — obeyed obeying
obfuscate — obfuscating obfuscation
obituary — obituaries
object — objected objecting objection objector
objectionable — objectionably
objective — objectively objectiveness objectivity
obligate — obligating obligation
obligatory
oblige — obliging obligingly
obligement
oblique — obliquely obliqueness/obliquity
obliterate — obliterating obliteration

oblivion
oblivious   obliviously
                               obliviousness
oblong
obloquy
obnoxious   obnoxiously
                               obnoxiousness
oboe   oboist
obscene   obscenely obscenities
                               obscenity
obscure   obscurely obscurity
obsequies (death rites)
obsequious (servile)   obsequiously
                               obsequiousness
observance
observant   observantly
observation
observatory   observatories
observe   observer observing
obsess   obsessed
obsession   obsessional
                               obsessionally
obsessive   obsessively
                               obsessiveness
obsidian
obsolescent   obsolescence
obsolete   obsoleteness
obstacle
obstetric   obstetrical
                               obstetrically
                               obstetrician
obstinacy   obstinacies
obstinate   obstinately
obstreperous   obstreperously
                               obstreperousness
obstruct   obstructed obstructing
                               obstruction
obstructive   obstructively
                               obstructiveness
obtain   obtained obtaining
obtainable   obtainability
obtrude   obtruding
obtrusion
obtrusive   obtrusively
                               obtrusiveness
obtuse   obtusely obtuseness
obverse   obversely

obviate   obviating
obvious   obviously obviousness
ocarina
occasion   occasional
                               occasionally
Occident   occidental
occlude   occlusion
occult   occultism
occupancy   occupancies
occupant
occupation   occupational
occupier
occupy   occupied occupier
                               occupies occupying
occur   occurred occurring
occurrence
ocean   oceanic
oceanography   oceanographer
                               oceanographic
ocelot
ochre
o'clock
octagon   octagonal
octahedron
octane
octant
octave
octet
October
octogenarian
octopus   octopuses
ocular
oculist
odd   odder oddest oddly
                               oddness
oddity   oddities
oddment
odds
ode
odious   odiously odiousness
odium
odorous   odorously
                               odorousness
odour   odourless
odyssey
oesophagus
offal

offbeat	
offcut	
offence	
offend	offended offender offending
offensive	offensively offensiveness
offer	offered offering
offertory	offertories
offhand	offhanded offhandedly offhandedness
office	officer
official	officially
officialdom	
officiate	officiating
officious	officiously officiousness
offing	
off-peak	
offset	offsetting
offshoot	
offshore	
offside	
offspring	
oft	
often	
ogle	ogling
ogre	
ogress	
ohm	
oil	oiled oiling
oily	oilier oiliest oilily oiliness
oink	oinked oinking
ointment	
okapi	
okra	
old	older oldest
olden	
oleaginous	oleaginously oleaginousness
olfactory	
oligarch	oligarchic oligarchies oligarchy
olive	
Olympic	Olympiad Olympian

ombudsman	ombudsmen
omelette/omelet	
omen	
ominous	ominously ominousness
omission	
omit	omitted omitting
omnibus	omnibuses
omnipotence	
omnipotent	omnipotently
omniscience	
omniscient	omnisciently
omnivore	
omnivorous	omnivorously omnivorousness
once	
one	oneness
onerous	onerously onerousness
oneself	
ongoing	
onion	
onlooker	
only	
onomatopoeia	onomatopoeic/ onomatopoetic
onset	
onslaught	
onus	onuses
onward/onwards	
onyx	
oodles	
ooze	oozing oozingly
opacity	
opal	
opalescent	opalescence
opaque	opaquely opaqueness/opacity
open	opened opener opening openly openness
opera	operatic operatically
operable	
operate	operating operation operator
operational	operationally
operative	
operetta	

ophthalmic
opiate
opinion   opinionated
opium
opossum
opponent
opportune   opportunely
opportunism   opportunist
opportunity   opportunities
oppose   opposer opposing
                        opposition
opposite   oppositely
                        oppositeness
oppress   oppressed oppresses
                        oppressing oppressor
oppression
oppressive   oppressively
                        oppressiveness
opprobrious   opprobriously
opprobrium
opt   opted opting
optic
optical   optically
optician
optimist   optimistic
                        optimistically
                        optimism
optimum   optimal
option   optional optionally
optometer
opulence
opulent   opulently
opus   opuses/opera
oracle
oracular
oracy
oral   orally
orange
orangeade
orang-utan/orang-outang
orate   orating oration
orator
oratorio
oratory   oratories
orb
orbit   orbited orbiting
orbital

orchard
orchestra   orchestral orchestrally
orchestrate   orchestrating
                        orchestration
orchid
ordain   ordained ordaining
                        ordination
ordeal
order   ordered ordering
orderly   orderlies orderliness
ordinance (an instruction)
ordinary   ordinaries ordinarily
                        ordinariness
ordination
ordnance (artillery)
ore
organ   organic organically
organisation
organise   organiser organising
organism
orgasm   orgasmic orgasmically
orgiastic
orgy   orgies
oriel
orient   oriental
orientate   orientating orientation
orienteer   orienteered
                        orienteering
orifice
origami
origin   original originally
originality   originalities
originate   originating origination
ormolu
ornament   ornamented
                        ornamenting
ornamental   ornamentally
ornamentation
ornate   ornately ornateness
ornithology   ornithological
                        ornithologist
orphan   orphaned orphaning
orphanage
orrery   orreries
orthodox   orthodoxies orthodoxy
orthography   orthographical
                        orthographically

orthopaedics/orthopedics

oscillate   oscillating oscillation
                          oscillator

osier

osmosis

osprey

ossification

ossify   ossified ossifies
                          ossifying

ostensible   ostensibly

ostentation

ostentatious   ostentatiously

osteopath   osteopathy

ostracise   ostracising ostracism

ostrich   ostriches

other

otherwise

otter

ought

oughtn't

Ouija (board)

ounce

our   ours

ourselves

oust   ousted ousting

out

outback

outbid

outboard

outbreak

outbuilding

outcast

outclass   outclassed outclasses
                         outclassing

outcome

outcry   outcries

outdated

outdid

outdo   outdid outdoes
                         outdoing outdone

outdoor

outdoors

outer

outface   outfaced outfaces
                          outfacing

outfall

outfit   outfitted outfitting

outfitter

outflank   outflanked outflanking

outfox   outfoxed outfoxes
                          outfoxing

outgoings

outgrew

outgrow   outgrowing outgrown

outgrowth

outhouse

outing

outlandish   outlandishly
                          outlandishness

outlast   outlasted outlasting

outlaw   outlawed outlawing

outlay

outlet

outline   outlined outlining

outlook

outlying

outmanoeuvre   outmanoeuvred
                          outmanoeuvring

outmoded

outnumber   outnumbered
                          outnumbering

outpace   outpacing

outpatient

outplay   outplayed outplaying

outpouring

output

outrage   outraging

outrageous   outrageously
                          outrageousness

outran

outreach   outreached outreaches
                          outreaching

outrider

outright

outrun   outran outrunning

outset

outside

outsider

outsize

outskirts

outsmart   outsmarted
                          outsmarting

outspoken   outspokenly
                          outspokenness

outspread	outspreading	**overdeveloped**	
outstanding	outstandingly	overdid	
outstay	outstayed outstaying	overdo	overdid overdoes
outstretched			overdoing overdone
outstrip	outstripped	overdose	overdosing
	outstripping	overdraft	
outswinger		overdraw	overdrew overdrawing
outward	outwardly		overdrawn
outwards		overdressed	
outweigh	outweighed	overdrive	
	outweighing	overdue	
outwit	outwitted outwitting	**overeager**	overeagerly
outwith			overeagerness
outworn		overeat	overate (ate too much)
ouzo			overeaten
oval	ovally ovalness	overemphasis	overemphases
ovary	ovarian ovaries	overemphasise	overemphasising
ovation		overestimate	overestimating
oven			overestimation
ovenproof		overexcite	overexciting
ovenware		overexcitement	
over	overly	**overflow**	overflowed overflowing
overact	overacted overacting	**overgrow**	overgrew overgrowing
overactive	overactively		overgrown
	overactivity	**overhand**	
overall		overhang	overhanging overhung
overalls		overhaul	overhauled
overanxious	overanxiously		overhauling
	overanxiousness/	overhead	
	overanxiety	overhear	overheard overhearing
overarm		overheat	overheated
overawe	overawing		overheating
overbalance	overbalancing	overhung	
overbear	overbearing	**overjoyed**	
overblown		**overkill**	
overboard		**overlaid**	
overbook	overbooked	overland	
	overbooking	overlap	overlapped
			overlapping
overcame		overlay	overlaid overlaying
overcast		overleaf	
overcloud	overclouded	overleap	overleaping overleapt
	overclouding	overload	overloaded
overcoat			overloading
overcome	overcame overcoming	overlook	overlooked
overconfidence			overlooking
overconfident	overconfidently	overlord	
overcrowded	overcrowding		

overnight
overpitch overpitched overpitches
overpitching
overpopulate overpopulating
overpopulation
overpower overpowered
overpowering
overpoweringly
overrate (assess too highly)
overreach overreached
overreaches
overreaching
overreact overreacted
overreacting
overreaction
override overridden overriding
overrode
overripe
overrule
overrun overran overrunning
oversee oversaw overseen
overshadow overshadowed
overshadowing
overshoe
oversight
oversleep oversleeping overslept
overspend overspending
overspent
overspill
overspread overspreading
overstaffed
overstate overstating
overstatement
overstay overstayed overstaying
overstep overstepped
overstepping
overstrung
overt overtly overtness
overtake overtaken overtaking
overtook
overthrow overthrew
overthrowing
overthrown
overtime
overtook
overture

overturn overturned
overturning

overweening
overweight
overwhelm overwhelmed
overwhelming
overwhelmingly

overwork
overwrought
overzealous overzealously
overzealousness

ovoid
ovulate ovulating ovulation
ovum ova
owe owing
owl owlet
own owned owning
owner ownership
ox oxen
oxide
oxtail
oxygen
oxygenate oxygenating
oxygenation

oxymoron
oyster
ozone

pace   pacing
pacific   pacifically
pacification
pacifism   pacifist
pacify   pacified pacifier
                        pacifies pacifying
pack   packed packer packing
package   packaged packaging
packet
pact
pad   padded padding
paddle   paddling
paddock
padlock   padlocked padlocking
padre
paediatrician/pediatrician
                        paediatrics/pediatrics
paella
pagan   paganism
page   pager paging
pageant   pageantry
pageboy
pagoda
paid
pail (bucket)
pain (feeling)   pained paining
painful   painfully painfulness
painkiller
painless   painlessly painlessness
painstaking   painstakingly
paint   painted painter
                        painting
pair (two)   paired pairing
pal (friend)
palace

palatable   palatableness/
                        palatability palatably
palate (roof of mouth)
                        palatal (concerning the
                        palate)
palatial (like a palace)
palaver
pale (whitish)   palely paleness paler
                        palest
palette (artist's board)
palindrome
paling
palisade
pall (lose interest; coffin cover)
pallid   pallidly
pallor
palm   palmed palming
palmistry   palmist
palomino
palpable
palpitate   palpitating palpitation
palsy   palsies
paltry   paltrier paltriest
                        paltriness
pampas
pamper   pampered pampering
pamphlet
pamphleteer   pamphleteered
                        pamphleteering
pan   panned panning
panacea (remedy)
panache (style)
pancake
pancreas
panda
pandemonium
pander   pandered pandering
pane (of glass)
panel   panelled panelling
                        panellist
pang
panic   panicked panicking
                        panicky
panic-stricken
pannier
panoply   panoplies
panorama   panoramic

pansy	pansies	**parcel**	parcelled parcelling
pant	panted panting	parch	parched parches
pantaloons			parching
pantheism	pantheistic	parchment	
panther		**pardon**	pardoned pardoning
pantomime	pantomimic	**pare** (to cut)	paring
pantry	pantries	parent	parentage parental
pants		parenthesis	parentheses
pap		parenthood	
papacy	papacies	**pariah**	
papal		parish	parishes
papaya/pawpaw		parishioner	
paper	papered papering	parity	parities
papier mâché		**park**	parked parking
papoose		parka	
paprika		**parlance**	
papyrus	papyruses/papyri	parley	parleyed parleying
par		parliament	parliamentarian
parable			parliamentary
parabola	parabolic	parlour	
paracetamol		parlous	
parachute	parachuted parachuting	**parochial**	parochially
parachutist			parochialism
parade	parading	parody	parodied parodies
paradise			parodying
paradox	paradoxes paradoxical	parole	
	paradoxically	paroxysm	
paraffin		**parquet**	parquetry
paragon		**parricide** (killing of either parent)	
paragraph			parricidal
parakeet		parrot	
parallel	paralleled paralleling	parry	parried parries
parallelogram			parrying
paralyse	paralysing	**parse** (grammar)	parsing
paralysis	paralyses paralytic	Parsee (Indian)	
parameter		parsimonious	parsimoniously
paramilitary			parsimoniousness
paramount		parsimony	
paranoid	paranoic	parsley	
parapet		parsnip	
paraphernalia		parson	parsonage
paraphrase	paraphrasing	**part**	parted parting
paraplegia	paraplegic	partake	partaken partaking
paraquat			partook
parasite	parasitic parasitical	partial	partiality partially
parasol		participant	
paratroops	paratrooper		

participate | participating
 | participation
participator | participatory
participle
particle
particular | particularity
 | particularly
partisan
partition | partitioned
 | partitioning
partly
partner | partnered partnering
partnership
partook
partridge
parturition
party | parties
paschal
pass | passed passes passing
passable | passably
passage
passenger
passer-by | passers-by
passim
passion
passionate | passionately
 | passionateness
passionless | passionlessly
 | passionlessness
passive | passively
 | passiveness/passivity
Passover
passport
password
past
pasta
paste | pasting
pastel
pastern
pasteurise | pasteurisation
 | pasteurising
pastiche
pastille
pastime
pastor | pastoral
pastrami
pastry | pastries

pasture | pasturing
pasty | pasties
pasty-faced
pat (to touch) | patted patting
patch | patched patches
 | patching
patchy | patchier patchiest
 | patchily patchiness
pate (top of head)
pâté (spread)
patella | patellae
patent | patented patenting
 | patently
paternal | paternalism
 | paternalistic paternally
paternity | paternities
path
pathetic | pathetically
pathology | pathological
 | pathologist
 | pathologically
pathos
pathway
patience
patient | patiently
patina
patio
patisserie
patois
patriarch | patriarchal
patriarchy | patriarchies
patrician
patricide (killing of father)
 | patricidal
patrimony | patrimonial
 | patrimonies
patriot | patriotic patriotically
 | patriotism
patrol | patrolled patrolling
patroller
patron | patronage
patronise | patronising
patronymic
patter | pattered pattering
pattern | patterned patterning
patty | patties
paucity

paunch	paunches		pedalo
pauper			pedant
pause	pausing		**peddle** (to sell)
pave	paving		**pedestal**
pavement			pedestrian
pavilion			
paw (animal's foot)	pawed pawing		**pedigree**
pawky	pawkier pawkiest		**pedlar**
	pawkily pawkiness		**pedometer**
pawn	pawned pawning		**peek** (peep)
pawnbroker			**peel** (to take skin off)
pawpaw/papaya			**peep**
pay	paid paying		
payable			**peer** (to look)
payee			peerage
payment			**peeved**
pea			peevish
peace (calm)	peaceable peaceably		**peewit/pewit**
peaceful	peacefully		**peg**
	peacefulness		**pejorative**
peach	peaches		**Pekingese/Pekinese**
peacock			**pelican**
peafowl			**pellet**
peahen			pell-mell
peak (summit)	peaked peaking		pellucid
peaky	peakier peakiest		
	peakily peakiness		
peal (to ring out)	pealed pealing		**pelmet**
peanut			**pelota**
pear (fruit)			**pelt**
pearl	pearly		**pelvis**
peasant			**pen**
pease (pudding)			**penal**
peat	peaty		penalise
pebble	pebbly		penalty
pecan			penance
peccadillo	peccadilloes/peccadillos		**pence/pennies**
peccary	peccaries		penchant
peck	pecked pecking		pencil
peckish	peckishly peckishness		**pendant**
pectoral			pending
peculiar	peculiarly		pendulous
peculiarity	peculiarities		
pecuniary			pendulum
pedagogue	pedagogical		**penetrate**
	pedagogics pedagogy		
pedal (to cycle)	pedalled pedalling		
			penguin

Right column expansions:

pedant	pedantic pedantically
peddle (to sell)	peddling
pedestrian	pedestrianisation pedestrianise
peek (peep)	peeked peeking
peel (to take skin off)	peeled peeler peeling
peep	peeped peeper peeping
peer (to look)	peered peering
peevish	peevishly peevishness
peg	pegged pegging
pejorative	pejoratively
pellucid	pellucidly pellucidness/pellucidity
pelt	pelted pelting
pelvis	pelvises/pelves
pen	penned penning pent
penalise	penalising penalisation
penalty	penalties
pencil	pencilled pencilling
pendulous	pendulously pendulousness
pendulum	pendulums/pendula
penetrate	penetrating penetratingly penetration

penicillin

peninsula	peninsular
penis	penises
penitence	
penitent	penitently
penitential	penitentially
penitentiary	penitentiaries
penknife	
pennant	
penniless	
penny	pennies/pence
pension	pensioned pensioning
pensionable	
pensioner	
pensive	pensively pensiveness
pentagon	pentagonal
pentathlon	pentathlete
Pentecost	Pentecostal
penthouse	
penultimate	
penurious	penuriously
	penuriousness
peony (flower)	peonies
people	
pep	pepped pepping
pepper	peppered peppering
peppermint	
peppery	
peptic	
perambulate	perambulating
	perambulation
perambulator/pram	
perceive	perceiving
per cent	
percentage	
percentile	
perceptible	perceptibility
	perceptibly
perception	
perceptive	perceptively
	perceptiveness
perch	perched perches
	perching
percipience	
percipient	percipiently
percolate	percolating percolator
percussion	percussionist

perdition
peregrination

peregrine	
peremptory	peremptorily
	peremptoriness
perennial	perennially
perestroika	
perfect	perfected perfecting
	perfection perfectly
perfectionist	
perfidious	perfidiously perfidy
perfidy	perfidies
perforate	perforating
	perforation
perforce	
perform	performed performer
	performing
performance	
perfume	perfumer
perfunctory	perfunctorily
	perfunctoriness
pergola	
perhaps	
peril	
perilous	perilously perilousness
perimeter	
period	periodic periodical
	periodically
peripatetic	peripatetically
peripheral	peripherally
periphery	peripheries
periscope	
perish	perished perishes
	perishing
perishable	perishableness
	perishably
periwinkle	
perjure	perjuring
perjury	perjuries
perk	perked perking
perky	perkier perkiest
	perkily perkiness
perm	
permafrost	
permanence	permanencies
	permanency
permanent	permanently

permeable | permeability
 | permeably
permeate | permeating permeation
permissible | permissibility
 | permissibly
permission |
permissive | permissively
 | permissiveness
permit | permitted permitting
permutate | permutating
 | permutation
pernicious | perniciously
 | perniciousness
pernickety |
peroxide |
perpendicular | perpendicularity
 | perpendicularly
perpetrate | perpetrating
 | perpetration
perpetrator |
perpetual | perpetually
perpetuate | perpetuating
 | perpetuation
perpetuity |
perplex | perplexed perplexes
 | perplexing
 | perplexingly
perplexity | perplexities
perquisite |
persecute | persecuting
 | persecution
persecutor |
perseverance |
persevere | persevering
persimmon |
persist | persisted persisting
persistence |
persistent | persistently
person | personal
 | (concerning a person)
 | personally
persona | personae
personable | personableness
 | personably
personage |
personalise |
personality | personalities

personification |
personify | personified personifies
 | personifying
personnel (staff) |
perspective |
perspicacious | perspicaciously
 | perspicacity
 | (understanding well)
perspicuous | perspicuously
 | perspicuity
 | (easy to understand)
perspiration |
perspire | perspiring
persuade | persuading
persuasion |
persuasive | persuasively
 | persuasiveness
pert | pertly pertness
pertain | pertained pertaining
pertinacious | pertinaciously
 | pertinacity
pertinence |
pertinent | pertinently
perturb | perturbed perturbing
perturbation |
peruse | perusal perusing
pervade | pervading
pervasive | pervasively
 | pervasiveness
perverse | perversely
 | perversity/perverseness
perversion |
pervert | perverted perverting
peseta |
pessimism | pessimist
pessimistic | pessimistically
pest |
pester | pestered pesterer
 | pestering
pesticide |
pestiferous |
pestilence |
pestilent | pestilential
 | pestilentially
pestle |
pet | petted petting
petal |

petard
peter   petered petering
petition   petitionary petitioner
petrel (bird)
petrifaction
petrify   petrified petrifies
                             petrifying
petrochemical
petrol (fuel)
petroleum
petticoat
pettifogger   pettifogging
petty   pettier pettiest pettily
                             pettiness

petulance
petulant   petulantly
petunia
pew
pewit/peewit
pewter
phalanx   phalanxes
phantasm   phantasmic
phantasmagoria   phantasmagoric
phantom
Pharaoh
Pharisee
pharmaceutical
pharmacist   pharmacies pharmacy
pharmacology   pharmacological
                             pharmacologically
                             pharmacologist
phase   phasing
pheasant
phenomenal   phenomenally
phenomenon   phenomena
phial
philander   philandered
                             philanderer
                             philandering
philanthropic   philanthropically
philanthropy   philanthropist
philately   philatelic philatelist
philharmonic
Philistine
philosopher
philosophic   philosophical
                             philosophically

philosophy   philosophies
phlegm
phlegmatic   phlegmatically
phobia   phobic
phoenix   phoenixes
phone   phoning
phonetic   phonetically
phonetics
phoney   phonier phoniest
                             phonily phoniness

phosphate
phosphorescence
phosphorescent   phosphorescently
phosphorus
photocopy   photocopied
                             photocopier
                             photocopies
                             photocopying

photogenic
photograph/photo   photographed
                             photographing
photographic   photographically
photography   photographer
Photostat
photosynthesis
phrase   phrasing
phraseology
phrenology   phrenologist
phylactery   phylacteries
phylum   phyla/phylums
physical   physicality physically
physician
physicist
physics
physiological   physiologically
physiology   physiologist
physiotherapy   physiotherapist
physique
pianissimo
pianist
piano/pianoforte
pibroch
picador
picaresque
piccalilli
piccolo
pick   picked picker picking

pickaxe
picket   picketed picketing
pickle   pickling
picnic   picnicked picnicker
                          picnicking
pictorial   pictorially
picture   picturing
picturesque   picturesquely
                          picturesqueness
piddle   piddler piddling
pidgin (form of language)
pie
piebald
piece (part)   piecing
piecemeal
pier (landing place for boats)
pierce   piercing piercingly
piety   pieties pious piously
piffle   piffling
pig   pigged pigging
pigeon (bird)
piggery   piggeries
piggyback
piglet
pigment   pigmented
                          pigmentation
pigmy/pygmy   pigmies/pygmies
pigtail
pike
pikestaff
pilau/pilaff/pilaw
pilchard
pile   piling
pilfer   pilfered pilferer
                          pilfering
pilgrim   pilgrimage
pill
pillage
pillar
pillion
pillory   pilloried pillories
                          pillorying
pillow   pillowed pillowing
pillowcase
pilot   piloted piloting
pimento
pimpernel

pimple
pin   pinned pinning
pinafore
pincer
pinch   pinched pinches
                          pinching
pine   pining
pineapple
ping   pinged pinging
pinion   pinioned pinioning
pink   pinked pinking
pinnacle
pint
pioneer   pioneered pioneering
pious   piety piously
pip (to defeat; seed) pipped pipping
pipe (tube)   piper piping
pipeline
pipistrelle
pippin
pipsqueak
piquancy
piquant   piquantly
pique
piranha
pirate   piracy pirating
piratical
pirouette
Pisces
pistachio
piste (ski run)
pistil (part of flower)
pistol (gun)
piston
pit   pitted pitting
pitch   pitched pitches
                          pitching
pitcher
pitchfork   pitchforked pitchforking
piteous   piteously piteousness
pitfall
pith
pithy   pithier pithiest pithily
                          pithiness
pitiable   pitiableness pitiably
pitiful   pitifully pitifulness
pitiless   pitilessly pitilessness

piton
pitta (bread)
pittance
pity   pitied pities pitying
pivot   pivotal pivoted
                                  pivoting

pixie
pizza   pizzeria
pizzicato
placard
placate   placating placatory
place (to put down)   placing
placebo
placement
placenta   placentae/placentas
placid   placidity placidly
                                  placidness

plagiarise   plagiariser plagiarising
plagiarism
plague   plaguing
plaice (fish)
plaid
plain (ordinary; clear) plainer plainest
                         plainly plainness
plaintiff (someone who brings a case in Court)
plaintive (mournful)   plaintively plaintiveness
plait (to fold hair)   plaited plaiting
plan (to prepare)   planned planner
                                  planning
plane (to glide; flat surface; tool)
                                  planing
planet   planetary
planetarium   planetariums/planetaria
plangent   plangently
plank   planked planking
plankton
plant   planted planter
                                  planting
plantain
plantation
plaque
plasma
plaster   plastered plasterer
                                  plastering
plastic   plastically plasticity
                                  plasticky
Plasticine

plate   plater plating
plateau   plateaus/plateaux
platform
platinum
platitude   platitudinous
                                  platitudinously

platonic
platoon
platter
platypus   platypuses
plaudits
plausible   plausibility plausibly
play   played player playing
playful   playfully playfulness
playground
playing-card
playwright
plaza
plea
plead   pleaded pleading
                                  pleadingly
pleasant   pleasantly pleasantness
pleasantry   pleasantries
please   pleasing pleasingly
pleasurable   pleasurableness
                                  pleasurably
pleasure   pleasuring
pleat   pleated pleating
pleb/plebeian
plebiscite
plectrum   plectrums/plectra
pledge   pledging
plenary
plenipotentiary   plenipotentiaries
plenitude
plenteous   plenteously
                                  plenteousness
plentiful   plentifully
                                  plentifulness
plenty
plethora
pleurisy
pliable   pliability pliably
pliancy
pliant   pliantly
pliers
plight   plighted plighting

plimsoll
plinth
plod — plodded plodder plodding
plonk — plonked plonking
plop — plopped plopping
plot — plotted plotter plotting
plough — ploughed ploughing
ploughman — ploughmen
plover
ploy
pluck — plucked plucking
plucky — pluckier pluckiest pluckily
plug — plugged plugging
plum (fruit) — plummier plummiest plummy
plumage
plumb (measure depth; act as plumber) — plumbed plumber plumbing
plume (to decorate) — pluming
plummet — plummeted plummeting
plump — plumply plumpness
plunder — plundered plunderer plundering
plunge — plunger plunging
pluperfect
plural — plurality plurally
pluralism
plus
plush — plushly
plushy — plushier plushiest plushily plushiness

Pluto
plutocracy — plutocracies plutocrat plutocratic
plutonium
ply — plied plies plying
plywood
pneumatic — pneumatically
pneumonia
poach — poached poacher poaches poaching

pocket — pocketed pocketing
pocketful
pock-mark — pock-marked
pod
podgy — podgier podgiest podgily podginess
podium — podiums/podia
poem
poet — poetic
poetess — poetesses
poetical — poetically
Poet Laureate
poetry
poignancy
poignant — poignantly
point — pointed pointedly pointedness pointer pointing
point-blank
pointillism — pointillist
pointless — pointlessly pointlessness
pointy — pointier pointiest
poise
poison — poisoned poisoning
poisonous — poisonously poisonousness
poke — poker poking
poky — pokiness
polar — polarities polarity
polarise — polarising polarisation
Polaroid
pole (stick, rod)
poleaxe — poleaxing
polecat
polemic — polemical polemically
pole-vault — pole-vaulted pole-vaulter pole-vaulting
police — policing
policeman — policemen
policewoman — policewomen
policy — policies
polio/poliomyelitis
polish — polished polisher polishes polishing
polite — politely politeness

political	politically	ponder	pondered pondering
politician		ponderable	ponderability
politicise	politicising	ponderous	ponderously
politics			ponderousness
polka		**pontiff**	
poll (to count votes)	polled polling	pontificate	pontificating
pollard	pollarded pollarding	pontoon	
pollen		**pony**	ponies
pollinate	pollinating pollination	**poodle**	
pollute	pollutant polluting	**pool**	pooled pooling
	pollution	**poop–deck**	
		poor (not good; not rich)	
polo			poorer poorest poorly
polonaise			poorness
polony	polonies	**pop** (to burst out)	popped popping
poltergeist		**pope** (religious figure)	
poly/polytechnic		**poplar**	
polyanthus	polyanthuses	poplin	
polychromatic		**poppadom**	
polychrome		poppy	poppies
polyester		**populace**	
polygamy	polygamist polygamous	popular	popularity popularly
	polygamously	popularise	popularising
polyglot			popularisation
polygon		populate	populating population
polyhedron		populous	populousness
polymath		**porage/porridge**	
polymer		**porcelain**	
polyp		porch	porches
polyphonic		porcupine	
polystyrene		**pore** (sweat gland)	
polysyllabic		**pork**	porker porky
polytechnic/poly		**pornography**	pornographer
polytheism	polytheistic		pornographic
polythene			pornographically
polyunsaturated		**porosity**	
polyurethane		porous	porousness
pomade		**porpoise**	
pomander		**porridge/porage**	
pomegranate		porringer	
pommel	pommelled pommelling	**port**	
pomp		portable	portability
pompon/pompom		portage	
pompous	pompously	Portakabin	
	pompousness/	portal	
	pomposity	portcullis	
poncho		portend	portended portending
pond			

portent	
portentous	portentously
	portentousness
porter	
portfolio	
porthole	
portico	
portion	portioned portioning
portly	portliness
portmanteau	portmanteaus/
	portmanteaux
portrait	portraitist portraiture
portray	portrayal portrayed
	portraying
pose	poser posing
poseur	
posh	posher poshest
	poshly poshness
position	positioned positioning
positive	positively positiveness
positron	
posse	
possess	possessed possesses
	possessing possessor
possession	
possessive	possessively
	possessiveness
possible	possibility possibly
possum/opossum	
post	posted posting
postage	
postal	
postcode	
poster	
posterior	
posterity	
postern	
postgraduate	
posthumous	posthumously
postilion	
postman	postmen
postmaster	
postmistress	postmistresses
post-mortem	
postpone	postponing
postponement	
postscript	

postulant	
postulate	postulating postulation
posture	
posy	posies
pot	potted potting
potable (drinkable)	potability
potage	
potash	
potassium	
potato	potatoes
poteen	
potency	potencies
potent	potently
potentate	
potential	potentially
pothole	potholer potholing
potion	
pot-pourri	
potter	pottered pottering
pottery	potteries
pouch	pouched pouchy
poulterer	
poultice	poulticing
poultry	
pounce	pouncing
pound	pounded pounding
poundage	
pour (to make flow)	poured pourer pouring
pout	pouted pouting
poverty	
powder	powdered powdering
	powdery
power	powered powering
powerful	powerfully
	powerfulness
powerless	powerlessly
	powerlessness
powwow	powwowed
	powwowing
practicable	practicability
	practicably
practical	practicality practically
practice (what you do)	
practise (to do)	practising
practitioner	
pragmatic	pragmaticality
	pragmatically

pragmatism pragmatist
prairie
praise praising
praiseworthy praiseworthily
 praiseworthiness

praline
pram/perambulator
prance prancing
prank prankster
prate prating
prattle prattler prattling
prawn
pray prayed praying
prayer
preach preached preacher
 preaches preaching

preamble
prearrange prearrangement
prebendary prebendaries
precarious precariously
 precariousness

precaution precautionary
precede preceding
precedence precedented
precedent
precentor
precept
precinct
preciosity
precious preciously preciousness
precipice
precipitate precipitately
 precipitating
 precipitation
precipitous precipitously
 precipitousness
précis (a summary)
precise (exact) precisely
 precision/preciseness
preclude precluding preclusion
precocious precociously
 precociousness/
 precocity
preconceive preconceiving
preconception
precondition
precursor precursory

predator predatory
predecessor
predestination
predestined
predetermine predetermining
 predetermination

predicament
predicate predicating predication
predict predicted predicting
 prediction
predictable predictability
 predictably
predispose predisposing
 predisposition
predominance
predominant predominantly
predominate predominately
 predominating

pre-eminence
pre-eminent pre-eminently
pre-empt pre-empted
 pre-empting
pre-emptive pre-emptively
preen preened preening
prefabricate prefabricating
 prefabrication
preface prefacing
prefect
prefer preferred preferring
preferable preferably
preference
preferential preferentially
prefix prefixes
pregnable
pregnancy pregnancies
pregnant
prehensile
prehistoric prehistorically
 prehistory
prejudge prejudging
prejudice prejudicing
prejudicial prejudicially
prelate
prelim
preliminary preliminaries
prelude
premarital

premature	prematurely
	prematureness/
	prematurity
premeditate	premeditating
	premeditation
premenstrual	
premier (prime minister)	
première (first night)	
premise/premiss (statement)	
	premises/premisses
premises (buildings)	
premium	
premonition	premonitory
preoccupation	
preoccupy	preoccupied
	preoccupies
	preoccupying
preparation	preparatory
prepare	preparing
prepay	prepaid prepaying
preponderance	
preponderant	preponderantly
preposition	
preposterous	preposterously
prerequisite	
prerogative	
presage	presaging
Presbyterian	
presbytery	presbyteries
prescience	
prescient	presciently
prescribe	prescribing
prescription (medicine suggested by doctor)	
prescriptive	prescriptively
	prescriptiveness
presence	
present	presented presenter
	presenting presently
presentable	presentability
	presentably
presentation	
presentiment	
preservation	preservative
preserve	preserving
preside	presiding
presidency	presidencies

president	presidential
	presidentially
press	pressed presses
	pressing pressingly
pressure	pressuring
pressurise	pressurising
	pressurisation
prestige	
prestigious	prestigiously
presto	
presumably	
presume	presuming
presumption	presumptive
	presumptively
presumptuous	presumptuously
	presumptuousness
presuppose	presupposing
	presupposition
pretence	
pretend	pretended pretender
	pretending
pretension	
pretentious	pretentiously
	pretentiousness
pretext	
pretty	prettier prettiest
	prettily prettiness
prevail	prevailed prevailing
prevalence	
prevalent	prevalently
prevaricate	prevaricating
	prevarication
prevent	prevented preventing
	prevention
preventive/preventative	
	preventively/
	preventatively
	preventiveness
preview	previewed previewing
previous	previously
prey	preyed preying
price	pricing
priceless	pricelessness
pricey/pricy	pricier priciest
prick	pricked pricker
	pricking
prickle	prickling

prickly	pricklier prickliest
	prickliness
pride	priding
prideful	pridefully pridefulness
priest	priesthood priestly
priestess	priestesses
prig	priggish priggishly
	priggishness
prim (very formal)	primmer primmest
	primly primness
primacy	primacies
primaeval/primeval	primaevally/primevally
primal	
primary	primaries primarily
primate	
prime (best; to prepare)	
	primer priming
primeval/primaeval	primevally/primaevally
primitive	primitively
	primitiveness
primitivism	
primordial	primordially
primp	primped primping
primrose	
primula	
Primus (stove)	
prince	princely
princess	princesses
principal (first, chief)	principally
principality	principalities
principle (rule)	
principled	
print	printed printer
	printing
prior	
prioress	prioresses
priority	priorities
priory	priories
prise (to open)	prising
prism	prismatic
prison	prisoner
prissy	prissier prissiest
	prissily prissiness
pristine	
privacy	
private	privately
privateer	

privation	
privatise	privatisation
	privatising
privet	
privilege	
privy	privies
prize (to value; a reward)	
	prizing
probability	probabilities
probable	probably
probation	probationary
	probationer
probe	probing
probity	
problem	problematic
	problematical
	problematically
proboscis	proboscises
procedure	procedural
	procedurally
proceed	proceeded proceeding
process	processed processes
	processor processing
procession	processional
	processionally
proclaim	proclaimed proclaimer
	proclaiming
proclamation	proclamatory
proclivity	proclivities
procrastinate	procrastinating
	procrastination
	procrastinator
procreate	procreating procreation
proctor	
procuration	procurator
procure	procuring
procurement	
prod	prodded prodding
prodigal	prodigality prodigally
prodigious	prodigiously
	prodigiousness
prodigy	prodigies
produce	producer producing
product	production
productive	productively
	productiveness
productivity	

profane	profanely profanities	projectionist	
	profanity	projector	
profess	professed professes	**proletarian**	proletariat/proletariate
	professing	proliferate	proliferating
profession			proliferation
professional	professionally	prolific	prolifically prolificness
	professionalism	prolix	prolixity prolixly
professor	professorial	prologue	
	professorially	prolong	prolonged prolonging
proffer	proffered proffering	prolongation	
proficiency	proficiencies	**promenade**	promenader
proficient	proficiently		promenading
profile	profiling	prominence	
profit	profited profiting	prominent	prominently
profitable	profitability profitably	promiscuous	promiscuities
profiteer	profiteered profiteering		promiscuity
profiterole			promiscuously
profligate	profligately	promise	promising promisingly
	profligacy/profligateness	promissory	
pro forma		promontory	promontories
profound	profoundly	promote	promoter promoting
	profoundness	promotion	promotional
profundity			promotionally
profuse	profusely profuseness	prompt	prompted prompter
profusion			prompting
progenitor		promptly	promptness
progeny		promulgate	promulgating
prognosis	prognoses		promulgation
prognosticate	prognosticating	**prone**	pronely proneness
	prognostication	prong	pronged
program (computers)	programmed	pronoun	
	programmer	pronounce	pronouncing
	programming	pronouncement	
programme (to arrange)		pronunciation	
	programmer	**proof**	
	programming	**prop**	propped propping
progress	progressed progresses	propaganda	propagandist
	progressing progression	propagandise	propagandising
progressive	progressively	propagate	propagating
	progressiveness		propagation
prohibit	prohibited prohibiting		propagator
	prohibition	propane	
prohibitive	prohibitively	propel	propelled propelling
	prohibitiveness	propellant (noun)	
project	projected projecting	propellent (adjective)	
	projection	propeller	
projectile		propensity	propensities

proper   properly
property   propertied properties
prophecy (something foretold)
                        prophecies
prophesy (to foretell) prophesied prophesies
                        prophesying
prophet   prophetic
                        prophetically
propinquity
propitiate   propitiating propitiation
propitious   propitiously
                        propitiousness
proponent
proportion   proportioned
proportional   proportionality
                        proportionally
proportionate   proportionately
proposal
propose   proposer proposing
proposition
propound   propounded
                        propounding
proprietary
proprietor   proprietorial
                        proprietorially
propriety   proprieties
propulsion
prosaic   prosaically prosaicness
proscenium   prosceniums/proscenia
proscribe   proscribing
proscription (exile)   proscriptive
                        proscriptively
prose
prosecute   prosecuting prosecution
                        prosecutor
prosody
prospect   prospected prospecting
                        prospector
prospective   prospectively
prospectus   prospectuses
prosper   prospered prospering
prosperity
prosperous   prosperously
                        prosperousness
prostate (gland)
prostitute   prostitution
prostrate (lying flat) prostrating prostration

prosy   prosier prosiest
                        prosily prosiness
protagonist
protect   protected protecting
                        protection protector
protective   protectively
                        protectiveness
protégé (male)   protégée (female)
protein
protest   protested
                        protester/protestor
                        protesting
Protestant   Protestantism
protestation
protocol
proton
prototype
protract   protracted protracting
                        protraction
protractor
protrude   protruding
protrusion   protrusive protrusively
proud   prouder proudest
                        proudly
prove   proven proving
provenance
proverb   proverbial proverbially
provide   provider providing
providence
provident   providently
providential   providentially
province   provincial provincially
provision   provisional provisionally
proviso
provocation
provocative   provocatively
provoke   provoking provokingly
provost
prow
prowess
prowl   prowled prowler
                        prowling
proximate   proximately
proximity
proxy   proxies
prude   pruderies prudery
prudence

prudent — prudently
prudential — prudentially
prudish — prudishly prudishness
prune — pruning
prurience
prurient — pruriently
prussic (acid)
pry — pried pries prying
psalm — psalmist
psalter
psephology — psephologist
pseudo
pseudonym
psyche
psychedelic
psychiatric — psychiatrical
psychiatrically
psychiatry — psychiatrist
psychic — psychical psychically
psychoanalyse — psychoanalysing
psychoanalysis — psychoanalyst
psychoanalytical — psychoanalytically
psychological — psychologically
psychology — psychologies
psychologist
psychopath — psychopathic
psychopathically
psychosis — psychoses psychotic
psychosomatic
pterodactyl
puberty — pubertal
pubescence
pubescent
pubic (part of body)
public (in clear view) — publicly
publican
publication
publicise — publicising publicist
publicity
publish — published publisher
publishes publishing
puck — puckish puckishly
puckishness
pucker — puckered puckering
pudding
puddle
puerile — puerilely puerility

puff — puffed puffer puffing
puffin
puffy — puffier puffiest
puffily puffiness
pug
pugilist — pugilism pugilistic
pugilistically
pugnacious — pugnaciously pugnacity
puissance
pull — pulled puller pulling
pullet
pulley
pullover
pullulate — pullulating pullulation
pulp — pulped pulping
pulpit
pulsar
pulsate — pulsating pulsation
pulse
pulverise — pulverising
pulverisation
puma
pumice
pummel — pummelled pummelling
pump — pumped pumping
pumpernickel
pumpkin
pun — punned punning
punch — punched puncher
punches punching
punctilious — punctiliously
punctiliousness
punctual — punctuality punctually
punctuate — punctuating
punctuation
puncture — puncturing
pundit
pungency
pungent — pungently
punish — punishable punished
punishes punishing
punishment
punitive — punitively
punnet
punt — punted punter
punting

puny	punier puniest punily puniness
pup	
pupa	pupae pupal
pupil	
puppet	puppeteer puppetry
puppy	puppies
purchase	purchasing
purdah	
pure	purely pureness/purity purer purest
purée	
purgation	
purgative	
purgatory	
purge	purging
purification	
purify	purified purifies purifying
purist	
puritan	puritanical puritanically
puritanism	
purity	
purl	purled purling
purloin	purloined purloining
purple	
purport	purported purporting
purpose	purposely purposing
purposeful	purposefully purposefulness
purposeless	purposelessly purposelessness
purr	purred purring
purse	pursing
purser	
pursuance	
pursuant	
pursue	pursuer pursuing
pursuit	
purvey	purveyed purveying purveyor
purview	
pus	
push	pushed pusher pushes pushing

pushy	pushier pushiest pushily pushiness
pusillanimity	pusillanimities
pusillanimous	pusillanimously
put (to place)	putting
putative	putatively
putrefaction	
putrefy	putrefied putrefies putrefying
putrid	putridly putridness
putt (move a golf ball)	
	putted putter putting
putty	putties
puzzle	puzzling puzzlingly
puzzlement	
pygmy/pigmy	pygmies/pigmies
pyjamas	
pylon	
pyramid	pyramidal
pyre	
pyrites	
pyromania	pyromaniac
pyrotechnic	pyrotechnical
pyrotechnics	
python	

Qq

quack quacked quacking
quad/quads (see quadruplet)
quadrangle
quadrant
quadraphonic/quadrophonic
quadraphonically/
quadrophonically
quadratic
quadrilateral
quadrille
quadriplegic quadriplegia
quadruped
quadruplet/quadruplets (see quad)
quagmire
quail
quaint quainter quaintest
quaintly quaintness
quake quaking
Quaker
qualification
qualify qualified qualifier
qualifies qualifying
qualitative qualitatively
quality qualities
qualm
quandary quandaries
quantify quantified quantifier
quantifies quantifying
quantitative quantitatively
quantity quantities
quantum quanta
quarantine
quarrel quarrelled quarreller
quarrelling
quarrelsome

quarry quarried quarries
quarrying
quart
quarter quartered quartering
quarterly quarterlies
quartet/quartette
quartile
quarto
quartz
quasar
quash quashed quashes
quashing
quaver quavered quavering
quaveringly
quay
queasy queasier queasiest
queasily queasiness
queen queenly
queer queerer queerest
queerly queerness
quell quelled quelling
quench quenched quenches
quenching
quern
querulous querulously
querulousness
query queries
quest quested questing
question questioned
questioning
questioningly
questionable questionably
questionnaire
queue queuing/queueing
queuer
quibble quibbling quibblingly
quiche
quick quicker quickest
quickly quickness
quicken quickened quickening
quiescence
quiescent quiescently
quiet quieter quietest
quietly quietness
quieten quietened quietening
quiff
quill

quilt   quilted quilting
quince
quinine
quintessence
quintessential quintessentially
quintet/quintette
quip   quipped quipping
quipster
quire
quirk
quirky   quirkier quirkiest
                 quirkily quirkiness

quisling
quit (to leave) quitter quitting
quite (almost)
quits
quiver   quivered quivering
                 quiveringly
quiz   quizzed quizzes
                 quizzing
quizzical   quizzically
quoits
quorum
quota
quotation
quote   quoting
quotient
Qur'an/Koran

Rr

rabbi
rabbit   rabbited rabbiting
rabble
rabid   rabidly rabidness
rabies
race   racer racing
racial   racially
racialism   racialist
racism   racist
rack   racked racking
racket (bat used in some games; noise)
racketeer   racketeered
                 racketeering
raconteur
racoon/raccoon
racquet/racket (bat used in some games)
racy   racier raciest racily
                 raciness
radar
radial   radially
radiance   radiancies radiancy
radiant   radiantly
radiate   radiating radiation
radiator
radical (fundamental) radicalism radically
radicle (root)
radio
radioactive   radioactivity
radiography   radiographer
radiology   radiologist
radish   radishes
radium
radius   radiuses/radii
raffia
raffle   raffling

raft
rafter
raga
ragamuffin
rage   raging
ragged   raggedly raggedy
raglan
ragout
raid   raided raider raiding
rail   railed railing
raillery
railway
raiment
rain (water from clouds)
                                rained raining
rainbow
raincoat
raindrop
rainy   rainier rainiest rainily
                                raininess
raise   raising
raisin
rajah/raja
rake   raking
rakish   rakishly rakishness
rallentando
rally   rallied rallies rallying
ram   rammed ramming
Ramadan
ramble   rambler rambling
                                ramblingly
ramekin
ramification
ramify   ramified ramifies
                                ramifying
ramp
rampage
rampant   rampantly
rampart
ramrod
ramshackle
ranch   ranched rancher
                                ranches ranching
rancid   rancidity rancidly
                                rancidness
rancour   rancorous rancorously
rand

random   randomly randomness
ranee/rani
rang
range   ranger ranging
rangy   rangier rangiest
                                rangily ranginess
rani/ranee
rank   ranked ranker ranking
rankle   rankling
ransack   ransacked ransacker
                                ransacking
ransom   ransomed ransoming
rant   ranted ranting
rap   rapped rapping
rapacious   rapaciously
                                rapaciousness/rapacity
rape   raping rapist
rapid   rapidity rapidly
rapier
rapport
rapprochement
rapscallion
rapt
rapture   rapturous rapturously
                                rapturousness
rare   rarely rareness rarer
                                rarest
rarebit
rarefy   rarefied rarefies
                                rarefaction
rarity   rarities
rascal   rascality rascally
rash   rasher rashes rashest
                                rashly rashness
rasher
rasp   rasped rasping
                                raspingly
raspberry   raspberries
Rastafarian/Rasta
rat   ratted ratter ratting
ratatouille
ratchet
rate   rating
rateable
rather
ratify   ratified ratifies
                                ratifying

ratio		**real**	
ration	rationed rationing	realign	realigned realigning
rational (sensible)	rationality rationally	realignment	
rationale (underlying purpose)		realisation	
rationalise	rationalisation	realise	realising
	rationalising	realism	
rationalism	rationalist	realist	realistic realistically
rattan		reality	realities
rattle	rattler rattling	really	
raucous	raucously raucousness	realm	
raunchy	raunchier raunchiest	**ream**	
	raunchily raunchiness	**reap**	reaped reaper reaping
ravage	ravager ravaging	reappear	reappeared reappearing
rave	raver raving	reappearance	
raven		reapply	reapplied reapplies
ravenous	ravenously		reapplying
	ravenousness	reappraisal	
ravine		reappraise	reappraising
ravioli		**rear**	reared rearing
ravish	ravished ravisher	rearm	rearmed rearming
	ravishes ravishing	rearmament	
	ravishingly	rearrange	rearranging
raw	rawer rawest rawly	rearrangement	
	rawness	**reason**	reasoned reasoning
ray		reasonable	reasonableness
rayon			reasonably
raze	razing	reassemble	reassembling
razor	razored razoring		reassembly
razzle-dazzle		reassert	reasserted reasserting
razzmatazz/razzamatazz		reassess	reassesses reassessed
reach	reached reaches		reassessing
	reaching	reassurance	
react	reacted reacting	reassure	reassuring reassuringly
	reaction	**rebarbative**	rebarbatively
reactionary	reactionaries		rebarbativeness
reactivate	reactivating	rebate	
reactive		**rebel**	rebelled rebelling
reactor		rebellion	
read	reader reading	rebellious	rebelliously
readable	readability readably		rebelliousness
readjust	readjusted readjusting	**rebirth**	
readjustment		**reborn**	
ready	readied readier	rebound	rebounded rebounding
	readies readiest	**rebuff**	rebuffed rebuffing
	readily readiness	rebuild	rebuilding rebuilt
	readying	rebuke	rebuking
reaffirm	reaffirmed reaffirming	rebus	rebuses

rebut — rebuttal rebutted rebutting

recalcitrance

recalcitrant — recalcitrantly

recall — recalled recalling

recant — recanted recanting

recap — recapped recapping

recapitulate — recapitulating recapitulation

recapture — recapturing

recast

recede — receding

receipt — receipted receipting

receive — receiver receiving

recent — recently

receptacle

reception — receptionist

receptive — receptively receptivity/receptiveness

recess — recessed recesses recessing

recession — recessional recessionary

recessive

recipe

recipient

reciprocal — reciprocally

reciprocate — reciprocating reciprocation

reciprocity — reciprocities

recital

recitative

recite — recitation reciting

reckless — recklessly recklessness

reckon — reckoned reckoning

reclaim — reclaimable reclaimed reclaiming reclamation

recline — reclining

recluse — reclusive

recognisance — recognisant

recognise — recognising

recognition

recoil — recoiled recoiling

recollect — recollected recollecting recollection

recommend — recommended recommending

recommendation

recompense — recompensing

reconcile — reconciling

reconciliation

recondite

recondition — reconditioned reconditioning

reconnaissance

reconnoitre — reconnoitring

reconsider — reconsideration reconsidered reconsidering

reconstitute — reconstituting reconstitution

reconstruct — reconstructed reconstruction

reconvene — reconvening

record — recorded recorder recording

recount (to tell a story)

re-count (to count again)

recoup — recouped recouping

recourse

recover (to regain) — recovered recovering

re-cover (to cover again)

recovery — recoveries

re-create — re-creating re-creation (creating again)

recreation (leisure) — recreational recreationally

recriminate — recriminating recrimination

recruit — recruited recruiting recruitment

rectangle — rectangular

rectification

rectify — rectified rectifies rectifying

rectitude

rector — rectorial

rectory — rectories

rectum — rectums/recta

recumbent — recumbently

recuperate — recuperating recuperation recuperative

recur — recurred recurring

recurrence
recurrent   recurrently
recusant
recycle   recycling
red   redder reddest redly
                            redness

redcurrant
redden   reddened reddening
reddish   reddishness
redeem   redeemed redeemer
                            redeeming
redemption
redeploy   redeployed redeploying
                            redeployment
redevelop   redeveloped
                            redeveloping
                            redevelopment

redid
rediscover   rediscovered
                            rediscovering
rediscovery   rediscoveries
redo   redid redoes redoing
                            redone
redolent
redouble   redoubling
redoubt
redoubtable
redress   redressed redresses
                            redressing
reduce   reducing
reduction
redundancy   redundancies
redundant   redundantly
reduplicate   reduplicating
                            reduplication
re-echo   re-echoed re-echoes
                            re-echoing

reed
reedy   reedier reediest
reef
reek (to smell)   reeked reeking
reel   reeled reeling
re-elect   re-elected re-election
re-enter   re-entered re-entering
re-examine   re-examination
                            re-examining
refectory   refectories

refer   referral referred
                            referring
referee   refereeing
reference   referent
referendum   referendums/referenda
referral
refill   refilled refilling
refine   refining
refinement
refinery   refineries
refit   refitted refitting
reflate   reflating reflation
reflect   reflected reflecting
                            reflectingly
reflection/reflexion
reflective   reflectively
                            reflectiveness
reflector
reflex   reflexes
reflexive   reflexively
reflexology
refloat   refloated refloating
reform   reformed reformer
                            reforming
reformation/Reformation
reformatory   reformatories
refract   refracting refraction
refractory
refrain   refrained refraining
refresh   refreshed refresher
                            refreshes refreshing
                            refreshingly
refreshment
refrigerate   refrigerating
                            refrigeration
refrigerator
refuel   refuelled refuelling
refuge (safe place)
refugee (someone taking refuge)
refulgence
refulgent   refulgently
refund   refunded refunding
refurbish   refurbished
                            refurbishes
                            refurbishing
                            refurbishment
refusal

refuse	refusing
refutation	
refute	refuting
regain	regained regaining
regal (royal)	regally
regale (entertain)	regaling
regalia	
regard	regarded regarding
regardless	
regatta	
regency	regencies
regenerate	regenerating
	regeneration
regent	
reggae	
regime (system of government)	
regimen (course of exercise, diet)	
regiment (unit of army)	
	regimental regimentally
region	regional regionally
register (list; to list)	registered registering
registrar (an official)	
registration	
registry	registries
regress	regressed regresses
	regressing regression
regret	regretted regretting
regretful	regretfully
	regretfulness
regrettable	regrettableness
	regrettably
regular	regularity regularly
regularise	regularising
	regularisation
regulate	regulating regulation
	regulator
regurgitate	regurgitating
	regurgitation
rehabilitate	rehabilitating
	rehabilitation
rehash	rehashed rehashes
	rehashing
rehearsal	
rehearse	rehearsing
reign (ruling)	reigned reigning
reimburse	reimbursing
reimbursement	

rein (control a horse)	reined reining
reincarnation	
reindeer	*plural* reindeer/
	reindeers
reinforce	reinforcing
reinforcement	
reinstate	reinstating
reinstatement	
reinvest	reinvested reinvesting
reinvestment	
reissue	reissuing
reiterate	reiterating reiteration
reject	rejected rejecting
	rejection
rejoice	rejoicing
rejoin	rejoined rejoining
rejoinder	
rejuvenate	rejuvenating
	rejuvenation
rekindle	rekindling
relapse	relapsing
relate	relating
relation	relationship
relative	relatively
relativity	relativities
relax	relaxed relaxes
	relaxing
relaxation	
relay	relayed relaying
release	releasing
relegate	relegating relegation
relent	relented relenting
relentless	relentlessly
	relentlessness
relevance	relevancy
relevant	relevantly
reliable	reliability reliably
reliance	
reliant	
relic	
relief	
relieve	relieving
religion	
religious	religiously religiousness
relinquish	relinquished
	relinquishes
	relinquishing

relish | relished relishes relishing
relive | reliving
relocate | relocating relocation
reluctance
reluctant | reluctantly
rely | relied relies relying
remain | remained remaining
remainder
remake | remade remaking
remand | remanded remanding
remark | remarked remarking
remarkable | remarkably
remarry | remarried remarries remarrying
remedial | remedially
remedy | remedies
remember | remembered remembering
remembrance
remind | reminded reminder reminding
remindful
reminisce | reminiscing
reminiscence
reminiscent | reminiscently
remiss
remission
remit | remitted remitting
remittance
remix | remixed remixes remixing
remnant
remonstrate | remonstrating remonstration
remorse
remorseful | remorsefully remorsefulness
remorseless | remorselessly remorselessness
remote | remotely remoteness remoter remotest
remould | remoulded remoulding
remount | remounted remounting
removable | removability
removal
remove | remover removing

remunerate | remunerating remuneration
renaissance/Renaissance
renal
rend | rending rent
render | rendered rendering
rendezvous | *plural* rendezvous
rendition
renegade
renege | reneging
renew | renewable renewed renewing
rennet
renounce | renouncing
renovate | renovating renovation
renown | renowned
rent | rented renting
rental
renunciation | renunciate renunciating
reoccupy | reoccupied reoccupies reoccupying
reoccur | reoccurred reoccurrence reoccurring
reorient | reoriented reorienting
reorientate | reorientating reorientation
repaid
repair | repaired repairing
reparable/repairable
reparation
repartee
repast
repatriate | repatriating repatriation
repay | repaid repaying
repeal | repealed repealing
repeat | repeatable repeated repeatedly repeating
repel | repelled repelling
repellent
repent | repented repenting
repentance
repentant | repentantly
repercussion
repertoire
repertory | repertories
repetition

repetitious — repetitiously, repetitiousness

repetitive — repetitively, repetitiveness

rephrase — rephrasing

replace — replacing

replacement

replay — replayed, replaying

replenish — replenished, replenishes, replenishing

replete — repletion

replica

replicate — replicating, replication

reply — replied, replies, replying

report — reported, reportedly, reporter, reporting

reportage

repose — reposing

repository — repositories

repossess — repossessed, repossesses, repossessing

repossession

repot — repotted, repotting

reprehend — reprehended, reprehending

reprehensible — reprehensibly

reprehension

represent — represented, representing

representation — representational

representative

repress — repressed, represses, repressing, repression

reprieve — reprieving

reprimand — reprimanded, reprimanding

reprint — reprinted, reprinting

reprisal

reproach — reproached, reproaches, reproaching

reprobate

reproduce — reproducing

reproduction

reproductive — reproductively, reproductiveness

reprographics

reproof (a rebuke)

reprove (to rebuke) — reproving, reprovingly

reptile

republic — republican, republicanism

repudiate — repudiating, repudiation

repugnance

repugnant — repugnantly

repulse — repulsing, repulsion

repulsive — repulsively, repulsiveness

reputable — reputably

reputation

repute — reputedly

request — requested, requesting

requiem/Requiem

require — requiring

requirement

requisite

requisition

requite — requiting

rescind — rescinded, rescinding

rescue — rescuer, rescuing

research — researched, researcher, researches, researching

reseat — reseated, reseating

resemblance

resemble — resembling

resent — resented, resenting, resentment

resentful — resentfully, resentfulness

reservation

reserve — reserving

reservist

reservoir

reset — resetting

reside — residing

residence

residency — residencies

resident — residential

residual

residue

resign — resigned, resignedly, resigning

resignation

resilience	
resilient	resiliently
resin	
resist	resisted resisting
	resistingly
resistance	
resistant	
resistible	resistibility resistibly
resistor	
resit	resat resitting
resolute	resolutely resoluteness
resolution	
resolve	resolving
resonance	
resonant	resonantly
resonate	resonating
resort	resorted resorting
resound	resounded resounding
	resoundingly
resource	
resourceful	resourcefully
	resourcefulness
respect	respected respecting
respectable	respectability
	respectably
respectful	respectfully
	respectfulness
respective	respectively
respiration	
respirator	respiratory
respite	
resplendence	
resplendent	resplendently
respond	responded responding
response	
responsible	responsibility
	responsibly
responsive	responsively
	responsiveness
rest	rested resting
restate	restating
restatement	
restaurant	restaurateur
restful	restfully restfulness
restitution	
restive	restively restiveness
restless	restlessly restlessness

restoration/Restoration	
restorative	
restore	restoring
restrain	restrained restraining
restraint	
restrict	restricted restricting
	restriction
restrictive	restrictively
	restrictiveness
restructure	restructuring
result	resulted resulting
resultant	
résumé (a summary)	
resume (to start again)	
	resuming
resumption	
resurgence	
resurgent	
resurrect	resurrected resurrecting
	resurrection
resuscitate	resuscitating
	resuscitation
retail	retailed retailer
	retailing
retain	retained retaining
	retention
retaliate	retaliating retaliation
retard	retarded retarding
retch	retched retches
	retching
retention	
retentive	retentively
	retentiveness
rethink	rethinking rethought
reticence	
reticent	reticently
retina	retinas/retinae
retinue	
retiral	
retire	retiring
retirement	
retort	retorted retorting
retouch	retouched retouches
	retouching
retrace	retracing
retract	retractable retracted
	retracting retraction

retractor		reviewer	
retreat	retreated retreating	revile	reviler reviling
retrench	retrenched retrenches	revilement	
	retrenching	revise	revising revision
retrenchment		revival	
retrial		revive	reviving
retribution		**revocation**	
retributive		revoke	revoking
retrieve	retrieval retrieving	revolt	revolted revolting
retriever			revoltingly
retrograde		revolution	revolutionaries
retrogress	retrogressed		revolutionary
	retrogresses	revolve	revolving
	retrogressing	revolver	
	retrogression	**revue** (an entertainment)	
retrogressive	retrogressively	revulsion	
retrospect	retrospection	**reward**	rewarded rewarding
retrospective	retrospectively	**rewind**	rewinding rewound
return	returned returning	rewire	rewiring
returnable		**rewrite**	rewriting rewritten
reunion			rewrote
reunite	reuniting	**rhapsody**	rhapsodies
revaluation		**rhea**	
revalue	revaluation revaluing	**rhetoric**	rhetorical rhetorically
revamp	revamped revamping	**rheumatic**	rheumatism
reveal	revealed revealing	**rhinoceros**	rhinoceroses/rhinoceros
	revealingly	**rhododendron**	
reveille		**rhombus**	rhombuses/rhombi
revel	revelled reveller	**rhubarb**	
	revelling	**rhumba/rumba**	
revelation		**rhyme** (in poetry)	rhymer rhyming
revelry	revelries	**rhythm**	rhythmic rhythmical
revenge	revenging		rhythmically
revenue		**rib**	ribbed ribbing
reverberate	reverberating	**ribald**	ribaldries ribaldry
	reverberation	**ribbon**	
revere (to admire)	revering	**rice**	
reverence		**rich**	richer riches richest
reverend			richly richness
reverent	reverently	**rick**	ricked ricking
reverie (a dream)		rickets	
reversal		rickety	ricketiness
reverse	reversing	rickshaw	
reversible	reversibility reversibly	**ricochet**	ricocheted/ricochetted
reversion			ricocheting/ricochetting
revert	reverted reverting	**rid**	ridding
review (to look over)	reviewed reviewing	**riddance**	

riddle	riddler riddling
ride	ridden rider riding
	rode
ridge	
ridicule	ridiculing
ridiculous	ridiculously
	ridiculousness
rife	
riffle (to flick through)	
	riffling
riff-raff	
rifle (gun)	rifling
rift	
rig	rigged rigger rigging
right	righted righting
	rightly rightness
righteous	righteously
	righteousness
rightful	rightfully rightfulness
rigid	rigidity rigidly
rigmarole	
rigorous	rigorously rigorousness
rigour	
rim	rimmed rimming
rime (frost)	
rind	
rindless	
ring	rang (a bell)
	ringed (put a ring on)
	ringing rung
ringer	
ringlet	ringleted
rink	
rinse	rinsing
riot	rioted rioter rioting
riotous	riotously riotousness
rip (to tear)	ripped ripping
ripe (ready to eat)	ripely ripeness riper
	ripest
ripen	ripened ripening
riposte	
ripple	rippling
rise	risen rising rose
riser	
risible	risibility risibly
risk	risked risking

risky (dangerous)	riskier riskiest riskily
	riskiness
risotto	
risqué (slightly shocking)	
rissole	
rite (a ceremony)	
ritual	ritually
rival	rivalled rivalling
rivalry	rivalries
river	
rivet	riveted riveting
Riviera/riviera	
rivulet	
roach	
road	
roadie	
roam	roamed roaming
roan (colour of horse's coat)	
roar	roared roaring
roast	roasted roasting
rob (to steal from)	robbed robber
	robbing
robbery	robberies
robe (to dress)	robing
robin	
robot	robotic
robust	robustly robustness
roc (legendary bird)	
rock (stone)	rocked rocking
rocker	
rockery	rockeries
rocket	rocketed rocketing
rocky	rockier rockiest
	rockiness
rococo	
rod	
rode	
rodent	
rodeo	
roe (deer; fish eggs)	
rogue	rogueries roguery
roguish	roguishly roguishness
role (part played by an actor)	
roll (to turn over)	rolled rolling
roller	
rollick	rollicked rollicking
	rollickingly

roly–poly
Roman
romance
romantic   romantically
romanticise   romanticising
                        romanticism
romp   romped romping
rompers
rondo
rood (crucifix; measure of land)
roof   roofed roofing
rook   rooked rooking
rookery   rookeries
rookie
room   roomed rooming
roomy   roomier roomiest
                        roominess
roost   roosted roosting
rooster
root (part of a plant) rooted rooting
rope   roping
Roquefort
rosary   rosaries
rose
roseate
rosemary
rosette
rosin   rosined rosining
roster
rostrum   rostrums/rostra
rosy   rosier rosiest rosily
                        rosiness
rot   rotted rotten rotting
rota
rotary
rotate   rotating rotation
rote (learned by repetition)
rotisserie
rotor (part of machine)
rotter (bad person)
Rottweiler
rotund   rotundity rotundly
rotunda
rouble (Russian coin)
rouge   rouging
rough   rougher roughest
                        roughly roughness

roughage
roughen   roughened
                        roughening
roulette
round   rounded rounder
                        roundest rounding
roundabout
rounders
roundly   roundness
rouse   rousing rousingly
rout (to defeat)   routed routing
route (road)   routed routeing
routine   routinely
roux
rove   rover roving rovingly
row (to move a boat; to quarrel)
                        rowed rower rowing
rowan (tree)
rowdy   rowdier rowdiest
                        rowdily rowdiness
rowlock
royal   royally
royalist
royalty   royalties
rub   rubbed rubbing
rubber
rubbish
rubble (small stones)
rubella
Rubicon (a place)
rubicund (ruddy-faced)
rubric
ruby   rubies
ruche (in curtains) ruching
ruck (in rugby)   rucked rucking
rucksack
ruction
rudd (fish)
rudder   rudderless
ruddy   ruddier ruddiest
                        ruddily ruddiness
rude (not polite)   rudely rudeness ruder
                        rudest
rudiments   rudimentary
rue (to regret)   ruing
rueful   ruefully ruefulness

ruff   ruffed ruffing
ruffian
ruffle   ruffling
rugby
rugged   ruggedly ruggedness
ruin   ruined ruining
ruination
ruinous   ruinously ruinousness
rule   ruler ruling
rum
rumba/rhumba
rumble   rumbling rumblingly
rumbustious   rumbustiously
                     rumbustiousness
ruminant
ruminate   ruminating rumination
                     ruminator
rummage   rummaging
rummy (card game)
rumour   rumoured
rump
rumpled
rumpus   rumpuses
run (to move fast) ran runner running
runaway
rune (old writing) runic
rung   runged
runny   runnier runniest
runt
runway
rupee
rupture   rupturing
rural   rurally
ruse
rush   rushed rushes rushing
rusk
russet   russety
rust   rusted rusting
rustic   rustically
rusticate   rusticating rustication
rustle   rustler rustling
rusty   rustier rustiest rustily
                     rustiness
rut   rutted rutting
ruthless   ruthlessly ruthlessness
rye

Ss

Sabbath
sabbatical
sable
sabotage   sabotaging
saboteur
sabre
saccharin (sweet substance)
saccharine (sweet, sugary)
sachet
sack   sacked sacking
sacrament   sacramental
                      sacramentally
sacred   sacredly sacredness
sacrifice   sacrificing
sacrificial   sacrificially
sacrilege
sacrilegious   sacrilegiously
                      sacrilegiousness
sacristy   sacristan sacristies
sacrosanct
sad   sadder saddest sadly
                      sadness
sadden   saddened saddening
saddle   saddler saddling
sadist   sadism sadistic
                     sadistically
safari
safe   safely safer safest
                     safety
safeguard
safety
saffron
sag   sagged sagging
saga
sagacious   sagaciously sagacity

sage
Sagittarius
sago
Sahara
sahib
said
sail (move by wind)   sailed sailing sailor
saint   sainted
saintly   saintlier saintliest
                      saintliness
sake
salaam
salacious   salaciously
                      salaciousness
salad
salamander
salami
salary   salaried salaries
sale (selling of goods)
saleable   saleability saleably
salesperson   salespeople
salient   saliently
saline
saliva
salivate   salivating salivation
sallow   sallowly sallowness
sally   sallied sallies sallying
salmon   plural salmon
salmonella
salon (room used by hairdresser or beautician)
saloon
salt   salted salting
saltire
saltpetre
salty   saltier saltiest saltiness
salubrious   salubriously
                      salubriousness
salutary (healthy, timely)
salutation
salute   saluting
salvage   salvageable salvaging
salvation
salve   salving
salver
salvo   salvos/salvoes
Samaritan
samba

same	sameness
samosa	
samovar	
sampan	
sample	sampling
samurai	
sanatorium	sanatoriums/sanatoria
sanctify	sanctified sanctifies
	sanctifying
sanctimonious	sanctimoniously
	sanctimoniousness
sanction	sanctioned sanctioning
sanctity	sanctities
sanctuary	sanctuaries
sanctum	
sand	sanded sanding
sandal	
sandpaper	
sandwich	sandwiches
sandy	sandier sandiest
	sandiness
sane	sanely saneness saner
	sanest
sang	
sang-froid	
sanguinary	sanguinarily
sanguine	sanguinely
	sanguineness
sanitary	
sanitation	
sanity	sanities
sank	
sap	sapped sapping
sapience	
sapient	sapiently
sapling	
sapper	
sapphire	
sappy	sappier sappiest
	sappily sappiness
sarcasm	
sarcastic	sarcastically
sardine	
sardonic	sardonically
sargasso	
sari/saree	
sarong	

sartorial	sartorially
sash	sashes
Sassenach	
Satan	Satanism Satanist
satanic	satanically
satchel	
satellite	
satiable	satiability satiably
satiate	satiating satiation
satin	satiny
satire (type of humour)	
	satirical satirically
	satirist
satisfaction	
satisfactory	satisfactorily
	satisfactoriness
satisfy	satisfied satisfies
	satisfying satisfyingly
satsuma	
saturate	saturating saturation
Saturday	
Saturn	
saturnine	
satyr (creature in Greek mythology)	
sauce	
saucer	
sauerkraut	
sauna	
saunter	sauntered sauntering
sausage	
sauté	
savable	
savage	savagely savaging
savagery	savageries
savannah/savanna	
save	saver saving
saviour (person who saves from danger)	
savoir faire	
savory (a plant)	
savour (taste)	savoured savouring
savourless	
savoury (a taste)	savouries savouriness
saw	sawed sawing sawn
sawdust	
saxifrage	
saxophone	saxophonist
say	said saying

scab	scabbed scabbing
scabbard	
scabby	scabbier scabbiest
	scabbily scabbiness
scabies (an infection)	
scabious (a plant)	
scabrous	scabrously
	scabrousness
scaffold	scaffolder scaffolding
scald	scalded scalding
	scaldingly
scale	scaling
scalene	
scallion	
scallop	
scallywag	
scalp	scalped scalping
scalpel	
scam	
scamp	
scamper	scampered scampering
scampi	
scan	scanned scanner
	scanning
scandal	
scandalise	scandalising
scandalous	scandalously
	scandalousness
scant	
scanty	scantier scantiest
	scantily scantiness
scapegoat	
scar	scarred scarring
scarab	
scarce	scarcely scarceness
scarcity	scarcities
scare	scaring
scarecrow	
scarf	scarfed scarfs/scarves
scarlet	
scathing	
scatter	scattered scattering
scatterbrain	scatterbrained
scavenge	scavenger scavenging
scenario	
scene	scenic scenically
scenery	sceneries

scent (smell)	scented scenting
sceptic (doubting)	sceptical sceptically
	scepticism
sceptre	
schedule	scheduling
schema	
schematic	schematically
scheme	schemer scheming
scherzo	
schism	schismatic
schizophrenia	schizophrenic
scholar	scholarly
scholarship	
scholastic	scholastically
school	schooled schooling
schoolboy	schoolboyish
schoolgirl	schoolgirlish
schoolmaster	
schoolmistress	schoolmistresses
schoolroom	
schoolteacher	
schoolwork	
schooner	
sciatica	
science	
scientific	scientifically
scientist	
scimitar	
scintilla	
scintillate	scintillating
	scintillatingly
	scintillation
scissor	scissored scissoring
scissors	
scoff	scoffed scoffer
	scoffing scoffingly
scold	scolded scolding
scone	
scoop	scooped scooping
scoot	scooted scooting
scooter	
scope	
scorch	scorched scorcher
	scorches scorching
score	scorer scoring
scoreboard	
scorn	scorned scorning

scornful   scornfully scornfulness
Scorpio
scorpion
scotch   scotched scotches
                scotching
scoundrel   scoundrelly
scour   scoured scourer
                scouring
scourge   scourging
scout   scouted scouting
scowl   scowled scowling
                scowlingly
scrabble
scraggy   scraggier scraggiest
                scragginess
scramble   scrambler scrambling
scrap (to throw away)
                scrapped scrapping
scrape (to mark, scratch)
                scraper scraping
scratch   scratched scratcher
                scratches scratching
scratchy   scratchier scratchiest
                scratchily scratchiness
scrawl   scrawled scrawling
scrawny   scrawnier scrawniest
                scrawniness
scream   screamed screamer
                screaming screamingly
scree
screech   screeched screeches
                screeching
screed
screen   screened screening
screw   screwed screwing
screwdriver
scribble   scribbler scribbling
scribe   scribing
scrimmage   scrimmaging
scrimp   scrimped scrimping
scrimshaw
script   scripted scripting
scripture   scriptural scripturally
scroll   scrolled scrolling
scrounge   scrounger scrounging
scrub   scrubbed scrubber
                scrubbing

scruff
scruffy   scruffier scruffiest
                scruffily scruffiness
scrum
scrummage   scrummaging
scrumptious   scrumptiously
                scrumptiousness
scruple
scrupulous   scrupulously
                scrupulousness
scrutinise   scrutinising
scrutiny   scrutineer scrutinies
scuba–diving scuba-diver
scud   scudded scudding
scuff   scuffed scuffing
scuffle   scuffling
scull (to row) sculled sculler
                sculling
scullery   sculleries
sculpt   sculpted sculpting
sculptor
sculptress   sculptresses
sculpture   sculpturing
scum
scummy   scummier scummiest
                scummily scumminess
scupper   scuppered scuppering
scurrilous   scurrilously
                scurrilousness
scurry   scurried scurries
                scurrying
scurvy   scurvier scurviest
                scurvily scurviness
scut
scuttle   scuttling
scythe   scything
sea (water)
seaboard
seaborne
seafarer   seafaring
seafood
seagoing
seagull
seal   sealed sealing
sealant
sea level
sealskin

seam (join in cloth; ledge of coal, etc.)
     seamed seaming
seaman   seamen (sailors)
seamanship
seance
seaplane
sear (to scorch)   seared searing
     searingly
search   searched searcher
     searches searching
     searchingly

seashore
seaside
season   seasoned seasoning
seasonable   seasonableness
     seasonably
seasonal   seasonally
seat   seated seating
seaway
seaweed
seaworthy   seaworthily
     seaworthiness
secateurs
secede   seceder seceding
secession
seclude   secluding
seclusion
second   seconded seconder
     seconding
secondary   secondarily
second-class
second-hand
second-rate
secrecy
secret (hidden)   secretly
secretary   secretarial secretaries
secrete (to hide; to make moist)
     secreting secretion
secretive   secretively
     secretiveness
sect   sectarian sectarianism
section   sectioned sectioning
sectional   sectionally
sectionalise   sectionalising
sector
secular
secure   securely securing

security   securities
sedan (chair)
sedate   sedately sedateness
     sedation sedative
sedge
sediment   sedimentary
sedition   seditious seditiously
seduce   seducer seducing
     seducingly seduction
seductive   seductively
     seductiveness
sedulous   sedulously
     sedulousness
see   saw seen seeing
seed   seeded seeding
seedless
seedling
seek   seeker seeking sought
seem (to give the impression)
     seemed seeming
     seemingly
seep   seepage seeped
     seeping
seer (a prophet)
seersucker
seesaw   seesawed seesawing
seethe   seething
segment   segmentation
     segmented
     segmenting
segmental   segmentally
     segmentary
segregate   segregating segregation
seismic
seize   seizing
seizure
seldom
select   selected selecting
     selection
selective   selectively
     selectiveness
selector
self   selves
selfhood
selfish   selfishly selfishness
selfless   selflessly selflessness
selfsame

sell	seller selling sold	sequential	sequentially
sellable		sequin	
Sellotape	sellotaping	**serenade**	serenading
selves		serendipity	
semaphore	semaphoring	serene	serenely serenity
semblance		**serf**	
semen (fluid)		**serge**	
semicircle	semicircular	sergeant	
semicolon		**serial** (in parts)	serially
seminar		serialise	serialisation serialising
semolina		series	*plural* series
senate	senator	serious	seriously seriousness
send	sender sending	**sermon**	
	sent (dispatched)	**serpent**	serpentine
senile	senility	**serrated**	serration
senior	seniority	serried	
sensation	sensational	**serum**	serums/sera
	sensationally	**servant**	
sensationalise	sensationalising	serve	server serving
	sensationalism	service	servicing
sense	sensing	serviceable	serviceableness
senseless	senselessly		serviceably
	senselessness	serviette	
sensible	sensibility sensibly	servile	servilely servility
sensitive	sensitively sensitivity	servitude	
sensory		**sesame**	
sensual	sensuality sensually	**session**	sessional sessionally
sensuous	sensuously	**set** (to put down)	set setting
	sensuousness	**sett** (a badger's burrow)	
sent (dispatched)		settee	
sentence	sentencing	setter	
sententious	sententiously	settle	settler settling
	sententiousness	settlement	
sentient		**seven**	seventh seventhly
sentiment	sentimental	seventeen	seventeenth
	sentimentally	seventy	seventies seventieth
sentinel		sever (to cut off)	severance severed
sentry	sentries		severing
separable	separableness separably	several	severally
separate	separately separateness	severe (strict, hard)	severely severity
	separating separation	**sew**	sewed sewing sewn
sepia		**sewage** (waste matter)	
September		**sewer**	sewerage (system of
septic (infected)	septicaemia/septicemia		drains)
sepulchre	sepulchral sepulchrally	**sex**	sexes sexing sexism
sequel			sexist
sequence		**sextant**	

sexton	
sexual	sexuality sexually
sexy	sexier sexiest sexily
	sexiness
shabby	shabbier shabbiest
	shabbily shabbiness
shack	
shackle	shackling
shade	shading
shadow	shadowed shadowing
shadowy	
shady	shadier shadiest
	shadily shadiness
shaft	shafted shafting
shag	
shaggy	shaggier shaggiest
	shaggily shagginess
shake	shaken shaking shook
shakeable/shakable	
shaky	shakier shakiest
	shakily shakiness
shale	
shall	
shallot	
shallow	shallower shallowest
	shallowly shallowness
shalom	
sham (false)	
shamble	shambling shamblingly
shame (humiliation)	
shameful	shamefully
	shamefulness
shameless	shamelessly
	shamelessness
shampoo	shampooed
	shampooing
shamrock	
shandy	shandies
shank	
shan't (shall not)	
shanty	shanties
shape	shaping
shapeless	shapelessly
	shapelessness
shapely	shapelier shapeliest
	shapeliness
shard	

share	sharing
shark	
sharp	sharper sharpest
sharpen	sharpened sharpener
	sharpening
sharply	sharpness
shatter	shattered shattering
	shatteringly
shave	shaven shaver
	shaving
shawl	shawled
sheaf	sheaves
shear (to cut, clip)	sheared shearer
	shearing shorn
shears	
sheath (close-fitting cover)	
sheathe (to put in a sheath)	
	sheathing
sheaves	
shed	shedding
sheen	
sheep	*plural* sheep sheepish
	sheepishly
	sheepishness
sheer (steep; to move away)	
	sheered sheering
sheet	sheeted sheeting
sheik/sheikh	sheikdom/sheikhdom
shelf (furniture)	shelves
shell	shelled shelling
she'll (she will)	
shellfish	shellfish/shellfishes
shelter	sheltered sheltering
sheltie (dog or pony)	
shelve (to put aside)	shelving
shelves	
shepherd	shepherded
	shepherding
sherbet	
sheriff	
sherry	sherries
shibboleth	
shied	
shield	shielded shielding
shies	
shift	shifted shifting
shiftless	shiftlessly shiftlessness

shifty	shiftier shiftiest
	shiftily shiftiness
shilling	
shilly-shally	shilly-shallied
	shilly-shallies
	shilly-shallying
shimmer	shimmered shimmering
	shimmeringly
shin (leg)	
shine (to glow)	shining shone
shingle	
Shinto	
shinty	
shiny	shinier shiniest shinily
	shininess
ship	shipped shipper
	shipping
shipbuilder	
shipment	
shipwreck	shipwrecked
	shipwrecking
shipwright	
shipyard	
shire	
shirk	shirked shirking
shirt	
shirty	shirtier shirtiest
	shirtily shirtiness
Shiva/Siva	
shiver	shivered shivering
	shivery
shoal	shoaled shoaling
shock	shocked shocker
	shocking shockingly
shoddy	shoddier shoddiest
	shoddily shoddiness
shoe (for foot)	shoeing
shoehorn	
shoelace	
shoemaker	
shoeshine	
shoestring	
shone	
shoo (to drive off)	shooed shooing
shook	
shoot	shot shooter shooting

shop	shopped shopper
	shopping
shore	shoring
shorn	
short	shorter shortest
	shortly shortness
shortage	
shortbread	
shortcomings	
shorten	shortened shortening
shorthand	
shot	
shotgun	
should	
shoulder	shouldered
	shouldering
shouldn't (should not)	
shout	shouted shouting
shove	shoving
shovel	shovelled shovelling
show	showed showing
showdown	
shower	showered showering
	showery
showroom	
showy	showier showiest
	showily showiness
shrank	
shrapnel	
shred	shredded shredder
	shredding
shrew	
shrewd	shrewder shrewdest
	shrewdly shrewdness
shrewish	shrewishly
	shrewishness
shriek	shrieked shrieking
shrill	shriller shrillest shrilly
	shrillness
shrimp	
shrine	
shrink	shrank shrinking
	shrunk
shrinkage	
shrivel	shrivelled shrivelling
shroud	shrouded shrouding
shrub	shrubbery shrubberies

shrug | shrugged shrugging
shrunk | shrunken
shudder | shuddered shuddering
 | shudderingly
shuffle | shuffling
shun | shunned shunning
shunt | shunted shunting
shut | shutting
shutter | shuttered shuttering
shuttle | shuttling
shuttlecock |
shy | shied shies shyer
 | shyest shying
shyly | shyness
sibilance | sibilant
sibling |
sick | sickness
sicken | sickened sickening
 | sickeningly
sickish |
sickle |
sickly | sicklier sickliest
 | sickliness
side | siding
sideboard |
sideline |
sidelong |
sideways |
sidle | sidling
siege |
siesta |
sieve | sieving
sift | sifted sifter sifting
sigh | sighed sighing
sight | sighted sighting
sightless | sightlessly
 | sightlessness
sightsee | sightseer sightseeing
sign | signed signer signing
signal | signalled signaller
 | signalling
signatory | signatories
signature |
signet |
significance |
significant | significantly

signify | signified signifies
 | signifying
Sikh | Sikhism
silage |
silence | silencer silencing
silent | silently
silhouette |
silica |
silicon (used in computer chips) |
silicone (plastic substance) |
silk | silken
silky | silkier silkiest silkily
 | silkiness
sill |
silly | sillier silliest sillily
 | silliness
silo |
silt | silted silting
silver | silveriness silvery
simian |
similar | similarities similarity
 | similarly
simile |
simmer | simmered simmering
simper | simpered simpering
 | simperingly
simple | simpler simplest
 | simply
simpleton |
simplicity |
simplification |
simplify | simplified simplifies
 | simplifying
simplistic | simplistically
simulate | simulating simulation
simulator |
simultaneous | simultaneity
 | simultaneously
sin (to do wrong) | sinned sinner sinning
since |
sincere | sincerely sincerity
sine (mathematics) |
sinecure |
sinew | sinewy
sinful | sinfully sinfulness
sing (to make music) | sang singer singing
 | singingly

singe (to burn)	singeing
single	singling singly
singlet	
singular	singularities
	singularity singularly
sinister	sinisterly
sink	sank sinking sunk
sinus	sinuses sinusitis
sip	sipped sipping
siphon/syphon	siphoned/syphoned
	siphoning/syphoning
sir (gentleman)	
sire (to father)	siring
siren	
sirloin	
sirocco	
sister	sisterly sisterliness
sisterhood	
sister-in-law	sisters-in-law
sit (to take a seat)	sat sitter sitting
sitar	
sitcom	
site (place)	siting
situate	situating situation
situational	
Siva/Shiva	
six	sixth sixthly
sixteen	sixteenth
sixty	sixties sixtieth
size	sizing
sizeable	sizeably
sizzle	sizzling sizzlingly
skate	skater skating
skateboard	skateboarder
	skateboarding
skein	
skeleton	skeletal
sketch	sketched sketches
	sketching
sketchy	sketchier sketchiest
	sketchily sketchiness
skew	skewed skewing
skewbald	
skewer	skewered skewering
ski	skied skier skies
	skiing
skid	skidded skidding

skiff	
skiffle	
skilful	skilfully skilfulness
skill	skilled
skim	skimmed skimmer
	skimming
skimp	skimped skimping
skimpy	skimpier skimpiest
	skimpily skimpiness
skin	skinned skinning
skinful	
skinless	
skinny	
skint	
skip	skipped skipping
skipper	
skirl	skirled skirling
skirmish	skirmished skirmishes
	skirmishing
skirt	skirted skirting
skit	
skitter	skittered skittering
skittish	skittishly skittishness
skittle	skittling
skua	
skulduggery	skulduggeries
skulk	skulked skulking
skull (head)	
skunk	
sky	skied skies skying
skylight	
skyscraper	
slab	slabbed slabbing
slack	
slacken	slackened slackening
slag	
slain	
slake	slaking
slalom	
slam	slammed slamming
slander	slandered slanderer
	slandering
slanderous	slanderously
slang	slanging
slangy	slangier slangiest
	slangily slanginess
slant	slanted slanting

slap   slapped slapping
slapdash
slapstick
slash   slashed slasher
                      slashes slashing
slat (strip of wood) slatted slatting
slate (roof-tile; to abuse)
                      slater slating
slattern   slatternliness
                      slatternly
slaughter   slaughtered slaughterer
                      slaughtering
slaughterhouse
slave   slaver slavery slaving
slaver   slavered slavering
                      slaveringly
slavish   slavishly slavishness
slay (to kill)   slain slayer slaying
                      slew
sleazy   sleazier sleaziest
                      sleazily sleaziness
sled
sledge   sledger sledging
sleek   sleekly sleekness
sleep   sleeping slept
sleepless   sleeplessly
                      sleeplessness
sleepy   sleepier sleepiest
                      sleepily sleepiness
sleet   sleetier sleetiest
                      sleety
sleeve
sleeveless
sleigh (sledge)
sleight of hand
slender   slenderer slenderest
                      slenderly slenderness
slept
sleuth   sleuthed sleuthing
slew   slewed slewing
slice   slicer slicing
slick   slicker slickest slickly
                      slickness
slid (glided)
slide (to glide)   slid slider sliding

slight   slighted slighter
                      slightest slighting
                      slightingly slightly
                      slightness
slim (to lose weight) slimly slimmed
                      slimmer slimmest
                      slimming slimness
slime (mud)
slimy   slimier slimiest slimily
                      sliminess
sling   slinging slung
slink   slinking slunk
slip   slipped slipping
slippage
slipper
slippery   slipperiness
slippy   slippier slippiest
                      slippily slippiness
slipshod
slipstream
slipway
slit   slitted slitting
slither   slithered slithering
                      slithery
sliver   slivered slivering
slob
slobber   slobbered slobberer
                      slobbering
sloe (berry)
slog   slogged slogger
                      slogging
slogan
sloop (ship)
slop (to spill)   slopped slopping
slope (incline; to move down)
                      sloping
sloppy   sloppier sloppiest
                      sloppily sloppiness
slosh   sloshed sloshes
                      sloshing
slot   slotted slotting
sloth
slothful   slothfully slothfulness
slouch   slouched slouches
                      slouching slouchingly
slouchy   slouchier slouchiest
slovenly   slovenliness

slow (not fast)   slowed slower
                             slowest slowing
slowly   slowness
slow-worm
sludge
slug   slugged slugger
                             slugging
sluggish   sluggishly sluggishness
sluice   sluicing
slum   slummed slumming
slumber   slumbered slumbering
                             slumberingly
slump   slumped slumping
slung
slunk
slur   slurred slurring
slurp   slurped slurping
slurry   slurries
slush   slushier slushiest
                             slushy
slut
sluttish   sluttishly sluttishness
sly   slyer slyest slyly
                             slyness
smack   smacked smacking
small   smallness
smallpox
smarm   smarmed smarming
smarmy   smarmier smarmiest
                             smarmily smarminess
smart   smarted smarter
                             smartest smarting
                             smartly smartness
smarten   smartened smartening
smash   smashed smasher
                             smashes smashing
smatter   smattering
smear   smeared smearing
smell   smelled/smelt smeller
                             smelling
smelly   smellier smelliest
                             smelliness
smile   smiler smiling
                             smilingly
smirk   smirked smirking
                             smirkingly

smite   smiting smitten
                             smote
smithereens
smithy   smithies
smitten
smock (frock)
smog
smoke (to give off fumes)
                             smoker smoking
smokeless
smooth   smoothed smoother
                             smoothes smoothest
                             smoothing
smoothly   smoothness
smorgasbord
smote
smother   smothered smothering
smoulder   smouldered
                             smouldering
smudge   smudging
smudgy   smudgier smudgiest
                             smudgily smudginess
smug   smugly smugness
smuggle   smuggler smuggling
smut
smutty   smuttier smuttiest
                             smuttily smuttiness
snack
snack bar
snaffle   snaffling
snag   snagged snagging
snail
snake   snaking
snaky   snakily snakiness
snap   snapped snapper
                             snapping
snappish   snappishly
                             snappishness
snappy   snappier snappiest
                             snappily snappiness
snare   snaring
snarl   snarled snarler
                             snarling snarlingly
snatch   snatched snatcher
                             snatches snatching
sneak   sneaked sneaking
sneakers

sneaky	sneakier sneakiest sneakily	**snub**	snubbed snubbing
sneer	sneered sneerer sneeringly	**snuff**	snuffed snuffer snuffing
sneeze	sneezer sneezing	snuffle	snuffling
snick	snicked snicking	**snug**	snugger snuggest snugly snugness
snicker	snickered snickering	snuggle	snuggled snuggling
snide	snidely snideness	**soak**	soaked soaker soaking
sniff	sniffed sniffer sniffing	**soap**	soaped soaping
sniffy	sniffier sniffiest sniffily sniffiness	soapy	soapier soapiest soapily soapiness
snigger	sniggered sniggering	**soar** (to rise up)	soared soaring
snip (to cut)	snipped snipping	**sob**	sobbed sobbing
snipe (bird; to shoot)	sniper sniping	**sober**	sobered sobering soberingly
snippet		soberly	soberness sobriety
snippy	snippier snippiest snippily	**sobriquet**	
snivel	snivelled sniveller snivelling snivelly	**soccer**	
snob	snobberies snobbery snobby	**sociable**	sociability sociably
snobbish	snobbishly snobbishness	social	socially
		socialise	socialising
snood		Socialism	socialist
snooker	snookered snookering	society	societies
snoop	snooped snooper snooping	sociology	sociologist
snooty	snootier snootiest snootily snootiness	**sock**	socked socking
snore	snorer snoring	socket	
snorkel	snorkelled snorkeller snorkelling	**sod**	
snort	snorted snorting	**soda**	
snotty	snottier snottiest snottily snottiness	**sodden**	
		sodium	
snout		**sofa**	
snow	snowed snowing	**soft**	softer softest softly softness
snowball	snowballed snowballing	soften	softened softener softening
snowdrift		software	
snowdrop		**soggy**	soggier soggiest soggily sogginess
snowflake		**soil**	soiled soiling
snowman	snowmen	**sojourn**	sojourned sojourning
snowplough		**solace**	
snowy	snowier snowiest snowily snowiness	solar	
		solarium	solaria/solariums
		sold	
		solder (to join metals)	soldered soldering

soldier (army person) soldiered soldiering
soldierly   soldierliness
sole (bottom of shoe; only; fish)
                           solely
solemn   solemnly
solemnity   solemnities
sol-fa
solicit   solicited soliciting
solicitation
solicitor
solicitous   solicitously
                           solicitousness/solicitude
solicitude
solid   solidity solidly
solidarity
solidify   solidified solidifies
                           solidifying
soliloquy   soliloquies
solitaire
solitary   solitarily solitariness
solitude
solo   soloist
solstice
soluble   solubility solubly
solution
solvable   solvability
solve   solving
solvency
solvent
sombre   sombrely sombreness
sombrero
some
somebody
somehow
someone
somersault   somersaulted
                           somersaulting
something
somewhat
somewhere
son (boy child)
sonar
sonata
song
songster
sonic
son-in-law   sons-in-law

sonnet
sonorous   sonorously
                           sonorousness/sonority
soon   sooner soonest
soot
soothe   soothing
sooty   sootier sootiest
                           sootily sootiness
sophisticated   sophistication
soporific
soppy   soppier soppiest
                           soppily soppiness
soprano   sopranos/soprani
sorbet
sorcerer
sorceress   sorceresses
sorcery   sorceries
sordid   sordidly sordidness
sore (hurt)   sorely soreness
sorrow   sorrowed sorrowing
sorrowful   sorrowfully
                           sorrowfulness
sorry   sorrier sorriest
sort   sorted sorter sorting
sortie
soufflé
sough   soughed soughing
sought
soul (inner nature)
soulful   soulfully soulfulness
soulless   soullessly soullessness
sound   sounded sounding
                           soundly
soundproof
soundtrack
soup   souped (up)
                           souping (up)
sour   soured souring sourly
                           sourness
source
souse   sousing
soutane
south   southern
southerly   southerlies
souvenir
sou'wester

sovereign	sovereignly
	sovereignties
	sovereignty
sow	sowed sower sowing
	sown
soy/soya	
spa	
space	spaced spacer
	spacing
spacial/spatial (about space)	
	spacially/spatially
spacious	spaciously spaciousness
spade	
spadeful	
spaghetti	
span	spanned spanning
spangle	spangling spangly
spaniel	
spank	spanked spanking
spanner	
spar (to box)	sparred sparring
spare (to show mercy)	
	sparing sparingly
sparely	spareness
spark	sparked sparking
	sparky
sparkle	sparkler sparkling
	sparkly
sparrow	
sparse	sparsely sparseness
spasm	
spasmodic	spasmodically
spastic	
spat (ejected from mouth)	
spatchcock	
spate (in flood)	
spatial/spacial	spatially/spacially
spatter	spattered spattering
spatula	
spawn	spawned spawning
spay	spayed spaying
speak	speaker speaking
	spoke spoken
spear	speared spearing
special (not usual)	specially
specialise	specialisation
	specialising

specialist	
speciality	specialities
species (type of)	*plural* species
specifiable	specifiably
specific	specifically
specify	specification specified
	specifies specifying
specimen	
specious (false)	speciously speciousness
speck	specked
speckle	
spectacle	spectacular
	spectacularly
spectate	spectating spectator
spectre	spectral
spectrum	spectra
speculate	speculating speculation
speculative	speculatively
sped (moved fast)	
speech	speeches
speechless	
speed (to move fast)	sped (moved fast)
	speeded (went beyond
	the speed limit)
	speeding
speedometer	
speedway	
speedy	speedier speediest
	speedily speediness
spell	spelled/spelt speller
	spelling
spellbind	spellbinding spellbound
spend	spender spending
	spent
sperm	
spermaceti	
spew	spewed spewing
sphere	spherical spherically
sphincter	
sphinx	sphinxes
spice	spicing
spick and span	
spicy	spicier spiciest spicily
	spiciness
spider	spidery
spike	spiking

spiky	spikier spikiest spikily spikiness
spill	spilled/spilt spilling
spillage	
spin (to twist)	spinner spinning spun
spinach	
spindle	spindly
spine (backbone)	spinal
spineless	spinelessly spinelessness
spinnaker	
spinster	spinsterish spinsterly
spinsterhood	
spiny	spinier spiniest spininess
spire	spiral spirally
spirit	spirited spiriting
spiritual	spirituality spiritually
spiritualist	spiritualism
spit (to eject from mouth)	
	spat spitter spitting
spite (a grudge)	
spiteful	spitefully spitefulness
spittle	
splash	splashed splashes splashing
splashy	splashier splashiest
splatter	splattered splattering
splay	splayed splaying
spleen	splenetic splenetically
splendid	splendidly splendidness/splendour
splendour	
splice	splicing
splint	splinted splinting
splinter	splintered splintering
split	splitting
splurge	splurging
splutter	spluttered spluttering
spoil	spoiled spoiler spoiling spoilt
spoilsport	
spoke	spoken
spokesman	spokesmen
spokesperson	
spokeswoman	spokeswomen

sponge	sponger sponging
spongy	spongier spongiest spongily sponginess
sponsor	sponsored sponsoring sponsorship
spontaneous	spontaneously spontaneousness spontaneity
spoof	
spook	spooky spookier spookiest spookily spookiness
spool	spooled spooling
spoon	spooned spooning
spoonerism	
spoonful	
spoor (animal tracks)	
sporadic	sporadically
spore (plant cell)	
sporran	
sport	sported sporting sportingly
sporty	sportier sportiest sportily sportiness
spot	spotted spotting
spotless	spotlessly spotlessness
spotlight	spotlighted spotlighting
spotty	spottier spottiest spottily spottiness
spouse	
spout	spouted spouting
sprain	sprained spraining
sprang	
sprat	
sprawl	sprawled sprawling
spray	sprayed spraying
spread	spreader spreading
spreadeagle	spreadeagling
spreadsheet	
spree	
sprig	
sprightly	sprightlier sprightliest sprightliness
spring	sprang springer springing sprung
springbok	

springy	springier springiest	squeal	squealed squealer
	springily springiness		squealing
sprinkle	sprinkler sprinkling	squeamish	squeamishly
sprint	sprinted sprinter		squeamishness
	sprinting	squeeze	squeezing
sprite		squelch	squelched squelches
sprocket			squelching
sprout	sprouted sprouting	squelchy	squelchier squelchiest
spruce	sprucely spruceness		squelchily
	sprucing		squelchiness
sprung		**squib**	
spry	spryer spryest spryly	squid	
	spryness	squint	squinted squinting
spume		squire	
spunk		squirm	squirmed squirming
spunky	spunkier spunkiest	squirrel	
	spunkiness	squirt	squirted squirter
spur	spurred spurring		squirting
spurious	spuriously	**stab**	stabbed stabbing
	spuriousness	stabilise	stabilisation stabiliser
spurn	spurned spurning		stabilising
spurt	spurted spurting	stability	
sputter	sputtered sputtering	stable	stably
spy	spied spies spying	**staccato**	
squabble	squabbling	stack	stacked stacker
squad			stacking
squadron		**stadium**	stadiums/stadia
squalid	squalidly	**staff**	staffed staffing
	squalidness/squalor	**stag** (deer)	
squall	squally	stage (to put on a show)	
squalor			staged staging
squander	squandered	stagger	staggered staggering
	squandering		staggeringly
square	squaring	stagnant	stagnantly
squarely	squareness	stagnate	stagnating stagnation
squash	squashed squashes	**staid** (dull)	staidly staidness
	squashing	stain	stained staining
squashy	squashier squashiest	stainless	
	squashily squashiness	stair	
squat	squatly squatness	staircase	
	squatted squatter	stairway	
	squatting	**stake** (wooden post) staking	
squaw		**stalactite**	
squawk	squawked squawking	stalagmite	
squeak	squeaked squeaking	stale	stalely staleness staler
squeaky	squeakier squeakiest		stalest
	squeakily squeakiness	stalemate	

stalk	stalked stalker stalking
stall	stalled stalling
stallion	
stalwart	stalwartly stalwartness
stamen	
stamina	
stammer	stammered stammerer stammering
stamp	stamped stamping
stampede	
stance	
stanchion	
stand	standing stood
standard	
standardise	standardisation standardising
standpoint	
standstill	
stang	
stank	
stanza	
staple	stapler stapling
star (in sky)	starred starring
starboard	
starch	starched starches starching
starchy	starchier starchiest starchily starchiness
stare (to look)	staring
stark	starkly starkness
stark naked	
starling	
starry	starrily starriness
start	started starter starting
startle	startling
starve	starvation starving
stash	stashed stashes stashing
state	stating
stateless	
stately	statelier stateliest stateliness
statement	
static	statically
station	stationed stationing

stationary (standing still)	
stationery (papers)	
statistic	statistical statistically
statistics	
statue	
statuesque	statuesquely statuesqueness
statuette	
stature	
status	
status (quo)	
statute	statutory
staunch	staunched staunches staunching staunchly
stave	staving stove
stay	stayed stayer staying
stead	
steadfast	steadfastly steadfastness
steady	steadier steadiest steadily steadiness
steak (food)	
steal	stealer stealing stole stolen
stealth	
stealthy	stealthier stealthiest stealthily stealthiness
steam	steamed steamer steaming
steamy	steamier steamiest steamily steaminess
steed	
steel	steeled steeling steely
steep	steeped steeper steepest steeping
steeple	
steeplechase	
steeplejack	
steeply	steepness
steer	steered steering
stellar	
stem	stemmed stemming
stench	stenches
stencil	stencilled stencilling
step	stepped stepping
stereo	
stereotype	

sterile	sterility	stocky	stockier stockiest
sterilise	sterilising sterilisation		stockily stockiness
sterling		stockyard	
stern	sternly	**stodge**	
steroid		stodgy	stodgier stodgiest
stethoscope			stodgily stodginess
stetson		**stoic**	stoical stoically
stew	stewed stewing		stoicism
steward		**stoke**	stoker stoking
stewardess	stewardesses	**stole**	
stick	sticker sticking stuck	**stomach**	
sticky	stickier stickiest	stomach-ache	
stiff	stiffly stiffness	stomp	stomped stomping
stiffen	stiffened stiffener	**stone**	stoning
	stiffening	stonewall	stonewalled
stifle	stifling		stonewalling
stigma	stigmas/stigmata	stonewashed	
stile (step)		stony	stonier stoniest
stiletto			stonily stoniness
still	stilled stilling	**stood**	
stilt	stilted	stooge	
stimulant		stook	
stimulate	stimulating	stool	
	stimulation	stoop (to bend)	stooped stooping
stimulus	stimuli	**stop** (to finish)	stopped stopper
sting	stinging stung		stopping
stingy	stingier stingiest	stopcock	
	stingily stinginess	stoppage	
stink	stank stunk stinking	stopwatch	stopwatches
stint	stinted stinting	**storage**	
stipend	stipendiary	store	storing
stipple	stippler stippling	storekeeper	
stipulate	stipulating stipulation	storeroom	
stir	stirred stirring	storey (floor in building)	
stirrup			*plural* storeys
stitch	stitched stitches	stork	
	stitching	storm	stormed storming
		stormy	stormier stormiest
stoat			stormily storminess
stock	stocked stocker	story (fiction)	stories
	stocking	storyteller	
stockade		**stout**	stouter stoutest
stockbroker			stoutly stoutness
stockholder		**stove**	
stockpile	stockpiling	**stow**	stowed stowing
stocks		stowaway	
stock-still		**straddle**	straddling

strafe	strafing	stress	stressed stresses
straggle	straggler straggling		stressing
straight (not curved)	straightly straightness	stressful	stressfully
straightaway			stressfulness
straightedge		stretch	stretched stretches
straighten	straightened		stretching
	straightener	stretcher	
	straightening	strew	strewed strewing
strain	strained strainer		strewn
	straining	**stricken**	
strait (channel)		strict	stricter strictest
straitjacket			strictly strictness
strand	stranded stranding	stricture	
strange	strangely strangeness	stride	striding stridden
	stranger strangest		strode
strangle	strangler strangling	stridency	stridencies
stranglehold		strident	stridently
strangulate	strangulating	strife (trouble)	
	strangulation	strike	striker striking struck
strap	strapped strapping	string	stringed stringing
strapless			strung
stratagem		stringency	
strategist		stringent	stringently
strategy	strategic strategically	stringy	stringier stringiest
	strategies		stringily stringiness
stratification		strip (to lay bare)	stripped (laid bare)
stratify	stratified stratifies		stripper stripping
	stratifying	stripe (band of colour)	
stratosphere	stratospheric	striped (banded)	
stratum	strata	striptease	
straw	strawy	stripy	stripily stripiness
strawberry	strawberries	strive (to try hard)	striven striving strove
stray	strayed straying	**strobe** (lighting)	
streak	streaked streaker	stroke	stroking
	streaking	stroll	strolled stroller
streaky	streakier streakiest		strolling
	streakily streakiness	strong	stronger strongest
stream	streamed streamer		strongly
	streaming		strongness/strength
streamlined		stronghold	
street		strongman	strongmen
strength		strong-minded	
strengthen	strengthened	strongroom	
	strengthener	strontium	
	strengthening	stroppy	stroppier stroppiest
strenuous	strenuously		stroppily stroppiness
	strenuousness	strove	

struck
structural   structurally
structure   structuring
strudel
struggle   struggling
strum   strummed strummer
                    strumming
strung
strut   strutted strutting
strychnine
stub   stubbed stubbing
stubble
stubborn   stubbornly
                    stubbornness
stubby   stubbier stubbiest
                    stubbily stubbiness
stucco   stuccoed stuccoing
stuck
stud   studded studding
student
studio
studious   studiously studiousness
study   studied studies
                    studying
stuff   stuffed stuffing
stuffy   stuffier stuffiest
                    stuffily stuffiness
stumble   stumbling stumblingly
stump   stumped stumping
stumpy   stumpier stumpiest
                    stumpily stumpiness
stun   stunned stunning
                    stunningly
stung
stunk
stunt
stupefaction
stupefy   stupefied stupefies
                    stupefying
                    stupefyingly
stupendous   stupendously
                    stupendousness
stupid   stupider stupidest
                    stupidly
                    stupidness/stupidity
stupor

sturdy   sturdier sturdiest
                    sturdily sturdiness
sturgeon
stutter   stuttered stutterer
                    stuttering stutteringly
sty   sties
style (way of doing something)
                    styling
stylish   stylishly stylishness
stylist
stylus   styluses/styli
suave   suavely
                    suaveness/suavity
subaltern
subaqua   subaquatic
                    subaquatically
subatomic
subconscious   subconsciously
                    subconsciousness
subcontract   subcontracted
                    subcontracting
                    subcontractor
subdivide   subdividing
subdivision
subdue   subduing
subgroup
subhuman
subject   subjected subjecting
                    subjection
subjective   subjectively subjectivity
subjugate   subjugating subjugation
subjunctive
sublieutenant
sublimate   sublimating sublimation
sublime   sublimely sublimity
subliminal   subliminally
submarine   submariner
submerge   submerging
submersible   submersibility
submersion
submission
submissive   submissively
                    submissiveness
submit   submitted submitting
subnormal
subordinate   subordinating
                    subordination

subscribe   subscriber subscribing
subscription
subsequent   subsequently
subservience
subservient   subserviently
subside   subsiding
subsidence
subsidiary   subsidiaries subsidiarily
  subsidiarity
subsidise   subsidisation
  subsidising
subsidy   subsidies
subsist   subsisted subsisting
subsistence
subsoil
substance   substantial
  substantially
substantiate   substantiating
  substantiation
substantive
substitute   substituting
  substitution
substratum   substrata
subterfuge
subterranean   subterraneously
subtitle (translation on film)
subtle (delicate, fine)   subtler subtlest subtly
subtlety   subtleties
subtotal
subtract   subtracted subtracting
  subtraction
suburb   suburban suburbia
subversion
subversive   subversively
subvert   subverted subverting
subway
succeed   succeeded succeeding
success   successes
successful   successfully
succession
successive   successively
successor
succinct   succinctly succinctness
succour   succoured succouring
succulent
succumb   succumbed succumbing
such

such-and-such
suchlike
suck   sucked sucker sucking
suckle   suckling
suction
sudden   suddenly suddenness
suds
sue   suing
suede (type of leather)
suet
suffer   suffered sufferer
  suffering
sufferable
sufferance
suffice
sufficiency   sufficiencies
sufficient   sufficiently
suffix   suffixes
suffocate   suffocating
  suffocatingly
  suffocation
suffrage
suffragette
suffuse   suffusing
Sufi   Sufism
sugar   sugariness sugary
suggest   suggested suggesting
  suggestion
suggestible   suggestibility
  suggestibleness
suggestive   suggestively
  suggestiveness
suicide   suicidal suicidally
suit (of clothes; to match)
  suited suiting
suitable   suitability suitably
suitcase
suite (of rooms, furniture)
suitor
sukiyaki
sulk   sulked sulking
sulky   sulkier sulkiest sulkily
  sulkiness
sullen   sullenly sullenness
sully   sullied sullies sullying
sulphate
sulphide

sulphur	sulphuric	superabundant	superabundantly
sultan		superannuate	superannuating
sultana			superannuation
sultry	sultrier sultriest	superb	superbly
	sultrily sultriness	supercilious	superciliously
sum	summed summing		superciliousness
summarise	summarising	superficial	superficiality
summary (brief outline)			superficially
	summaries summarily	superfluous	superfluously
summation			superfluousness/
summer	summeriness		superfluity
	summery (like summer)	superglue	
summit		supergrass	
summon	summoned	superhuman	superhumanly
	summoning	superimpose	superimposition
summons	summonses	superintendent	
sumo (wrestling)		superior	superiority superiorly
sump		superlative	superlatively
sumptuous	sumptuously		superlativeness
	sumptuousness	superman	
sun	sunned sunning	supermarket	
sunbathe	sunbather sunbathing	supernatural	supernaturally
sunbeam			supernaturalness
sunburn	sunburned/sunburnt	supernova	supernovae/supernovas
sunburst		supernumerary	supernumeraries
sundae (dessert)		supersede	superseding
Sunday (day of the week)		supersonic	supersonically
sundial		superstition	superstitious
sundry	sundries		superstitiously
sunflower		supervise	supervising supervision
sung		supervisor	supervisory
sunglasses		**supine**	supinely supineness
sunk	sunken	**supper** (meal)	
sunlight	sunlit	supplant	supplanted supplanter
Sunna			supplanting
Sunni		supple	suppleness supply
sunny	sunnier sunniest	supplement	supplementary
	sunnily sunniness	suppliant	suppliantly
sunrise		supplicant	
sunset		supplicate	supplicating
sunshine	sunshiny		supplicatingly
sunspot			supplication
sunstroke		supply	supplied supplier
suntan	suntanned suntanning		supplies supplying
sup	supped supper supping	support	supported supporter
super (very good; better than)			supporting
superabundance			

supportable	supportableness	**surtax**	
	supportably	**surveillance**	
supportive	supportively	survey	surveyed surveying
suppose	supposedly supposing	surveyor	
	supposition	survivable	survivability
suppress	suppressed suppresses	survival	
	suppressing	survive	surviving survivor
	suppression	**susceptible**	susceptibility
suppressor			susceptibly
suppurate	suppurating	**sushi**	
	suppuration	**suspect**	suspected suspecting
supremacy	supremacies	suspend	suspended suspending
supreme	supremely		suspension
	supremeness	suspender	
supremo		suspense	
surcharge	surcharging	suspicion	suspicious suspiciously
sure	surely sureness surer	**sustain**	sustained sustaining
	surest	sustainable	sustainability
surety	sureties		sustainably
surf	surfed surfer surfing	sustenance	
surface	surfacing	**suture**	
surfeit	surfeited surfeiting	**svelte**	
surge	surging	**swab**	swabbed swabbing
surgeon		**swaddle**	swaddling
surgery	surgeries	**swag**	
surgical	surgically	swagger	swaggered swaggerer
surly	surlier surliest surlily		swaggering
	surliness		swaggeringly
surmise	surmiser surmising	**swallow**	swallowed swallower
surmount	surmounted		swallowing
	surmounting	**swam**	
surname		swami	
surpass	surpassed surpasses	swamp	swamped swamping
	surpassing	**swan**	swanned swanning
	surpassingly	swanlike	
surplice (priest's garment)		swannery	swanneries
surplus (excess)	surpluses	**swap/swop**	swapped/swopped
surprise	surprising surprisingly		swapping/swopping
surreal	surrealism surrealist	**swarm**	swarmed swarming
	surrealistically	**swastika**	
surrender	surrendered	**swat**	swatted swatting
	surrendering	swatch	
surreptitious	surreptitiously	swathe	
	surreptitiousness	**sway**	swayed swaying
surrogate	surrogacy	**swear**	swearer swearing
surround	surrounded		swore sworn
	surrounding		

sweat | sweated sweater
 | sweating
sweaty | sweatier sweatiest
 | sweatiness
swede (vegetable)
sweep | sweeper sweeping
 | sweepingly swept
sweepstake
sweet | sweeter sweetest
 | sweetly sweetness
sweeten | sweetened sweetener
 | sweetening
sweetheart
sweet pea
sweet-tempered
sweet william
swell | swelled swelling
 | swollen
swept
swerve | swerver swerving
swift | swifter swiftest
 | swiftly swiftness
swig | swigged swigging
swill | swilled swilling
swim | swam swimmer
 | swimming swum
swimmingly
swimsuit
swindle | swindler swindling
swine | swineries swinery
swing | swinger swinging
 | (from side to side)
 | swung
swingeing (severe) | swingeingly
swinish | swinishly swinishness
swipe | swiping
swirl | swirled swirling
swish | swished swishes
 | swishing
switch | switched switches
 | switching
switchback
switchboard
swivel | swivelled swivelling
swollen
swoon | swooned swooning
 | swooningly

swoop | swooped swooping
swop/swap | swopped/swapped
 | swopping/swapping
sword
swordsmanship
swore
sworn
swot | swotted swotting
swum
swung
sycamore
sycophancy
sycophant | sycophantic
 | sycophantically
syllable | syllabic syllabically
syllabub/sillabub
syllabus | syllabuses/syllabi
syllogism | syllogistic
 | syllogistically
sylph | sylphlike
symbiosis | symbiotic
symbol | symbolic symbolically
 | symbolism
symbolise | symbolising
symmetry | symmetries
 | symmetrical
 | symmetrically
sympathetic | sympathetically
sympathise | sympathiser
 | sympathising
sympathy | sympathies
symphony | symphonic
 | symphonies
symposium | symposiums/symposia
symptom | symptomatic
 | symptomatically
synagogue
synchronise | synchronisation
 | synchronising
synchronous | synchronously
 | synchronousness
 | synchrony
syncopate | syncopation
syndicate | syndication
syndrome
synod

synonym	synonymous
	synonymously
	synonymousness
synopsis	synopses synoptic
	synoptically
syntax	syntactical
	syntactically syntaxes
synthesis	syntheses
synthesise	synthesiser
	synthesising
synthetic	synthetically
syphon/siphon	
syringe	
syrup	syrupy
system	systematic
	systematically
systematise	systematisation
	systematiser
	systematising

Tt

tab	
tabby	tabbies
tabernacle	
table	tabling
tableau	tableaus/tableaux
tablecloth	
tablespoon	
tablet	
tabloid	
taboo	
tabular	tabularly
tabulate	tabulating tabulation
	tabulator
tachograph	
tacit	tacitly tacitness
taciturn	taciturnity taciturnly
tack	tacked tacking
tackle	tackling
tacky	tackier tackiest tackily
	tackiness
tact	
tactful	tactfully tactfulness
tactic	tactical tactically
tactics	
tactile	tactility
tactless	tactlessly tactlessness
tadpole	
taffeta	
tag	tagged tagging
tail (part of animal; to follow)	
	tailed tailing
tailback	
tailor	tailored tailoring
tailor-made	
tailpiece	

tailspin
taint tainted tainting
take taken taker taking
took
take-away
talc/talcum
tale (story)
talent talented
talisman *plural* talismans
talk talked talker talking
talkative talkatively
talkativeness
tall taller tallest tallness
tallow
tally tallied tallies tallying
Talmud Talmudic Talmudical
talon
tambourine
tame tamely tameness
tamer tamest taming
tammy tammies
tam-o'-shanter
tamper tampered tampering
tampon
tan tanned tanner
tanning

tandem
tandoori
tang
tangent tangential tangentially
tangerine
tangible tangibility tangibly
tangle tangling
tanglement
tango
tank tanker
tankard
tannery tanneries
tannin tannic
Tannoy
tantalise tantalising tantalisingly
tantamount
tantrum
Taoism Taoist
tap (pipe; to draw off)
tapped tapper
tapping

tape (strip of material)
taping
taper (to thin out) tapered tapering
tapestry tapestries
tapioca
tapir (animal)
tar tarred tarring
tarantula
tardy tardier tardiest tardily
tardiness
target targeted targeting
tariff
tarmacadam/tarmac
tarmacked tarmacking
tarn
tarnish tarnished tarnishes
tarnishing

tarot
tarpaulin
tarragon
tarry tarried tarries tarrying
tart tartly tartness
tartan
tartar
tartlet
task
taskmaster
tassel tasselled tasselling
taste tasting
taste bud
tasteful tastefully tastefulness
tasteless tastelessly tastelessness
tasty tastier tastiest tastily
tastiness
tatter tattered tattering
tattoo tattooed tattooing
taught (gave instruction)
taunt taunted taunting
tauntingly

Taurus
taut (stretched tight) tauter tautest tautly
tautness
tautology tautologies
tavern
tawdry tawdrier tawdriest
tawdrily tawdriness

tawny	tawnier tawniest
	tawniness
tawse	
tax	taxed taxes taxing
taxable	taxability taxably
taxation	
tax–deductible	
tax–exempt	
taxi	taxied taxiing/taxying
	taxis
taxidermy	taxidermist
taxpayer	
tea (drink)	
teach	taught teacher
	teaches teaching
teacup	
teak	
teal	
team (group; to group together)	
	teamed teaming
teamwork	
teapot	
tear	tearing tore torn
tearful	tearfully tearfulness
tease	teaser teasing
	teasingly
teashop	
teaspoon	
teat	
technical	technicality technically
technician	
technicolour	technicoloured
technique	
technological	technologically
technology	technologies
	technologist
tedious	tediously tediousness
tedium	
tee (support for golf-ball)	
	teeing
teem (be abundant; to pour)	
	teemed teeming
teen	
teenage	teenager
teeter	teetered teetering
	teeteringly
teeth (plural of 'tooth')	

teethe (to cut teeth)	teething
teetotal	teetotaller
telecommunication	
telegram	
telegraph	telegraphed
	telegrapher
	telegraphing
telegraphic	telegraphically
telepathy	telepathic
	telepathically
telephone	telephonic
telephonist	
teleprinter	
telescope	telescopic telescopically
teletext	
telethon	
televise	televising
television	
telex	telexes
tell	teller telling told
tell-tale	
temerity	
temper	tempered tempering
temperament	temperamental
	temperamentally
temperance	
temperate	temperately
	temperateness
temperature	
tempest	
tempestuous	tempestuously
	tempestuousness
template	
temple	
tempo	
temporal	temporally
temporary	temporarily
	temporariness
temporise	temporiser temporising
tempt	tempted tempter
	tempting temptingly
temptation	
temptress	temptresses
ten	tenth
tenable	tenability tenably
tenacious	tenaciously
	tenaciousness

tenacity		
tenancy	tenancies	
tenant		
tend	tended tending	
tendency	tendencies	
tendentious	tendentiously	
	tendentiousness	
tender	tendered tendering	
	tenderly tenderness	
tenderise	tenderising	
tendon		
tendril		
tenement		
tenet		
tennis		
tenor		
tense	tensing tension	
tensely	tenseness tensity	
tent	tented tenting	
tentacle		
tentative	tentatively	
	tentativeness	
tenterhooks		
tenuous	tenuously tenuousness	
tenure		
tepee		
tepid	tepidity tepidly	
	tepidness	
term	termed	
terminal	terminally	
terminate	terminating termination	
terminology	terminologies	
terminus	terminuses/termini	
termite		
tern (bird)		
terrace		
terracotta		
terrain		
terrapin		
terrazzo		
terrestrial	terrestrially	
terrible	terribleness terribly	
terrier		
terrific	terrifically	
terrify	terrified terrifies	
	terrifying terrifyingly	
terrine		

territorial	territoriality territorially
territory	territories
terror	
terrorise	terrorisation terrorising
	terrorism terrorist
terse	tersely terseness
	terser tersest
tessellate	tessellating tessellation
test	tested tester testing
testament	
testicle	
testify	testified testifies
	testifying
testimonial	
testimony	testimonies
test tube	
testy	testier testiest testily
	testiness
tetanus	
tetchy	tetchier tetchiest
	tetchily tetchiness
tether	tethered tethering
text	textual textually
textbook	
textile	
texture	textured
than	
thank	thanked thanking
thankful	thankfully thankfulness
thankless	thanklessly
	thanklessness
thanksgiving	
that	
thatch	thatched thatcher
	thatches thatching
thaw	thawed thawing
the	
theatre	
theatrical	theatricality
	theatrically
theft	
their (belonging to)	
theism	theist theistic
them (others)	themselves
theme (subject)	thematic thematically
then	
thence	

theological   theologically
theology   theologian   theologies
theorem
theoretical   theoretically
theorise   theorising
theory   theories
therapeutic   therapeutically
therapy   therapies   therapist
there (in that place)
thereabouts
thereafter
thereby
therefore
therewith
therm   thermal
thermometer
thermonuclear
thermostat
thesaurus   thesauruses/thesauri
these (things nearby)
thesis (piece of writing)
                        theses
they   they'd   they'll   they're
                        they've
thick   thicker   thickest
                        thickly   thickness
thicken   thickened   thickener
                        thickening
thicket
thick-skinned
thief (noun)   thieves
thieve (verb)   thievery   thieving
thievish   thievishly   thievishness
thigh
thimble
thin   thinned   thinner
                        thinnest   thinning
thing
think   thinker   thinking
                        thought
thinkable
thinly   thinness
thin-skinned
third   thirdly
thirl   thirled   thirling
thirst   thirsted   thirsting

thirsty   thirstier   thirstiest
                        thirstily   thirstiness
thirteen   thirteenth
thirty   thirties   thirtieth
this
thistle
thither
thole   tholing
thong
thorax   thoraxes
thorn
thorny   thornier   thorniest
                        thorniness
thorough (out and out, complete)
                        thoroughly
                        thoroughness
thoroughbred
thoroughfare
thoroughgoing
those
thou (old form of 'you')
though (even if)
thought
thoughtful   thoughtfully
                        thoughtfulness
thoughtless   thoughtlessly
                        thoughtlessness
thousand   thousandth
thrall   thraldom/thralldom
thrash   thrashed   thrashes
                        thrashing
thread   threaded   threader
                        threading
threadbare
threat
threaten   threatened   threatening
                        threateningly
three
three-quarter
thresh   threshed   thresher
                        threshes   threshing
threshold
threw (past of 'throw')
thrice
thrift
thrifty   thriftier   thriftiest
                        thriftily   thriftiness

thrill	thrilled thriller
	thrilling thrillingly
thrive	thrived/throve thriving
throat	throatily throatiness
	throaty
throb	throbbed throbbing
	throbbingly
throes (violent pangs)	
thrombosis	thromboses
throne	
throng	
throttle	throttling
through (by way of)	
throughout	
throve	
throw (toss)	threw throwing
	thrown
throw-in	
thrush	thrushes
thrust	thrusting
thud	thudded thudding
thug	thuggery
thuggish	thuggishly
	thuggishness
thumb	thumbed thumbing
thumbmark	
thumbnail	
thumbscrew	
thump	thumped thumper
	thumping
thunder	thundered thundering
	thunderingly
thunderbolt	
thunderclap	
thunderous	thunderously
thunderstorm	
thunderstruck	
thundery	
Thursday	
thus	
thwart	thwarted thwarting
thyme (herb)	
thyroid	
thyself	
tiara	
tibia	tibiae/tibias
tic (nervous movement in face)	

tick (regular sound)	ticked ticker ticking
ticket	ticketed ticketing
ticket-office	
tickle	tickling tickly
ticklish	ticklishly ticklishness
tiddler	
tiddlywink	
tide	tidal
tidemark	
tidings	
tidy	tidied tidier tidies
	tidiest tidily tidiness
	tidying
tie	tying
tie-break	tie-breaker
tie-pin	
tier (to put in rows)	tiered tiering
tiff	
tiger	
tigerish	tigerishly tigerishness
tiger lily	
tight	tighter tightest
	tightly tightness
tighten	tightened tightening
tigress	
tile (to cover with tiles)	
	tiler tiling
till (cash register; to cultivate)	
	tilled tilling
tiller	
tilt	tilted tilting
timber (wood)	timbered timbering
timbre (quality of sound)	
time (duration; to measure by clock)	
	timer timing
timeless	timelessly timelessness
timely	
timeous	timeously
timepiece	
timeshare	
timetable	timetabling
timid	timidity timidly
timorous	timorously
	timorousness
timpani/tympani	timpanist/tympanist
tin (metal; put in to can)	
	tinned tinning

tincture
tinder
tinderbox　　　　　tinderboxes
tine (spike of fork)
tinge　　　　　　tingeing
tingle　　　　　　　tingling　tingly
tinsel　　　　　　tinselled　tinselly
tinsmith
tint　　　　　　　tinted　tinting
tiny　　　　　　　tinier　tiniest　tininess
tip　　　　　　　tipped　tipper　tipping
tipple
tipsy　　　　　　tipsier　tipsiest　tipsily
　　　　　　　　　　tipsiness
tiptoe　　　　　　tiptoeing
tiptop
tirade
tire (to become weary)
　　　　　　　　　　tiredness　tiring
tireless　　　　　　tirelessly　tirelessness
tiresome　　　　　　tiresomely
　　　　　　　　　　tiresomeness
tissue
tissue paper
tit
titanium
titbit
tithe
titillate　　　　　titillating　titillation
titivate　　　　　　titivating　titivation
title (name)
titleholder
title page
title role
titmouse　　　　　titmice
titter　　　　　　tittered　titterer
　　　　　　　　　　tittering
tittle (smallest amount)
titular
toad
toad
toadstool
toady　　　　　　　toadied　toadies
　　　　　　　　　　toadying
toast　　　　　　toasted　toaster
　　　　　　　　　　toasting
tobacco　　　　　tobacconist

toboggan　　　　　tobogganed
　　　　　　　　　　tobogganing
today (this day)
toddle　　　　　　toddler　toddling
toddy (hot drink)　　toddies
toe　　　　　　　toeing
toenail
toffee
tofu
toga
together　　　　　togetherness
toggle
toil　　　　　　　toiled　toiler　toiling
toilet
toilet roll
toiletry　　　　　　toiletries
token
told
tolerable　　　　　tolerability　tolerably
tolerance
tolerant　　　　　　tolerantly
tolerate　　　　　　tolerating　toleration
toll　　　　　　　tolled　tolling
tomahawk
tomato　　　　　　tomatoes
tomb
tombola
tomboy
tombstone
tome
tomfoolery　　　　tomfooleries
tomorrow
tom-tom
ton (imperial measure of weight)
tonal　　　　　　tonality　tonally
tone (sound; to alter) toning
tongs
tongue　　　　　　tonguing
tonic
tonight
tonnage
tonne (metric measure of mass)
tonsil　　　　　　tonsillitis
too (in addition; very)
took
tool　　　　　　　tooled　tooling
toot　　　　　　　tooted　tooting

tooth	teeth toothed
toothache	
toothbrush	
toothless	toothlessly
	toothlessness
toothpaste	
toothpick	
toothsome	toothsomeness
toothy	toothier toothiest
	toothily toothiness
top	topped topper
	topping
topaz	
top-hat	
top-heavy	
topiary	
topic	topical topicality
	topically
topless	toplessness
topmost	
topple	toppling
topsail	
topside	
topspin	
topsy-turvy	
Torah	
torch	torched torches
	torching
torch-bearer	
torchlight	
tore	
toreador	
torment	tormented tormentor
	tormenting
	tormentingly
torn	
tornado	tornadoes
torpedo	torpedoes
torpid	torpidly torpor
torque	
torrent	torrential torrentially
torrid	torridly torridness
torso	
tortilla	
tortoise	
tortoiseshell	

tortuous	tortuously tortuousness
torture	torturer torturing
toss	tossed tosses tossing
tot (to add up)	totted totting
total	totality totally
tote (to carry)	toting
totem	
totter	tottered tottering
	totteringly
toucan	
touch (to feel)	touched touches
	touching touchingly
touchable	touchableness
	touchably
touché (a hit in fencing)	
touch judge	
touchpaper	
touchstone	
touch-type	touch-typing
	touch-typist
touchy	touchier touchiest
	touchily touchiness
tough	tougher toughest
	toughly toughness
toughen	toughened toughening
toupee	
tour	toured tourer touring
tourist	tourism touristic
tournament	
tourniquet	
tousled	
tout (to seek business)	
	touted touting
tow	towed towing
toward	towards
towbar	
towel	towelled towelling
tower	towered towering
	toweringly
town	
township	
townsman	
toxic	
toxin	
toy	toyed toying
trace	tracer tracing
traceable	traceability traceably

tracery | traceries
trachea | tracheitis
track | tracked tracker
| tracking
tract |
tractable | tractability tractably
traction |
tractor |
trade | trader trading
trademark |
tradesman | tradesmen
tradeswoman | tradeswomen
tradition | traditional traditionalist
| traditionally
traffic | trafficked trafficker
| trafficking
traffic lights |
tragedy | tragedies
tragic | tragically
trail | trailed trailer trailing
train | trained trainer training
trainee |
trait |
traitor |
traitorous | traitorously
| traitorousness
trajectory | trajectories
tram |
tramcar |
trammel | trammelled
| trammelling
tramp | tramped tramper
| tramping
trample | trampling
trampoline |
trance |
tranquil | tranquillity tranquilly
tranquillise | tranquilliser
| tranquillising
transact | transacted transacting
| transaction
transcend | transcended
| transcending
transcendence | transcendency
transcendent | transcendently
transcendental |
transcontinental |

transcribe | transcriber transcribing
transcript | transcription
transfer | transference
| transferred transferring
transferable | transferability
| transferably
transfigure | transfiguring
| transfiguration
transfix | transfixed transfixes
| transfixing transfixion
transform | transformed
| transforming
transformation |
transformer |
transfuse | transfusing transfusion
transgress | transgressed
| transgresses
| transgressing
| transgression
transgressor |
transience |
transient | transiently
transistor |
transit |
transition |
transitory | transitorily
| transitoriness
translate | translating translation
| translator
translucency |
translucent | translucently
transmission |
transmit | transmitted
| transmitter
| transmitting
transmute | transmuting
| transmutation
transnational |
transparency | transparencies
transparent | transparently
transpire | transpiring
transplant | transplanted
| transplanting
transport | transportation
| transported
| transporter
| transporting

transpose	transposing
	transposition
transverse	transversely
transvestite	
trap	trapped trapper
	trapping
trapeze	
trapezium	trapezia/trapeziums
trappings	
trash	
trashy	trashier trashiest
	trashily trashiness
trauma	traumas/traumata
	traumatic
	traumatically
traumatise	
travel	travelled traveller
	travelling
travelogue	
traverse	traversing
travesty	travesties
trawl	trawled trawler
	trawling
tray	
treacherous	treacherously
	treacherousness
treachery	treacheries
treacle	treacliness treacly
tread	treading trod trodden
treadle	
treadmill	
treadwheel	
treason	
treasonable	treasonably
treasonous	
treasure	treasurer treasuring
treasury	treasuries
treat	treated treating
treatable	treatably
treatise	
treatment	
treaty	treaties
treble	trebling trebly
tree	
treeless	
treetop	

trek	trekked trekker
	trekking
trellis	trellised
tremble	trembling
tremendous	tremendously
	tremendousness
tremolo	
tremor	
tremulous	tremulously
	tremulousness
trench	trenched trenches
	trenching
trenchancy	
trenchant	trenchantly
trench coat	
trend	
trendy	trendier trendiest
	trendily trendiness
trepidation	
trespass	trespassed trespasser
	trespasses trespassing
tress	tresses
trestle	
trews	
triad	
trial	trialist
triangle	triangular triangularity
	triangularly
tribe	tribal tribalism tribally
tribulation	
tribune	tribunal
tributary	tributaries
tribute	
triceps	
trick	tricked tricker tricking
trickery	trickeries
trickle	trickling trickly
trickster	
tricky	trickier trickiest
	trickily trickiness
tricolour	tricoloured
tricycle	tricyclist
trident	
tried	
triennial	triennially
triffid	
trifle	trifling triflingly

trigger   triggered   triggering
trigonometry
trilby   trilbies
trill   trilled   trilling
trillion
trilobite
trilogy   trilogies
trim   trimmed   trimmer
     trimmest   trimming
trimly   trimness
trinity   trinities
trinket
trio
trip   tripped   tripper
     tripping   trippingly
tripartite   tripartism
tripe
triplane
triple   triply
triplet
triplicate
tripod
triptych
trireme
trite   tritely   triteness
triumph   triumphed   triumphing
triumphal   triumphalism
     triumphally
triumphant   triumphantly
trivia   trivial   triviality
     trivially
trod
trodden
troglodyte
troika
troll
trolley
trombone   trombonist
troop (to march; group of soldiers)
     trooped   trooper
     trooping
troopship
trophy   trophies
tropic   tropical   tropically
trot   trotted   trotter
     trotting
troubadour

trouble   troubling
troubleshooter
troublesome   troublesomely
     troublesomeness
trough
trounce   trouncing
troupe (group of actors)
trousers
trousseau   trousseaus/trousseaux
trout
trowel
truancy   truancies
truant   truanted   truanting
truce
truck   trucked   trucker
     trucking
truculence
truculent   truculently
trudge   trudging
true   truly
truffle
trump   trumped   trumping
trumpery   trumperies
trumpet   trumpeted   trumpeter
     trumpeting
truncate   truncating   truncation
truncheon
trundle   trundling
trunk
truss   trussed   trusses
     trussing
trust   trusted   trusting
trustee
trustful   trustfully   trustfulness
trustless   trustlessly
     trustlessness
trustworthy   trustworthily
     trustworthiness
trusty   trustier   trustiest
     trustily   trustiness
truth
truthful   truthfully   truthfulness
truthless   truthlessly
     truthlessness
try   tried   trier   tries   trying
tryst   trysting
tsar/czar

tub (barrel)
tuba (musical instrument)
tubby   tubbier tubbiest
                              tubbily tubbiness
tube (cylinder)   tubular
tuber (part of plant)   tuberous
tuberculosis   tubercular
tuck   tucked tucking
Tuesday
tuft   tufted
tug   tugged tugging
tuition
tulip
tumble   tumbling
tumbler
tumbrel/tumbril
tummy   tummies
tumour/tumor   tumorous
tumult
tumultuous   tumultuously
                              tumultuousness

tun (cask)
tuna
tundra
tune (melody)   tuning
tuneful   tunefully tunefulness
tuneless   tunelessly
                              tunelessness

tungsten
tunic
tuning-fork
tunnel   tunnelled tunnelling
tup
turban (head-dress)
turbid   turbidly
                              turbidness/turbidity
turbine (engine)
turbocharger   turbocharged
turbot
turbulence
turbulent   turbulently
tureen
turf   turfs/turves
turgid   turgidity turgidly
turkey
turmeric
turmoil

turn (move round a point)
                   turned turner turning
turnip
turnover
turnstile
turntable
turn-up
turpentine
turquoise
turret   turreted
turtle
turtleneck
turves
tusk   tusked
tussle   tussling
tussock
tut   tutted tutting
tutelage
tutor   tutored tutoring
tutorial
tutti
tutti-frutti
tutu
tuxedo
twang   twanged twanging
tweak   tweaked tweaking
tweed
tweedy   tweedier tweediest
                              tweedily tweediness
tweet
tweezers
twelfth
twelve
twenty   twenties twentieth
twerp
twice
twiddle   twiddling
twig
twilight   twilit
twill   twilled
twin (one of two)   twinned twinning
twine (string; to twist around)
                              twining
twinge
twinkle   twinkling
twirl   twirled twirling

twist	twisted twister
	twisting
twit	twitted twitting
twitch	twitched twitches
	twitching
twitchy	twitchier twitchiest
	twitchily twitchiness
twitter	twittered twittering
	twitteringly
two	
two-edged	
twofold	
two-headed	
two-seater	
two-sided	
two-stroke	
two-timer	
two-tone	
two-wheeled	
tycoon	
tympani/timpani	tympanist/timpanist
type	typing typist
typecast	
typeface	
typewriter	typewritten
typhoid	
typhoon	
typhus	
typical	typicality typically
typify	typified typifies
	typifying
typography	typographer
	typographic
	typographically
tyrannical	tyrannically
tyrannous	tyrannously
tyranny	tyrannies
tyrant	
tyre (tube)	

Uu

ubiquitous	ubiquitously ubiquity
udder	
UFO	UFOs
ugly	uglier ugliest uglily
	ugliness
ukulele	
ulcer	ulcerous
ulcerate	ulcerating ulceration
ulterior	ulteriorly
ultimate	ultimately
ultimatum	ultimatums/ultimata
ultrasound	
ultraviolet	
ululate	ululating ululation
umbilical	
umbrage	
umbrella	
umpire	
umpteen	
unabashed	
unable	
unanimous	unanimity unanimously
unawares	
unbecoming	
uncanny	uncannier uncanniest
	uncannily uncanniness
uncertainty	uncertainties
uncle	
unconscious	unconsciously
	unconsciousness
uncouth	uncouthly uncouthness
unction	
unctuous	unctuously
	unctuousness
undaunted	

under
underachieve   underachiever
                           underachieving
underachievement
underage
undercarriage
underclothes
undercoat   undercoated
                           undercoating
undercurrent
undercut   undercutting
underdone
underestimate   underestimating
underexposed
underfoot
undergarment
undergo   undergoes undergoing
                           undergone underwent
undergraduate
underground
undergrowth
underhand   underhandedly
                           underhandedness
underlay   underlaid
underlie   underlying
undermine   undermining
underneath
underpaid
underpants
underpass
underpin   underpinned
                           underpinning
underrate   underrating
underscore   underscoring
undersized
underskirt
understand   understanding
                           understood
understandable   understandability
                           understandably
understood
understudy   understudied
                           understudies
                           understudying
undertake   undertaken
                           undertaking undertook
undertaker

undertone
underwear
underwent
underwrite   underwriter
                           underwriting
                           underwritten
                           underwrote
undeserved   undeservedly
undo   undid undoes
                           undoing undone
undress   undressed undresses
                           undressing
undue   unduly
undulate   undulating undulation
undying
unemployed   unemployment
uneven   unevenly unevenness
unfit
unforeseen
unfortunate   unfortunately
ungainly   ungainlier ungainliest
                           ungainliness
unhappy   unhappily unhappiness
unhealthy   unhealthily
                           unhealthiness
unhygienic
unicorn
unicycle
unification
uniform   uniformity
unify   unified unifies
                           unifying
unilateral   unilaterally
union
unionise   unionisation unionising
unionism   unionist
unique   uniquely uniqueness
unisex
unison
unit (single item)   unitary
unite (to join together)
                           uniting
unity   unities
universal   universality universally
universe
university   universities
unjust   unjustly

unkempt	unkemptly	uproarious	uproariously
	unkemptness		uproariousness
unkind	unkindly unkindness	uproot	uprooted uprooting
unknown		**upset**	upsetting
unless		**upshot**	
unlikely	unlikelier unlikeliest	**upside down**	
	unlikelihood	**upstage**	
	unlikeliness	upstairs	
unmistakeable		upstanding	
unpopular	unpopularity	upstart	
unravel	unravelled unravelling	upstream	
unremitting	unremittingly	**uptake**	
unrest		**upthrust**	
unruly		**uptight**	
untie		**upturn**	upturned upturning
until		**upward**	upwardly upwardness
unwary	unwarily unwariness	upwards	
unwieldy	unwieldily	**uranium**	
	unwieldiness	Uranus	
unwitting	unwittingly	**urban** (belonging to the city)	
	unwittingness	urbane (smooth in manner)	
up	upped upping		urbanely urbanity
	upmost/uppermost	**urchin**	
upbeat		**Urdu**	
upbraid	upbraided upbraiding	**urge**	urging
upbringing		urgency	
update	updating	urgent	urgently
upend	upended upending	**urinal**	
upheaval		urinate	urinating urination
upheld		urine	urinary
uphill		**urn**	
uphold	upheld upholding	**usable**	usability usably
upholster	upholstered	**usage**	
	upholsterer	**use**	user using
	upholstering	**useful**	usefully usefulness
upholstery		**useless**	uselessly uselessness
upkeep		**U-shaped**	
uplift	uplifted uplifting	**usher**	
up-market		**usual**	usually usualness
upmost/uppermost		**usurp**	usurped usurper
upon			usurping
upper		usury	usurer usuries
uppity		**utensil**	
upraise	upraising	**uterus**	
upright	uprightly uprightness	**utilise**	utilising utilisation
uprising		utilitarian	
uproar		utility	utilities

utmost
Utopia
utter   uttered uttering
        utterly

utterance
uttermost
U-turn
uvula   uvulae uvular
uxorious   uxoriously
        uxoriousness

vacancy   vacancies
vacant   vacantly
vacate   vacating
vacation
vaccinate   vaccinating
       vaccination

vaccine
vacillate   vacillating vacillation
vacuous   vacuously vacuousness
vacuum
vagabond
vagary   vagaries
vagina
vagrancy   vagrancies
vagrant
vague   vaguely vagueness
       vaguer vaguest
vain (proud) vainly vainness/vanity
vainglorious vaingloriously
       vaingloriousness

vainglory
valance
vale (valley)
valediction valedictory
valentine
valet   valeted valeting
valiant   valiantly
valid   validity validly
valley
valorous   valorously
       valorousness/valour

valour
valuable   valuableness valuably
valuation
value   valuer valuing

valve	
vamp	vamped vamping
vampire	vampiric vampirism
van	
vandal	
vandalise	vandalising vandalism
vane (weathercock)	
vanguard	
vanilla	
vanish	vanished vanishes
	vanishing vanishingly
vanity	vanities
vanquish	vanquished vanquishes
	vanquishing
vanquishable	
vantage	
vapid	vapidly
	vapidness/vapidity
vaporise	vaporising
vapour	vaporous
variable	variability variably
variance	
variant	
variation	
varicose	
variegated	variegation
variety	varieties
various	variously variousness
varnish	varnished varnishes
	varnishing
vary	varied varies varying
vase	
Vaseline	
vassal	
vast	vastly vastness
vat	
Vatican	
vaudeville	
vault	vaulted vaulter
	vaulting
vaunt	vaunted vaunting
veal	
vector	
Veda	Vedantic Vedic
veer	veered veering
vegan	
vegetable	

vegetarian	vegetarianism
vegetate	vegetating vegetation
vehemence	
vehement	vehemently
vehicle	vehicular
veil (to cover)	veiled veiling
vein (part of the body, having veins)	
	veined veining
Velcro	
veld/veldt	
vellum	
velocity	velocities
velodrome	
velvet	velvety
venal	venality venally
vendetta	
vending	
vendor	
veneer	veneered veneering
venerable	venerability venerably
venerate	venerating veneration
vengeance	
vengeful	
venial	veniality venially
venison	
venom	
venomous	venomously
	venomousness
vent	vented venting
ventilate	ventilating ventilation
ventilator	
ventriloquist	ventriloquism
venture	venturing
venturesome	
venue	
Venus	Venusian
veracious (truthful)	veraciously veracity
veranda/verandah	
verb	
verbal	verbally
verbalisation	
verbalise	verbalising
verbatim	
verbose	verbosely
	verboseness/verbosity
verdancy	
verdant	verdantly

verdict
verdigris
verdure
verge   verging
verger
verification
verify   verifiable   verified
          verifies   verifying
verity   verities
vermicelli
vermilion
vermin   verminous
vermouth
vernacular
vernal   vernally
verruca   verrucas/verrucae
versatile   versatilely   versatility
verse   versing
versification
versify   versified   versifier
          versifies   versifying
version
versus
vertebra   vertebrae
vertebrate
vertex   vertices
vertical   verticality   vertically
vertiginous   vertiginously
          vertiginousness
vertigo
verve
very
vespers
vessel
vest   vested   vesting
vestibule   vestibular
vestige
vestment
vestry   vestral   vestries
vesture
vet   vetted   vetting
vetch
veteran
veterinary
veto   vetoed   vetoes   vetoing
vex   vexed   vexes   vexing
          vexingly

vexation
vexatious   vexatiously
          vexatiousness
via
viable   viability   viably
viaduct
vial/phial
vibes
vibrancy
vibrant   vibrantly
vibrate   vibrating   vibration
vibrato
vicar   vicarage
vicarious   vicariously
          vicariousness
vice
vice versa
vicinity   vicinities
vicious   viciously   viciousness
vicissitude
victim
victimisation
victimise   victimising
victor
Victoria   Victorian
victorious   victoriously
          victoriousness
victory   victories
victual   victualler
video   videoed   videoing
videotape
vie   vying
view   viewed   viewer
          viewing
vigil
vigilance
vigilant   vigilantly
vignette
vigorous   vigorously   vigorousness
vigour
vile   vilely   vileness   viler
          vilest
vilification
vilify   vilified   vilifier   vilifies
          vilifying
villa
village   villager

villain
villainous — villainously
villainy — villainies
vinaigrette
vindicate — vindicating vindication
vindictive — vindictively
vindictiveness

vine
vinegar — vinegarish vinegary
vineyard
vintage
vinyl
viola
violate — violating violation
violator
violence
violent — violently
violet
violin — violinist
violoncello/cello
viper — viperish viperishly
viperishness
viperous — viperously
viperousness

virago
virgin — virginity
virginal — virginally
Virgo
virile — virilely virility
virtual — virtually
virtue
virtuoso — virtuosity
virtuous — virtuously virtuousness
virulence
virulent — virulently
virus — viral viruses
visa
visage
vis-à-vis
viscera
viscose (material)
viscount
viscountess
viscous (sticky) — viscousness/viscosity
Vishnu
visible — visibility visibly
vision — visionaries visionary

visit — visited visiting visitor
visitation
visor
vista
visual — visually
visualisation
visualise — visualising
vital — vitality vitally
vitamin
vitiate — vitiating vitiation
vitreous
vitriol — vitriolic
vituperate — vituperating
vituperation
vituperative

vivacious — vivaciously vivacity
vivid — vividly vividness
vivisect — vivisected vivisecting
vivisection

vixen
vizier
vocabulary — vocabularies
vocal — vocally
vocalisation
vocalise — vocalising
vocalist
vocation — vocational vocationally
vociferous — vociferously
vociferousness

vodka
vogue
voice — voicing
void
volatile
vol-au-vent
volcanic
volcano — volcanoes
vole
volition
volley — volleyed volleying
volleyball
volt
voltage
voluble — volubility volubly
volume
volumetric

voluminous | voluminously
 | voluminousness/
 | voluminosity
voluntary | voluntarily
 | voluntariness
volunteer | volunteered
 | volunteering
voluptuous | voluptuously
 | voluptuousness
vomit | vomited vomiting
voodoo
voracious | voraciously
 | voraciousness/voracity
vortex | vortices/vortexes
vote | voter voting
vouch | vouched vouches
 | vouching
voucher
vouchsafe | vouchsafing
vow | vowed vowing
vowel
voyage | voyager voyaging
voyeur | voyeurism
vulgar | vulgarities vulgarity
 | vulgarly
vulnerable | vulnerability
 | vulnerably
vulture

Ww

wad | wadded wadding
waddle | waddling
wade | wader wading
wafer | wafery
waffle | waffling
waft | wafted wafting
wag (to shake) | wagged wagging
wage (payment; to fight)
 | waging
wager
wagon/waggon
wagtail
waif
wail | wailed wailing
waist (part of body) | waisted
waistband
waistcoat
wait | waited waiting
waiter
waitress | waitresses
waive (to let go) | waiver waiving
wake | waking
wakeful | wakefully wakefulness
waken | wakened wakening
walk | walked walker
 | walking
Walkman
wall | walled walling
wallaby | wallabies
wallet
wallflower
wallow | wallowed wallowing
wallpaper
walnut
walrus | walruses

waltz	waltzed waltzer	wasteful	wastefully
	waltzes waltzing		wastefulness
wan	wanly wanness	wastepaper	
wand		waste pipe	
wander	wandered wanderer	**watch**	watched watcher
	wandering wanderingly		watches watching
wane	waning	watchable	
wangle	wangler wangling	watchdog	
want	wanted wanting	watchful	watchfully
wanton	wantonly wantonness		watchfulness
war	warred warring	watchmaker	
warble	warbler warbling	watchword	
ward	warded warding	**water**	watered watering
warden		watercolour	
warder		watercress	
wardrobe		waterfall	
warehouse		waterlog	waterlogged
wares		watermark	
warfare		waterproof	
warhead		watershed	
warlock		watertight	
warm	warmed warmer	waterway	
	warmest warming	watery	wateriness
	warmly	**watt**	wattage
warmth		wattle	
warn	warned warning	**wave** (to signal)	waving
	warningly	waver (to hesitate)	wavered waverer
warp	warped warping		wavering waveringly
warrant	warranted warranting	**wax**	waxed waxes waxing
warrantable	warrantability	**waxen**	
	warrantably	**waxy**	waxier waxiest
warranty	warranties		waxiness
warren			
warrior		**way**	
warship		**wayfarer**	
wart	warty	wayfaring	
wary	warier wariest warily	**waylay**	waylaid waylaying
	wariness	**wayside**	
was	wasn't	**wayward**	waywardly
wash	washed washer		waywardness
	washes washing	**weak** (feeble)	weaker weakest
washable	washability		weakly weakness
wasp		weaken	weakened weakening
waspish	waspishly waspishness	weakling	
wassail		**weal** (mark on skin)	
wastage		wealth	wealthier wealthiest
waste (rubbish)	waster wasting		wealthily wealthy
		wean	weaned weaning

weapon	weaponry
wear	wearer wearing wore worn
weary	wearier weariest wearily weariness
weasel	weaselly
weather	weathered weathering
weather-beaten	
weathercock	
weatherproof	
weave	weaver weaving wove woven
web	webbed webbing
web-footed	
wed	wedded wedding
wedding-ring	
wedge	wedging
wedlock	
Wednesday	
weed	weeded weeding
weedkiller	
week (seven days)	weekly
weekday	
weekend	
weep	weeping wept
weepy	weepier weepiest weepily weepiness
weft	
weigh	weighed weighing
weight	weighted weighting
weightless	weightlessly weightlessness
weightlifting	weightlifter
weighty	weightier weightiest weightily weightiness
weir	
weird	weirdly weirdness
welcome	welcoming
weld	welded welder welding
welfare	
well	welled welling
we'll (we will/we shall)	
	we're (we are)
	we've (we have)
wellbeing	
wellington boots	

well-off	
welter	weltered weltering
wench	wenches
wend	wended wending
wept	
were	
werewolf	werewolves
west	western
westerly	westerlies
westward	westwardly
westwards	
wet	wetter wettest wetting wetly wetness
whack	whacked whacking
whale	whaler whaling
whalebone	
wham	whammed whamming
wharf	wharves
what	
whatsoever	
wheat	wheaten
wheedle	wheedling wheedlingly
wheel (round disc)	wheeled wheeling
wheelbarrow	
wheelchair	
wheelwright	
wheeze	wheezed wheezes wheezing
wheezy	wheezier wheeziest wheezily wheeziness
whelk	
whelp	whelped whelping
when	
whence	
whenever	
where	
whereabouts	
whereas	
whereby	
wherefore	
wherefrom	
wherein	
whereof	
whereupon	
wherever	
wherewith	

wherewithal		whither	
whet	whetted whetting	whiting	
whether		whitlow	
whetstone		whittle	whittling
whey		**whiz/whizz**	whizzed whizzing
whey-faced		**who**	
which		**whodunit/whodunnit**	
whichever		**whoever**	
whiff	whiffed whiffing	**whole**	wholly wholeness
while		wholefood	
whilst		wholehearted	wholeheartedly
whim		wholemeal	
whimper	whimpered whimpering	wholesale	wholesaler
	whimperingly	wholesome	
whimsical	whimsicality	**whom**	
	whimsically	**whoop**	whooped whooping
whimsy/whimsey	whimsies/whimseys	**whorl**	whorled
whine (noise)	whiner whining	**whose**	
whinge	whingeing	**why**	
whinny	whinnied whinnies	**wick**	
	whinnying	wicked	wickedly wickedness
whip	whipped whipping	wicker	
whipcord		wickerwork	
whiplash		wicket	
whippersnapper		**wide**	widely wideness
whippet			wider widest width
whirl	whirled whirling	wide-open	
whirligig		wide-ranging	
whirlpool		widespread	
whirlwind		**widow**	widowed widower
whirr/whir	whirred whirring	**width**	
whisk	whisked whisking	**wield**	wielded wielding
whisker		**wife**	wives
whisky/whiskey	whiskies	**wig**	wigged
whisper	whispered whisperer	**wiggle**	wiggling
	whispering	**wigwam**	
whist		**wild**	wilder wildest wildly
whistle	whistler whistling		wildness
white	whitely whiteness	wildebeest	
	whiter whitest	wilderness	
white-collar		wildlife	
white-hot		**wile**	wilily wiliness
whiten	whitened whitener	**wilful**	wilfully wilfulness
	whitening	**will**	willed willing willingly
whitewash	whitewashed		willingness
	whitewashes	will-o'-the-wisp	
	whitewashing	willow	willowy

willy-nilly
wilt   wilted wilting
wily   wilier wiliest wilily
                          wiliness
win   winner winning
                          winningly won
wince   wincing
winch   winched winches
                          winching
wind   winded (knocked
                          breath out of)
                          winding
                          wound (coiled)

windcheater
windfall
windmill
window
windowledge
window-shopping
windowsill
windscreen
windsurf   windsurfed windsurfer
                          windsurfing
windswept
windy   windier windiest
                          windily windiness
wine (drink)   wining
winery   wineries
wing   winged winger
                          winging
wingless
wink   winked winking
winkle   winkling
winnow   winnowed winnowing
winsome   winsomely
                          winsomeness
winter   wintered wintering
wintry   wintriness
wipe   wiper wiping
wire   wiring
wiry   wirier wiriest wirily
                          wiriness
wisdom
wise   wisely wiseness
wisecrack   wisecracked
                          wisecracking

wish   wished wishes
                          wishing
wishful   wishfully wishfulness
wishy-washy
wisp   wisped wisping
wispy   wispier wispiest
                          wispily wispiness
wisteria/wistaria
wistful   wistfully wistfulness
wit   witted witting
                          wittingly
witch   witches witching
witchcraft
witch doctor
witchery   witcheries
witch hazel
with
withdraw   withdrawing
                          withdrawn withdrew
withdrawal
wither   withered withering
                          witheringly
withers
withhold   withheld withholding
within
without
withstand   withstanding
                          withstood
witless   witlessly witlessness
witness   witnessed witnesses
                          witnessing
witticism
witty   wittier wittiest wittily
                          wittiness
wives
wizard   wizardries wizardry
wizened
woad
wobble   wobbling
woe
woebegone
woeful   woefully woefulness
woggle
wok
wolf   wolfed wolfing
                          wolves
wolfhound

wolfish	wolfishly wolfishness	**work**	worked worker working
wolverine		workable	workability workably
woman	women	workaholic	
womanhood		workbook	
womanish	womanishly womanishness	workforce	
womankind	womenkind	workhorse	
womanly	womanliness	workhouse	
womb		workmanlike	
wombat		workmanship	
women		workmate	
won		workout	
wonder	wondered wondering wonderingly	work-shy	
wonderful	wonderfully wonderfulness	worktop	
		world	
wonderment		worldly	worldliness
wonderstruck		worldly-wise	
wondrous	wondrously wondrousness	worldwide	
		worm	wormed worming
won't		worm-eaten	
woo	wooed wooer wooing wooingly	wormy	wormier wormiest wormily worminess
wood	wooded wooden woodenly woodenness	**worn**	
woodcarver	woodcarving	worn-out	
woodchip		**worry**	worried worries worrier worrying worryingly
woodcraft			
woodcut	woodcutter woodcutting	**worse**	
		worsen	worsened worsening
wooden		worship	worshipped worshipper worshipping
woodpecker		worshipful	worshipfully worshipfulness
woodshed			
woodwind		worst (least good)	
woodwork	woodworker woodworking	worsted (fine wool)	
		worth	
woodworm		worthless	worthlessly worthlessness
woodyard			
woof		worthwhile	
wool	woollen	worthy	worthier worthiest worthily worthiness
woolly	woollier woolliest woolliness		
		would	
woozy	woozily wooziness	**wound**	wounded wounding
word	worded wording	**wove**	woven
wordy	wordier wordiest wordily wordiness	**wrack**	
		wraith	
wore		**wrangle**	wrangler wrangling

wrap　　　　　　wrapped　wrapper
　　　　　　　　　wrapping
wrath
wrathful　　　　　wrathfully
　　　　　　　　　wrathfulness
wreak (to cause)　wreaked　wreaking
wreath (for a funeral)
wreathe (to coil round)
　　　　　　　　　wreathed　wreathing
wreck　　　　　wrecked　wrecker
　　　　　　　　　wrecking
wreckage
wren
wrench　　　　　　wrenched　wrenches
　　　　　　　　　wrenching
wrest　　　　　wrested　wresting
wrestle　　　　　　wrestler　wrestling
wretch　　　　　wretched　wretchedly
　　　　　　　　　wretches
wriggle　　　　　wriggling
wring　　　　　wringer　wringing
　　　　　　　　　wrung
wrinkle　　　　　　wrinkling
wrist　　　　　　wristy
wristlet
writ
write　　　　　　　writer　writing　written
　　　　　　　　　wrote
writhe　　　　　　writhing
wrong　　　　　wronged　wronging
　　　　　　　　　wrongly
wrongdoing　　　　wrongdoer
wrongful　　　　　wrongfully
　　　　　　　　　wrongfulness
wrong-headed　　　wrong-headedly
　　　　　　　　　wrong-headedness
wrote
wrought (made, shaped)
wrung
wry　　　　　　wryer/wrier
　　　　　　　　　wryest/wriest
wryly　　　　　wryness
wurst (sausage)

xenophobia　　　xenophobic
xerox　　　　　xeroxed　xeroxes
　　　　　　　　　xeroxing
Xmas
X-ray　　　　　X-rayed　X-raying
xylophone

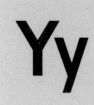

yacht yachting
yacht-club
yachtsman yachtsmen
yachtswoman yachtswomen
yack (idle chat) yacked yacking
yak (animal)
yam
yank yanked yanking
yap yapped yapping
yard yardage
yarmulka/yarmulke
yarn
yashmak
yaw yawed yawing
yawl
yawn yawned yawning
year yearly
yearling
yearn yearned yearning
yearningly

yeast
yeasty yeastier yeastiest
yeastiness
yell yelled yelling
yellow yellowed yellower
yellowest yellowing
yellowish
yelp yelped yelping
yen
yeoman yeomen
yes
yeshiva/yeshivah yeshivahs/yeshivoth
yesterday
yet
yeti

yew
Yiddish Yiddisher
yield yielded yielding
yieldingly
yodel yodelled yodeller
yodelling
yoga yogi yogism
yoghurt/yoghourt/yogurt
yoke (to tie together) yoked yoking
yokel
yolk (yellow of egg)
Yom Kippur
yonder
york yorked yorker yorking
you
you'll you're (you are)
you've (you have)
young younger youngest
youngster
your (belonging to you)
yours
yourself yourselves
youth
youthful youthfully
youthfulness
yowl yowled yowling
yo-yo
yucca
yule yuletide
yuppie

Zz

zabaglione	
zany	zanier zaniest zanily zaniness
zap	zapped zapping
zeal	zealous zealously
zealot	
zebra	
Zen	
zenith	
zephyr	
zero	zeroed zeroes zeroing
zest	
zigzag	zigzagged zigzagging
zinc	
zing	zinged zinging
Zion	Zionism Zionist
zip	zipped zipper zipping
zip (fastener)	
zither	
zodiac	zodiacal
zombie	
zone	zonal zoned zoning
zoo	
zoology	zoological zoologically zoologist
zoom	zoomed zooming

Appendices

Contents

The Appendices to **A Spelling Dictionary** give in clear detail the rules which govern the spelling of English. Each rule is accompanied by examples and a list of the most common words which follow or are exceptions to that particular rule.

This will show that the spelling of English is much more regular than is popularly supposed. Most of the words that confuse people follow straightforward rules which can be explained and learned. Furthermore, the total number of words involved in any given rule is much smaller and more manageable then expected.

This should have the pleasing effect of reducing people's worries about spelling and help make the teaching of it more systematic and effective.

We have made a feature of including lists of words at every opportunity. The purpose of this is to let the users of the **Appendices** see, all together in one section, words sharing a common feature, for example, starting with 'ps', or containing a double 'l' or 'm', or ending with '-que' or '-ment'.

The reader, by passing his or her eye over these lists from time to time, will unconsciously absorb and internalise their shape and form. It would take literally years of reading, involving thousands of pages of print, to encounter all of the words which these lists provide at a glance.

Of course, lists can never be a substitute for the actual discovery of words in sentences but they are a useful tool of learning if carefully and selectively used.

Forming Plurals

1. **To form the plural of a word you normally add 's'.**

   Examples

bat	bats
pencil	pencils
sun	suns
toffee	toffees

2. **You add 'es' when the word ends in 'o', 's', 'x', 'ch', 'sh'.**

a) **Words ending in 'o'**

   Examples

halo	haloes
motto	mottoes
potato	potatoes
tomato	tomatoes

   Exceptions

cuckoo	cuckoos
kangaroo	kangaroos
patio	patios
piano	pianos
ratio	ratios
studio	studios
tobacco	tobaccos

   Either/or

fresco	frescos/frescoes
memento	mementos/mementoes
salvo	salvos/salvoes

b) **Words ending in 's'**

   Examples

address	addresses
bus	buses
business	businesses
class	classes
goddess	goddesses
walrus	walruses

   Either/or

cactus	cactuses/cacti
octopus	octopuses/octopi
syllabus	syllabuses/syllabi
terminus	terminuses/termini

c) **Words ending in 'x'**

   Examples

box	boxes
climax	climaxes
fox	foxes
ibex	ibexes
hoax	hoaxes
telex	telexes

d) **Words ending in 'ch' or 'sh'**

   Examples

coach	coaches
match	matches
crash	crashes
lash	lashes
parish	parishes

3.

a) Words ending in 'y' after a consonant change the 'y' to 'ie' before adding 's'.

Examples

agony	agonies
body	bodies
century	centuries
company	companies
copy	copies
country	countries
dairy	dairies
diary	diaries
lily	lilies
melody	melodies
nursery	nurseries
story	stories
victory	victories

For other examples see page 233.

b) Words ending in 'y' after a vowel keep the 'y' and add 's'.

Examples

boy	boys
donkey	donkeys
key	keys
monkey	monkeys
play	plays
quay	quays
tray	trays
toy	toys

Exception

money	monies/moneys

4. Words ending in 'f' or 'fe' usually change the 'f' or 'fe' to 've' before adding 's'.

Examples

calf	calves
half	halves
leaf	leaves
loaf	loaves
wolf	wolves
knife	knives
life	lives
sheaf	sheaves
thief	thieves
wife	wives

Exceptions

belief	beliefs
chief	chiefs
grief	griefs
proof	proofs
roof	roofs

Either/or

dwarf	dwarfs/dwarves
scarf	scarfs/scarves
hoof	hoofs/hooves

5. **Unusual Plurals**

a) 'is' becomes 'es' in plural

Examples

basis	bases
crisis	crises
diagnosis	diagnoses
emphasis	emphases
oasis	oases
thesis	theses

b) 'um' becomes 'a' in plural

Examples

datum/data	data
emporium	emporia/emporiums
maximum	maxima/maximums
medium	media/mediums
minimum	minima/minimums
phylum	phyla/phylums
spectrum	spectra
stadium	stadia/stadiums
stratum	strata

c) 'us' becomes 'i'

Examples

fungus	fungi/funguses
gladiolus	gladioli/gladioluses
radius	radii/radiuses

d) 'a' becomes 'ae'

Examples

formula	formulae/formulas

e) 'eau' adds 's' or 'x'

Examples

chateau	chateaux
gateau	gateaus/gateaux
plateau	plateaus/plateaux

6. Some words change their spelling in the plural.

Examples

child	children
foot	feet
goose	geese
louse	lice
man	men
mouse	mice
ox	oxen
tooth	teeth
woman	women

7. Some words stay the same for singular and plural.

Examples

deer	deer
fish	fish/fishes
reindeer	reindeer/reindeers
rendezvous	rendezvous
salmon	salmon
series	series
sheep	sheep
species	species

8. To form the plural of some compound words you make the first word plural.

Examples

brother-in-law	brothers-in-law
court martial	courts martial
sister-in-law	sisters-in-law

Vowels and Vowel Clusters

1. 'ie'/'ei'

Rule: 'i' comes before 'e', except after 'c' when the sound is 'ee' as in 'see' or 'bee'; in all other cases 'e' comes before 'i'.

a) In the following words the sound is 'ee' and does not follow 'c', so the spelling is 'ie'.

achieve	aggrieved	believe
brief	chief	diesel
field	fiend	fierce
grief	niece	piece
priest	relieve	retrieve
shield	siege	thief
tier	wield	yield

Exceptions

protein	seize	weir
weird		

b) In the following words the sound is 'ee' and follows 'c', so it is 'ei'.

Examples

ceiling	conceit	conceive
deceit	deceive	perceive
receipt	receive	

There are *no* exceptions to this.

c) When the sound is *not* 'ee', then the 'e' usually comes before the 'i'.

abseil	deign	eight
feign	feint	feisty
foreign	height	heir
leisure	neigh	neighbour
reign	sleigh	their
veil	vein	weight

Exceptions

friend	view

Note:

i) 'either' and 'neither' have alternative pronunciations ('ee' or 'eye').

ii) In a number of other words where you find 'ie' they are pronounced as *two syllables* and don't involve the above rule.

alien	anxiety	audience
client	conscience	diet
dubiety	fiery	hosiery
lenient	notoriety	orient
society	soldier	variety

2. 'ea'

There are a large number of words with 'ea' in them. Here are some of the most common ones.

already	appear	beneath
bread	breakfast	deaf
each	eagle	easy
heal	heaven	increase
instead	jealous	meal
meant	measles	neat
peace	peak	pleasure
really	reason	seat
sergeant	speak	steady
thread	wealth	

3. **'ui'**

   This vowel cluster can cause problems in spelling. Fortunately there are not too many words with 'ui' in them.

biscuit	bruise	build
circuit	fluid	fortuitous
fruit	guide	guilt
juice	nuisance	penguin
recruit	ruin	sluice
suicide	suit	tuition

4. **'ou'**

   There are a large number of words with 'ou' in them, sometimes as part of a larger cluster, e.g. 'ough', 'ought', 'our' and 'ous'.

a) **'-ou-'**

account	council	courage
cousin	double	doubt
house	louse	mount
mouse	rouse	rout
route	should	shoulder
souvenir	thousand	tour
trouble	would	wound

b) **'-ough'**

although	bough	cough
dough	enough	plough
rough	thorough	though
through	tough	trough

c) **'-ought'**

bought	brought	drought
fought	ought	sought
thought		

d) **'-our'**

candour	clamour	colour
detour	endeavour	favour
flavour	flour	four
glamour	honour	hour
rancour	rigour	rumour
savour	splendour	valour
vapour	vigour	

e) **'-iour'**

behaviour	saviour

f) **'-ous'**

barbarous	callous	covetous
dangerous	enormous	fabulous
famous	generous	glamorous
humorous	jealous	ludicrous
marvellous	monstrous	nervous
numerous	odorous	ominous
perilous	prosperous	ravenous
ridiculous	rigorous	ruinous
scrupulous	treacherous	tremendous
tyrannous	unanimous	vigorous
wondrous		

g) **'-ious'**

anxious	capacious	cautious
conscientious	conscious	copious
curious	delicious	delirious
devious	egregious	envious
glorious	gracious	harmonious
hilarious	ignominious	illustrious
industrious	infectious	judicious
mysterious	nutritious	obnoxious
obvious	odious	officious
pernicious	precarious	punctilious
rebellious	religious	repetitious
studious	tedious	tenacious
various	vicious	victorious
vivacious		

h) '-uous'

ambiguous	arduous	conspicuous
contemptuous	continuous	fatuous
impetuous	incongruous	innocuous
sensuous	strenuous	sumptuous
superfluous	tortuous	tumultuous
unctuous	vacuous	voluptuous

i) '-eous'

advantageous	beauteous	contemporaneous
courageous	courteous	erroneous
extemporaneous		extraneous
gaseous	gorgeous	herbaceous
hideous	igneous	instantaneous
miscellaneous	outrageous	piteous
plenteous	righteous	simultaneous

5. 'au'

a) 'au'

applause	assault	auburn
auction	augment	August
aunt	author	automatic
autumn	beauty	because
bureau	cauldron	cauliflower
cause	caution	chauffeur
daub	exhaust	fault
fraud	gauge	gaunt
gauze	haul	haunt
launch	laundry	laurel
pause	restaurant	saucer
saunter	sausage	taunt

b) 'augh'/'aught'

caught	daughter	draught
laugh	laughter	naughty
slaughter	taught	

6. 'eu'

amateur	deuce	feud
lieutenant	milieu	neuralgia
neuter	neutral	neutron
neutrino	pasteurise	pneumatic
raconteur	rheumatism	sleuth

7. 'ua'

actual	casual	gradual
graduate	guard	truant
valuable	virtual	visual
usual		

8. 'eo'

cameo	chameleon	dungeon
galleon	leopard	leotard
meteorite	neon	people
pigeon	surgeon	truncheon
video		

Consonants and Consonant Clusters

Doubling the Final Consonant

Words which end in a single consonant sometimes double the consonant before an ending or suffix beginning with a vowel.

Here are the rules for doing this.

P

1.

a) You *double* the final 'p' in one-syllable words which have a single vowel before the 'p' when followed by an ending or suffix beginning with a vowel.

Examples

cho**p** + **e**d = chopped
tri**p** + **e**r = tripper
wra**p** + **i**ng = wrapping

Other words like this are:

cap	capped	capping	
dip	dipped	dipper	dipping
drip	dripped	dripping	
drop	dropped	dropping	
flap	flapped	flapper	flapping
lap	lapped	lapping	
map	mapped	mapping	
mop	mopped	mopping	
pop	popped	popping	
rip	ripped	ripping	
slip	slipped	slipping	
sip	sipped	sipping	
skip	skipped	skipping	

slap	slapped	slapping	
slip	slipped	slipping	
snap	snapped	snapping	
stop	stopped	stopper	stopping
strip	stripped	stripping	
tap	tapped	tapping	
trap	trapped	trapper	trapping

b) You also *double* the final 'p' in words of more than one syllable when there is a single vowel before the 'p' and the stress falls on the final syllable.

Examples

equi**p** + ed = equipped
equi**p** + ing = equipping

2.

a) You *do not double* the final 'p' when there are two vowels before the 'p'.

Examples

ke**ep** + er = keeper
so**ap** + ed = soaped
lo**op** + ing = looping

Other words like this are:

bleep	bleeped	bleeper	bleeping
creep	creeper	creeping	
droop	drooped	drooping	
heap	heaped	heaping	
leap	leaping		
peep	peeped	peeping	
reap	reaped	reaper	reaping
scoop	scooped	scooping	
sleep	sleeper	sleeping	
snoop	snooped	snooper	snooping
stoop	stooped	stooping	
sweep	sweeper	sweeping	
swoop	swooped	swooping	
weep	weeping		

b) You *do not double* the final 'p' in words ending in a single vowel before the 'p' if the stress *does not* fall on the last syllable.

Example

develop + ed = developed

Other words like this are:

develop	developer	developing
gallop	galloped	galloping
hiccup	hiccuped	hiccuping

Exception

kidnap	kidnapped	kidnapper	kidnapping

R

1.

a) You *double* the 'r' in one-syllable words which have a single vowel before the 'r' when followed by an ending beginning with a vowel.

Examples

bar + ed = barred
spur + ing = spurring

Other words like this are:

bar	barred	barring
blur	blurred	blurring
char	charred	charring
ear	earring	
jar	jarred	jarring
mar	marred	marring
scar	scarred	scarring
spur	spurred	spurring
star	starred	starring
stir	stirred	stirring
tar	tarred	tarring

b) You also *double* the final 'r' in words of more than one syllable when there is a single vowel before the 'r' and the stress falls on the final syllable.

Examples

defer + ed = deferred
refer + ing = referring

Other words like this are:

concur	concurred	concurring
confer	conferred	conferring
defer	deferred	deferring
deter	deterred	deterring
incur	incurred	incurring
infer	inferred	inferring
inter	interred	interring
prefer	preferred	preferring
recur	recurred	recurring
transfer	transferred	transferring

2.

a) You *do not double* the final 'r' when there are two vowels before the 'r'.

Examples

near + ed = neared
forbear + ance = forbearance

Other words like this are:

appear	appearance	appeared	appearing
bear	bearer	bearing	
clear	cleared	clearer	clearing
despair	despaired	despairing	
devour	devoured	devouring	
fear	feared	fearing	
flour	floured		
hear	hearer	hearing	
jeer	jeered	jeering	
moor	moored	mooring	
pair	paired	pairing	
peer	peered	peering	
pour	poured	pourer	pouring
rear	reared	rearing	
roar	roared	roaring	
scour	scoured	scourer	scouring
sheer	sheered	sheering	
sneer	sneered	sneering	
sour	soured	souring	
tear	tearing		
tour	toured	touring	tourist
wear	wearer	wearing	

b) You *do not double* the final 'r' in words ending in a single vowel before the 'r' if the stress *does not* fall on the last syllable.

Example

badger + ed = badgered
pester + ing = pestering

Other words like this are:

answer	answered	answering
batter	battered	battering
border	bordered	bordering
cater	catered	catering
chatter	chattered	chattering
cluster	clustered	clustering
clutter	cluttered	cluttering
conquer	conquered	conquering
consider	considered	considering
cover	covered	covering
encounter	encountered	encountering
enter	entered	entering
foster	fostered	fostering
gather	gathered	gathering
hammer	hammered	hammering
hover	hovered	hovering
linger	lingered	lingering
offer	offered	offering
order	ordered	ordering
pester	pestered	pestering
prosper	prospered	prospering
quiver	quivered	quivering
scatter	scattered	scattering
splutter	spluttered	spluttering
thunder	thundered	thundering
utter	uttered	uttering
whimper	whimpered	whimpering

N

1.

a) You *double* the final 'n' in one syllable words which have a single vowel before the 'n' when followed by an ending beginning with a vowel.

Examples

ban + ed = banned
run + er = runner

Other words like this are:

can	canned	canning
dim	dimmed	dimming
fan	fanned	fanning
grin	grinned	grinning
gun	gunned	gunning
pin	pinned	pinning
run	runner	running
scan	scanned	scanning
sin	sinned	sinning
spin	spinner	spinning
stun	stunned	stunning
tan	tanned	tanning

b) You also *double* the final 'n' in words of more than one syllable when there is a single vowel before the 'n' and the stress falls on the final syllable.

Examples

begin + er = beginner
begin + ing = beginning

2.

a) You *do not double* the final 'n' when there are two vowels before the 'n'.

Examples

lean + ing = leaning
rain + ed = rained

Other words like this are:

bargain	bargained	bargaining	
captain	captained	captaining	
chain	chained	chaining	
contain	contained	container	containing
detain	detained	detaining	
gain	gained	gaining	
groan	groaned	groaning	
join	joined	joiner	joining
moan	moaned	moaner	moaning
obtain	obtained	obtaining	
open	opened	opener	opening
pain	pained	paining	
preen	preened	preening	
rain	rained	raining	
refrain	refrained	refraining	
remain	remained	remaining	
stain	stained	staining	
train	trained	trainer	training

b) You *do not double* the final 'n' in words ending in a single vowel before the 'n' if the stress *does not* fall on the last syllable.

Examples

garden + er = gardener
iron + ing = ironing

Other words like this are:

awaken	awakened	awakening
brighten	brightened	brightening
harden	hardened	hardening
jettison	jettisoned	jettisoning
orphan	orphaned	
reason	reasoned	reasoning
straighten	straightened	straightening
sweeten	sweetened	sweetener sweetening
thicken	thickened	thickening
tighten	tightened	tightening
toughen	toughened	toughening

T

1.

a) You *double* the final 't' in one-syllable words which have a single vowel before the 't' when followed by an ending or suffix beginning with a vowel.

bat + ed = batted
cut + ing = cutting

Other words like this are:

bat	batted	batting
bet	betting	
chat	chatted	chatting
cut	cutter	cutting
dot	dotted	dotting
fret	fretted	fretting
jet	jetted	jetting
knit	knitted	knitting
knot	knotted	knotting
let	letter	letting
pat	patted	patting
pet	petted	petting
put	putting	
quit	quitted	quitting
set	setting	
shut	shutting	
sit	sitting	
spot	spotted	spotting
trot	trotted	trotting

b) You also *double* the final 't' in words of more than one syllable when there is a single vowel before the 't' and the stress falls on the final syllable.

Examples

commit + ed = committed
forget + ing = forgetting

Other words like this are:

babysit	babysitter	babysitting	
commit	committed	committing	
forget	forgetting		
outwit	outwitted	outwitting	
regret	regretted	regretting	
remit	remittance	remitted	remitting
submit	submitted	submitting	

2.

a) You *do not double* the final 't' when there are two vowels before the 't'.

Examples

l<u>oo</u>t + ed = l<u>oo</u>ted
s<u>ea</u>t + ing = s<u>ea</u>ting

Other words like this are:

coat	coated	coating	
defeat	defeated	defeating	
eat	eaten	eating	
entreat	entreated	entreating	
fleet		fleeting	
float	floated	floating	
heat	heated	heater	heating
meet		meeting	
riot	rioted	rioting	
root	rooted	rooting	
scout	scouted	scouting	
seat	seated	seating	
spout	spouted	spouting	
sprout	sprouted	sprouting	
treat	treated	treating	

b) You *do not double* the final 't' in words ending in a single vowel before the 't' if the stress *does not* fall on the last syllable.

Examples

c<u>o</u>sset + ed = c<u>o</u>sseted
pr<u>o</u>fit + ing = pr<u>o</u>fit<u>i</u>ng

Other words like this are:

ballot	balloted	balloting	
benefit	benefited	benefiting	
budget	budgeted	budgeting	
carpet	carpeted	carpeting	
credit	credited	creditor	crediting
deposit	deposited	depositing	
edit	edited	editor	editing
exhibit	exhibited	exhibitor	exhibiting
fillet	filleted	filleting	
limit	limited	limiting	
market	marketed	marketing	

plummet	plummeted	plummeting
profit	profited	profiting
prohibit	prohibited	prohibiting
rocket	rocketed	rocketing
target	targeted	targeting
tatter	tattered	
visit	visited	visiting

Exception

<u>ou</u>tfit + ed = <u>ou</u>tfit<u>t</u>ed
<u>ou</u>tfit + ing = <u>ou</u>tfit<u>t</u>ing

1. You *double* the final 'l' after a single vowel before an ending or suffix beginning with a vowel no matter where the stress is in the word.

Examples

patr<u>o</u>l + <u>e</u>d = patr<u>o</u>l<u>l</u>ed
grov<u>e</u>l + <u>i</u>ng = grov<u>e</u>l<u>l</u>ing

Other words like this are:

appal	appalled	appalling	
cancel	cancelled	cancelling	
compel	compelled	compelling	
control	controlled	controller	controlling
dispel	dispelled	dispelling	
distil	distilled	distilling	
equal	equalled	equalling	
excel	excelled	excellent	excelling
jewel	jewelled	jewellery	jewelling
label	labelled	labelling	
level	levelled	levelling	
model	modelled	modelling	
panel	panelled	panelling	
parcel	parcelled	parcelling	
pencil	pencilled	pencilling	
propel	propelled	propeller	propelling
repel	repelled	repelling	
rival	rivalled	rivalling	
signal	signalled	signalling	
towel	towelled	towelling	
travel	travelled	traveller	travelling
tunnel	tunnelled	tunnelling	

2. You *do not double* the final 'l' when there are two vowels before the 'l'.

Examples

appe<u>a</u>l + <u>i</u>ng = appealing
<u>o</u>il + <u>e</u>d = oiled

Other words like this are:

appeal	appealed	appealing	
bail	bailed	bailing	
boil	boiled	boiler	boiling
coil	coiled	coiling	
conceal	concealed	concealing	
cool	cooled	cooler	cooling
curtail	curtailed	curtailing	
deal	dealer	dealing	
detail	detailed	detailing	
fail	failed	failing	
feel	feeler	feeling	
foil	foiled	foiling	
fool	fooled	fooling	
hail	hailed	hailing	
heal	healed	healing	
kneel	kneeler	kneeling	
mail	mailed	mailing	
oil	oiled	oiling	
pool	pooled	pooling	
retail	retailed	retailing	
reveal	revealed	revealing	
soil	soiled	soiling	
steal	stealing		
toil	toiled	toiling	
veil	veiled	veiling	
wheel	wheeled	wheeling	

Exception

d<u>ia</u>l + <u>e</u>d = dialled
d<u>ia</u>l + <u>i</u>ng = dialling

M

1.
a) You *double* the final 'm' in one-syllable words which have a single vowel before the 'm' when followed by an ending or suffix beginning with a vowel.

Examples

cr<u>a</u>m + <u>e</u>d = crammed
sk<u>i</u>m + <u>i</u>ng = skimming

Other words like this are:

chum	chummed	chumming	
cram	crammed	cramming	
dim	dimmed	dimming	
drum	drummed	drummer	drumming
gum	gummed	gumming	
hum	hummed	humming	
ram	rammed	ramming	
rim	rimmed	rimming	
skim	skimmed	skimming	
slim	slimmed	slimmer	slimming
stem	stemmed	stemming	
strum	strummed	strumming	
swim	swimmer	swimming	
trim	trimmed	trimming	

2.
a) You *do not double* the final 'm' when there are two vowels before the 'm'.

Examples

<u>ai</u>m + <u>e</u>d = aimed
scr<u>ea</u>m + <u>i</u>ng = screaming

Other words like this are:

aim	aimed	aiming	
beam	beamed	beaming	
bloom	bloomed	blooming	
deem	deemed	deeming	
dream	dreamed	dreamer	dreaming
gleam	gleamed	gleaming	
groom	groomed	grooming	
maim	maimed	maiming	
redeem	redeemed	redeemer	redeeming
room	roomed	rooming	
scream	screamed	screaming	
seem	seemed	seeming	
team	teamed		
zoom	zoomed	zooming	

b) You *do not double* the final 'm' in words ending in a single vowel before the 'm' if the stress *does not* fall on the last syllable.

Examples

blossom	blossomed	blossoming
custom	customer	
ransom	ransomed	ransoming
venom	venomous	

B

You *double* the final 'b' after a vowel when it is followed by an ending or suffix beginning with a vowel.

Examples

rob + ed = robbed
scrub + ing = scrubbing

Other words like this are:

bob	bobbed	bobbing	
club	clubbed	clubbing	
dab	dabbed	dabbing	
fib	fibbed	fibber	fibbing
jab	jabbed	jabbing	
grab	grabbed	grabbing	
lob	lobbed	lobbing	
rib	ribbed		
rub	rubbed	rubber	rubbing
scrub	scrubbed	scrubbing	
stab	stabbed	stabbing	
swab	swabbed	swabbing	
throb	throbbed	throbbing	

G

You *double* the final 'g' after a vowel when it is followed by an ending or suffix beginning with a vowel.

Examples

big + er = bigger
drag + ing = dragging

Other words like this are:

bag	bagged		
beg	beggar	begged	begging
big	bigger	biggest	
brag	braggart	bragged	bragging
dog	dogged	dogging	
dig	digger	digging	
drag	dragged	dragging	
drug	drugged	druggist	drugging
flag	flagged	flagging	
flog	flogged	flogging	
gag	gagged	gagging	
hug	hugged	hugging	
jog	jogged	jogger	jogging
mug	mugged	mugger	mugging
nag	nagged	nagging	
plug	plugged	plugging	
sag	sagged	sagging	
shrug	shrugged	shrugging	
slog	slogged	slogging	
snag	snagged	snagging	
wag	wagged	wagging	

S

There are very few words which end in the letter 's' after a vowel. Here is a list of the most important ones with the allowed alternatives. They can be confusing so watch out.

bus + es = buses
gas + es = gases
gas + ed = gassed
gas + ing = gassing
focus + ed = focused
focus + ing = focusing

1. You *double* the final 'd' in one-syllable words which have a single vowel before the 'd' when followed by an ending or suffix beginning with a vowel.

Examples

wed + ing = wedding
red + er = redder

Other words like this are:

bed	bedded	bedding
bid	bidder	bidding
bud	budded	budding
gad	gadded	gadding
hid	hidden	
red	redder	reddest
shred	shredded	shredding
stud	studded	studding
thud	thudded	thudding
wed	wedded	wedding

2. You *do not double* the final 'd' when there are two vowels before the 'd'.

Examples

wood + en = wooden
tread + ing = treading

Other words like this are:

bead	beaded	beading
behead	beheaded	beheading
bleed	bleeding	
breed	breeding	
dread	dreaded	dreading
exceed	exceeded	exceeding
feed	feeder	feeding
head	headed	heading
heed	heeded	heeding
hood	hooded	hooding
lead	leaden	leading
loud	louder	loudest
need	needed	needing
proceed	proceeded	proceeding
raid	raided	raider	raiding

read	reader	reading
seed	seeded	seeding
speed	speeded	speeding
thread	threaded	threading
tread	treading	

There are few words which end in 'f' after a vowel. All are words with two vowels before the 'f' and so do not double the 'f' before a following vowel.

Here are the main examples

deaf	deafen	
leaf	leafed	leafing
loaf	loafed	loafing
roof	roofed	roofing

The few words which end in 'k' after a vowel generally have two vowels before the 'k' and so do not double the final 'k'.

Here are the main examples

beak	beaked	beaker
creak	creaked	creaking
croak	croaked	croaking
leak	leaked	leaking
reek	reeked	reeking
seek	seeker	seeking
squeak	squeaked	squeaking
weak	weaker	weakest

Note:

trek	trekked	trekking

Words Ending in Silent 'e'

There are a very large number of words which end in a silent or unpronounced 'e'. When you add an ending which starts with a vowel to these words you drop the 'e'.

Examples

write + ing = writing
fame + ous = famous
value + able = valuable
excite + ed = excited
separate + ed = separated
compare + ing = comparing

The number of words like these is too numerous to list here.

Exceptions to this rule are:

a) Certain words ending in 'ge' or 'ce' and followed by '-able', '-ous' or '-ance'. These keep the 'e' when followed by an ending which starts with a vowel.

Examples

courage + ous = courageous
peace + able = peaceable
advantage + ous = advantageous
knowledge + able = knowledgeable

For other words ending in 'ce' or 'ge' followed by '-able', see page 235.

b) Words ending in 'e' after a vowel keep the 'e' when followed by 'ing'.

shoe + ing = shoeing
canoe + ing = canoeing
tiptoe + ing = tiptoeing

Words Ending in 'y'

1. In words ending in 'y' *after a vowel* the 'y' remains unchanged before all additional endings.

Examples

boy + s = boys
buy + ing = buying
enjoy + ment = enjoyment

Other words like this are:

employ	employed	employment
joy	joyful	joyous
pay	paying	payment
play	played	playing
pray	prayed	prayer	praying
say	saying	
stay	stayed	staying
stray	strayed	straying
toy	toyed	toying

Exceptions

In some words the 'y' after a vowel becomes 'i' before a following consonant.

Examples

day + ly = daily
gay + ly = gaily
pay + d = paid
say + d = said

2. Words ending in 'y' *after a consonant* change the 'y' to 'ie' before a following 's'.

a) This happens when forming *plurals*.

Examples

baby + s = babies
bakery + s = bakeries
fly + s = flies

For other examples see Forming Plurals on page 219.

b) You do this also when forming the third person singular, present tense, of verbs ending in 'y' after a consonant.

Examples

accompany + s = accompanies
apply + s = applies

Other words like this are:

certify	certifies
copy	copies
deny	denies
identify	identifies
satisfy	satisfies
vary	varies

c) Verbs ending in 'y' after a consonant change the 'y' to 'ie' before a following 'd' in the past tense.

Examples

apply + d = applied
dry + d = dried

Other words like this are:

bury	buried
carry	carried
hurry	hurried
marry	married
purify	purified
reply	replied
sky	skied
supply	supplied
verify	verified
worry	worried

d) Words ending in 'y' after a consonant keep the 'y' before a following 'i'.

Example

deny + ing = denying
try + ing = trying

Other words like this are:

ally	allying
apply	applying
certify	certifying
copy	copying
cry	crying
defy	defying
fry	frying
marry	marrying
pry	prying
vary	varying
verify	verifying

e) Words ending in 'y' after a consonant change the 'y' to an 'i' when an ending is added other than 's' or 'd'.

Examples

beauty + ful = beautiful
busy + ly = busily
easy + er = easier
merry + est = merriest

Other words like this are:

brawny	brawnier	brawniest		
breezy	breezily			
bulky	bulkier	bulkiest		
bushy	bushier	bushiest		
crazy	crazier	craziest	crazily	craziness
duty	dutiful			
easy	easier	easiest	easily	easiness
icy	icier	iciest	icily	iciness
lazy	lazier	laziest	lazily	laziness
lucky	luckier	luckiest	luckily	luckiness
mercy	merciful	merciless		
noisy	noisier	noisiest	noisily	
pity	pitiful	pitiless		
plenty	plentiful			
ready	readily	readiness		
silly	sillier	silliest	silliness	
sunny	sunnier	sunniest	sunniness	
wily	wilier	wiliest	wilily	wiliness

Exceptions

In a small number of words ending in 'y' after a consonant you change the 'y' to an 'e' before '-ous'.

beauty + ous = beauteous
pity + ous = piteous

Suffixes

1. '-able'

There are a large number of words which take the suffix '-able'. Here are the rules for adding this suffix to a root word.

a) After words ending in a consonant you simply add the suffix.

Example

accept + able = acceptable

Other words like this are:

acceptable	approachable	attainable
avoidable	beatable	comfortable
considerable	creditable	dependable
detestable	enjoyable	fashionable
favourable	lamentable	laughable
presentable	questionable	reasonable
remarkable	suitable	thinkable
understand-able		

b) After words ending in a silent 'e' you drop the 'e' before adding '-able'.

Example

admire + able = admirable

Other words like this are:

advisable	arguable	comparable
curable	debatable	deplorable
desirable	excusable	imaginable
measurable	notable	practicable
savable	solvable	usable
valuable		

Alternative spellings

These words can either keep the 'e' before 'able' or drop it. The commoner usage is given first:

lovable/loveable
moveable/movable
shakeable/shakable

c) Words ending in 'y' after a consonant change the 'y' to an 'i'.

Example

certify + able = certifiable

Other words like this are:

enviable	notifiable	pitiable
pliable	variable	verifiable

d) Words ending in 'ee' simple add '-able'.

Example

agree + able = agreeable

e) Words ending in 'ge' or 'ce' keep the 'e' before '-able'.

Example

notice + able = noticeable
knowledge + able = knowledgeable

Other words like this are:

changeable	manageable	marriageable
peaceable	serviceable	traceable

f) Here is a list of words where the suffix has become inseparable from the original root.

abominable	affable	amicable
applicable	capable	despicable
durable	equable	formidable
hospitable	inimitable	inscrutable
irritable	miserable	negotiable
operable	portable	satiable
sociable	tolerable	

2. '–ible'

In a number of words you add '-ible' rather than '-able'. In almost all of these words the '-ible' has become inseparable from the root word.

Here is a list of such words:

accessible	audible	collapsible
combustible	compatible	corruptible
credible	defensible	digestible
divisible	edible	eligible
exhaustible	flexible	forcible
gullible	horrible	illegible
impossible	incomprehensible	
intelligible	legible	negligible
ostensible	perceptible	
permissible	plausible	possible
responsible	risible	sensible
tangible	terrible	

3. In all the '-able'/'-ible' words you form nouns and adverbs as in the examples given below.

Adjective	Noun	Adverb
advisable	advisability	advisably
credible	credibility	credibly

There are no exceptions to this.

4. '–ly'

You add '-ly' to an adjective to form an adverb. In most cases you simply add '-ly' to the previous word.

Examples

cruel + ly = cruelly
sincere + ly = sincerely
beautiful + ly = beautifully
dangerous + ly = dangerously

There are a number of exceptions to this rule.

a) **When the adjective ends in 'y' you change the 'y' to 'i' before adding '-ly'.**

Example

busy + ly = busily

Others words like this are:

breezily	cosily	easily
heartily	jauntily	lazily
luckily	noisily	readily

b) **In the words 'true' and 'due' you drop the final 'e' before adding 'ly'.**

true + ly = truly
due + ly = duly

c) **In words ending in 'le' you drop the final 'le' before adding 'ly'**

Example

gentle + ly = gently

Other words like this are:

i) Words like bristly, prickly, tickly.
ii) All the '-able'/'-ible' words when forming adverbs (see 3 above).

5. '–ment'

a) When you add '-ment' to a verb to make it into a noun, the rules are the same whether the verb ends in a consonant or a vowel. You simply add '-ment' to the root word.

Example

abandon + ment = abandonment
abate + ment = abatement

Other words like this are:

adornment	advancement	advertisement
agreement	alignment	allotment
amusement	announcement	appointment
arrangement	astonishment	attainment
bereavement	commitment	confinement
department	government	instalment
payment	placement	postponement
puzzlement	settlement	statement
treatment		

Exceptions

argument

Either/or

judgement/judgment
acknowledgement/acknowledgment

b) There are a number of words where the root word and the suffix '-ment' have become inseparable.

Here is a list of the useful ones:

armament	casement	compartment
detriment	environment	figment
fitment	implement	increment
medicament	oddment	ointment
pavement	sacrament	sediment
segment	sentiment	supplement
tenement	testament	tournament

6. '-ance'/'-ant', '-ence'/'-ent'

a) There are a number of words which end in **'-ance'** to form a noun. These words take the ending **'-ant'** to form the adjective.

Here is a list of the more useful ones:

Noun	Adjective
abundance	abundant
arrogance	arrogant
assistance	assistant
attendance	attendant
brilliance	brilliant
dominance	dominant
elegance	elegant
extravagance	extravagant
exuberance	exuberant
flamboyance	flamboyant
fragrance	fragrant
ignorance	ignorant
importance	important
instance	instant
observance	observant
radiance	radiant
relevance	relevant
reluctance	reluctant
repugnance	repugnant
resistance	resistant
significance	significant
vigilance	vigilant

b) Here is a list of words ending in **'-ant'** which are *nouns*.

accountant	applicant	assailant
assistant	attendant	celebrant
defendant	elephant	emigrant
immigrant	inhabitant	lieutenant
merchant	militant	occupant
peasant	restaurant	sergeant
stimulant		

c) There are a number of words which end in **'-ence'**. These words take the ending **'-ent'** to form the adjective.

Here is a list of the more useful ones:

Noun	Adjective
abhorrence	abhorrent
absence	absent
affluence	affluent
benevolence	benevolent
coherence	coherent
confidence	confident
dependence	dependent
difference	different
diligence	diligent
eminence	eminent
impudence	impudent
innocence	innocent
intelligence	intelligent
negligence	negligent
obedience	obedient
patience	patient
penitence	penitent
permanence	permanent
persistence	persistent
presence	present
prominence	prominent
prudence	prudent
recurrence	recurrent
residence	resident
reverence	reverent
silence	silent
turbulence	turbulent
violence	violent
vehemence	vehement

7. '-ense'

Here is a list of the most useful words which end in **'-ense'**.

dense	expense	immense
incense	license (verb)	nonsense
recompense	sense	suspense
tense		

8. '-tion'

Here is a list of words ending in **'-tion'**.

action	addition	ammunition
assassination	caution	celebration
communication	compensation	competition
composition	condition	conjunction
consolation	conversation	correction
creation	deception	description
destruction	detention	direction
distinction	education	emotion
examination	exception	exclamation
execution	exhibition	faction
fiction	fraction	function
illustration	intention	invention
mention	nation	observation
operation	opposition	persecution
petition	population	position
prevention	qualification	question
reception	recognition	reputation
restriction	satisfaction	sensation
situation	station	suggestion
superstition	temptation	transformation

9. '-sion'

Here is a list of useful words ending in **'-sion'**.

collision	comprehension	compulsion
conclusion	confusion	conversion
corrosion	decision	delusion
dimension	diversion	division
erosion	evasion	exclusion
explosion	expulsion	extension
illusion	invasion	mansion
occasion	persuasion	provision
subversion	transfusion	vision

Note: suspicion

10. '-ssion'

Here is a list of useful words ending in **'-ssion'.**

admission	commission	compassion
concession	concussion	depression
emission	expression	impression
mission	obsession	omission
passion	permission	procession
succession	transmission	

11. '-ful'

a) You add '-ful' to the end of many words to make adjectives.

Examples

boast + ful = boastful
care + ful = careful

Here is a sample of other words like this:

artful	bashful	cheerful
colourful	delightful	dreadful
faithful	fearful	forceful
graceful	grateful	harmful
hopeful	joyful	lawful
mournful	peaceful	purposeful
resentful	rightful	shameful
sorrowful	successful	thankful
thoughtful	truthful	useful
wasteful	wrongful	youthful

Exceptions

skill + ful = skilful
will + ful = wilful

b) When you add '-ful' to words ending in 'y', you change the 'y' to an 'i'.

Example

pity + ful = pitiful

Other words like this are:

beautiful	dutiful	fanciful
merciful	pitiful	plentiful

c) When you add '-ly' to a word ending in '-ful' to make an adverb you will, of course, have two 'll's.

Examples

careful	carefully
faithful	faithfully
merciful	mercifully
successful	successfully
thoughtful	thoughtfully
useful	usefully

12. '-less'

Here is a list of useful words which end in **'-less'.**

artless	boundless	careless
ceaseless	changeless	cheerless
colourless	countless	doubtless
faceless	faultless	fruitless
hopeless	harmless	lawless
listless	matchless	nameless
needless	noiseless	painless
priceless	reckless	ruthless
senseless	soulless	tactless
tasteless	thoughtless	tireless
useless	weightless	worthless

When you add '-less' to a word ending in 'y', you change the 'y' to an 'i' before adding '-less'.

Examples

pity + less = pitiless
mercy + less = merciless

13. '-some'

Here is a list of words ending in **'-some'.**

awesome	cumbersome	fearsome
frolicsome	gruesome	handsome
quarrelsome	tiresome	toothsome
troublesome	venturesome	winsome

14. '-ary', '-ery', '-ory'

a) Here is a list of words which end in **'-ary'**.

adversary	anniversary	beneficiary
capillary	commentary	coronary
documentary	dromedary	dictionary
dispensary	elementary	emissary
exemplary	extemporary	extraordinary
fragmentary	glossary	hereditary
imaginary	infirmary	momentary
monetary	necessary	ordinary
primary	sanitary	secondary
secretary	stationary (standing still)	
temporary		

b) Here is a list of words which end in **'-ery'**.

adultery	battery	brewery
confectionery	crockery	discovery
distillery	embroidery	jewellery
knavery	imagery	machinery
periphery	recovery	
stationery (papers)		

c) Here is a list of words which end in **'-ory'**.

category	compulsory	condemnatory
conservatory	cursory	derogatory
directory	factory	inventory
lavatory	mandatory	obligatory
observatory	promontory	repertory

15. '-al', ' -el', ' -il'

a) Here is a list of useful words which end in **'-al'**.

'-al'

accidental	animal	cereal
crystal	decimal	educational
eternal	fatal	formal
general	hospital	jackal
identical	incidental	journal
local	logical	musical
mineral	national	petal
principal	rascal	rehearsal
several	signal	total
typical	vandal	vertical

'-ial'

aerial	circumstantial	confidential
crucial	essential	facial
impartial	judicial	special

'-ual'

casual	eventual	habitual
individual	manual	usual

b) Here is a list of useful words which end in **'-el'**.

angel	apparel	barrel
camel	channel	chapel
chisel	colonel	duel
easel	enamel	fuel
hazel	hostel	hotel
jewel	label	lapel
laurel	level	lintel
mackerel	model	navel
nickel	novel	panel
parcel	pastel	personnel
quarrel	rebel	spaniel
tinsel	towel	travel
vessel		

c) Here is a list of useful words which end in **'-il'**.

pupil	stencil	tendril
tonsil	utensil	vigil

16. '-or', '-ar', '-er'

a) Here is a list of useful words which end in **'-or'**.

actor	author	calculator
competitor	conductor	conjuror
conspirator	décor	director
doctor	exterior	factor
indicator	inferior	inspector
instructor	investigator	major
manor	minor	mirror
moderator	motor	narrator
operator	professor	projector
prosecutor	radiator	refrigerator
sailor	sponsor	suitor
survivor	tenor	traitor
tutor	victor	

b) Here is a list of useful words which end in **'-ar'**.

altar (in church)		beggar
burglar	calendar	caterpillar
cellar	circular	collar
familiar	grammar	guitar
irregular	particular	peculiar
perpendicular	pillar	popular
registrar	regular	scholar
similar	singular	solar
sonar	vinegar	

c) Here is a list of useful words which end in **'-er'**.

Occupations/People

announcer	baker	carpenter
carrier	cashier	coroner
employer	farmer	foreigner
gardener	mariner	passenger
soldier	traveller	

Others

alter (change)	answer	bitter
butter	character	conquer
cylinder	hammer	ladder
leather	manner	order
pepper	register	remember
saucer	slaughter	spider
surrender	terrier	tower
weather		

More Letter Clusters

This section contains lists of words which might give difficulty, or are in common use, which contain consonant clusters, i.e. two or more consonants together.

1. 'tt'

attack	attain	attempt
attention	attitude	attract
battle	better	bottle
bottom	butter	button
cigarette	confetti	cottage
cotton	ditto	gazette
glitter	glutton	jetty
kitten	latter	launderette
litter	matter	mutton
omelette	otter	platter
regatta	serviette	shutter
titter	totter	twitter
utter	vendetta	wattle

2. 'pp'

appalling	apparatus	apparent
appeal	appear	appetite
apple	apply	appoint
appreciate	approach	approve
approximately	cripple	dapper
disappearance	disapproval	happen
happy	hippopotamus	opponent
oppose	opposite	oppress
pepper	puppet	ripple
sapphire	stoppage	supper
supple	supply	support
suppose	suppress	topple
upper	whippet	

3. 'll'

a) Here is a list of useful words which have '-ll' at the end of the word.

ball	bell	bill
bull	call	cell
doll	dull	dwell
fell	fill	full
mill	pill	pull
quell	roll	shall
smell	spell	still
stroll	tell	trill
will		

b) Here is a list of useful words which have '-ll-' in the middle of the word.

alley	allow	ally
ballad	ballet	balloon
ballot	billiards	brilliant
bullet	cello	challenge
chilly	collect	college
dolly	fellow	follow
gallon	gazelle	gorilla
Halloween	hollow	holly
illustration	intellect	jelly
jolly	killer	lollipop
lullaby	mellow	miller
parallel	pellet	penicillin
pulley	rally	rebellion
shallow	stallion	sullen
thriller	trolley	umbrella
valley	vanilla	village
villain	volley	wallet
willow	yellow	

4. 'ss'

a) Here is a list of useful words which have '**-ss**' at the end of the word.

abbess	abscess	assess
baroness	bless	bliss
bypass	caress	chess
class	compass	confess
countess	digress	dismiss
duchess	embarrass	excess
express	fortress	goddess
harass	harness	hiss
impress	kiss	laundress
morass	poetess	progress
stress	success	surpass
toss	trespass	unless

b) Here is a list of useful words which have '**-ss-**' in the middle of the word.

assassin	assault	assemble
assign	assist	blossom
casserole	cassette	crevasse
croissant	delicatessen	dissect
dissuade	embassy	finesse
fissure	fossil	glossary
gossamer	hassle	incessant
lasso	lesson	massacre
massage	massive	message
missile	mission	mousse
necessity	obsessed	possess
rissole	russet	session

5. 'rr'

arrange	arrears	arrest
arrive	arrow	barrel
barren	barrier	barrow
burrow	carriage	carrot
carry	correct	correspond
corrupt	currant (fruit)	
current (electricity)		curriculum
curry	earring	embarrass
error	ferry	furrow
garrison	herring	horrid
horrified	horror	marriage
merry	mirror	narrative
narrow	occurrence	purr
quarry	resurrection	sparrow
squirrel	surrender	surround
terrace	terrible	terrier
terrify	terror	tomorrow
warren	warrior	worry

6. 'cc'

accelerate	accept	accessory
accident	acclaim	accommodation
accomplish	accordingly	accumulation
accurate	broccoli	eccentric
hiccup	impeccable	moccasin
piccolo	occasion	occupy
occur	succeed	success
succulent	tobacco	vaccinate

7. 'mm'

accommodation	ammonia	ammunition
comma	command	commend
comment	commitment	common
commotion	flammable	gammon
glimmer	grammar	hammer
immediate	immense	immune
mammal	recommend	simmer
summary	summer	summit
summon		

8. 'dd'

add	adder	address
befuddle	bladder	cuddle
fiddle	giddy	huddle
ladder	middle	muddle
paddle	pudding	puddle
oddity	redden	riddle
rudder	shudder	sudden
swaddle	twiddle	udder
waddle	wedding	

9. 'ff'

a) Here is a list of useful words which have '–ff' at the end of the word.

bluff	cliff	dandruff
gruff	midriff	sheriff
sniff	staff	stuff
tiff	whiff	

b) Here is a list of useful words which have '–ff–' in the middle of the word.

affair	affection	afflict
affix	afford	baffling
buffalo	buffer	buffet
coffee	coffin	daffodil
difficult	efface	effort
giraffe	muffler	offend
offer	office	paraffin
raffle	ruffian	ruffle
scaffold	scruffy	scuffle
suffer	suffice	suffix
suffocate	toffee	traffic
waffle		

10. 'nn'

anniversary	announce	annoy
annual	banner	bunny
cannibal	cannon	cannot
channel	connection	flannel
funnel	funny	inner
kennel	innocent	madonna
mannequin	manner	mayonnaise
minnow	nanny	personnel
questionnaire	runner	spanner
tennis	tunnel	uncanny
winnow		

11. 'bb'

abbey	abbot	babble
bobbin	bubble	cabbage
chubby	dabble	dribble
ebb	flabby	gibbon
gobble	hobble	hobby
jabber	nibble	pebble
rabbi	rabbit	rabble
ribbon	robber	rubber
rubbish	rubble	shabby
squabble	stubble	stubborn

12. 'gg'

aggravate	aggression	baggage
beggar	dagger	exaggerate
giggle	groggy	haggard
haggis	juggler	luggage
maggot	nugget	reggae
rugged	smuggle	stagger
struggle	suggest	swagger
toboggan	trigger	wriggle

13. 'zz'

blizzard	buzz	dazzle
dizzy	drizzle	embezzled
fizzy	frizzle	fuzzy
guzzled	jazz	muzzled
nozzle	nuzzle	pizza
puzzle	quizzical	sizzle

14. 'sc'

a) **pronounced 'ss'**

abscess	ascend	Ascension
crescent	discern	disciple
fascinate	miscellaneous	reminiscence
scene	science	scissors

b) **pronounced 'sk'**

biscuit	discus (sport)	discuss (to talk)
escape	manuscript	mascara
mascot	scarce	scratch
screen	scripture	

c) pronounced 'sh'

| conscience | conscientious | crescendo |

15. 'gh'

a) 'gh'

aghast	although	borough
bough	burgh	cough
dinghy	dough	enough
ghastly	ghetto	ghost
ghoul	high	laugh
plough	rough	sigh
sleigh	thigh	thorough
though	through	tough
trough	weigh	

b) 'ght'

almighty	alright	blight
bought	bright	brought
caught	daughter	distraught
draught	drought	eight
fight	flight	fought
freight	haughty	height
knight	light	lightning
might	mighty	naughty
nought	onslaught	ought
plight	right	sight
slaughter	slight	sought
straight	taught	thought
tight	tonight	twilight
upright	uptight	weight

16. 'gu'

a) 'gu-'

| guarantee | guard | guess |
| guest | guillotine | |

b) '-gu-'

baguette	beguile	distinguish
extinguish	language	languid
languor		

c) '-gue'

catalogue	colleague	dialogue
fatigue	harangue	intrigue
league	monologue	morgue
plague	prologue	rogue
synagogue	tongue	travelogue

17. 'wh-'

whale	whack	wheat
wheedle	wheel	when
wherever	where	whet
which	whiff	while
whim	whimper	whine
whinge	whip	whisk
whisker	whisky	whisper
whist	white	whiz/whizz
who	whoever	whale
wholesome	whom	whose
why		

18. 'qu'

a) 'qu-'

quaint	qualify	quality
quantity	quarrel	quarter
queen	queer	quench
question	questionnaire	queue
quick	quiet	quite
quiz	quotation	

b) '-qu-'

bequeath	bequest	delinquent
equal	eloquent	equator
frequent	liquid	mosquito
relinquish	request	requiem
sequel	sequin	squabble
square	squash	squawk
squeeze	squid	squint
tranquil	vanquish	ventriloquist

c) '-que'

antique	boutique	cheque
clique	grotesque	mosque
mystique	oblique	opaque
physique	picturesque	pique
statuesque	technique	unique

19. 'ph'

a) 'ph-'

phantom	pharmacy	pheasant
phenomenal	philosophy	phoenix
phone	phosphorus	photograph
physical	physician	physics

b) '-ph-'

alphabet	amphibian	atmosphere
biography	catastrophe	decipher
elephant	emphasis	geography
hemisphere	hyphen	metaphor
microphone	morphine	nephew
orphan	pamphlet	prophet
siphon	sphere	sulphate
sulphur	symphony	telephone
typhoid	typhoon	

c) '-ph'

cenotaph	epitaph	paragraph
photograph	telegraph	triumph

20. '-dge'

badge	bridge	cartridge
dodge	dredge	edge
fridge	fudge	grudge
hedge	knowledge	ledge
lodge	nudge	partridge
pledge	porridge	ridge
sledge	sludge	smudge
stodge	trudge	

21. '-le'

a) '-gle'

angle	bangle	bungle
dangle	eagle	gargle
jingle	jungle	mangle
mingle	ogle	rectangle
shingle	single	smuggle
spangle	struggle	tangle
triangle	wangle	wriggle

b) '-ple'

couple	maple	multiple
participle	people	pimple
principle	purple	sample
scruple	staple	steeple
temple		

c) '-pple'

apple	nipple	ripple
stipple	supple	tipple

d) '-cle'

bicycle	cycle	icicle
manacle	muscle	obstacle
receptacle	tentacle	treacle

e) '-kle'

sparkle	sprinkle	twinkle
winkle	wrinkle	

f) '-ckle'

pickle	prickle	shackle
sickle	speckle	suckle
tackle	tickle	trickle

g) '-dle'

bundle	candle	cradle
curdle	dandle	doodle
girdle	handle	hurdle
idle	ladle	needle
noodle	poodle	spindle
swindle		

h) '-ddle'

cuddle	fiddle	fuddle
huddle	meddle	middle
paddle	peddle	riddle
saddle	straddle	twiddle
waddle		

i) '-tle'

beetle	bristle	castle
dismantle	gentle	jostle
rustle	startle	subtle
thistle	title	whistle
wrestle		

j) '-ttle'

battle	bottle	fettle
kettle	rattle	scuttle
settle	shuttle	skittle
throttle	wattle	

k) '-ble'

(See pages 235 and 236 for all the -able/-ible words.)

able	cable	gable
gamble	garble	humble
jumble	marble	mumble
nimble	noble	ramble
rumble	scramble	stable
stumble	syllable	thimble
tremble	trouble	tumble
warble		

l) '-bble'

babble	bubble	gabble
gobble	hobble	nibble
pebble	rabble	rubble
scribble	squabble	wobble

22. '-tch-'

batch	butcher	catch
clutch	ditch	etch
hatch	hatchet	hitch
hutch	itch	ketch
ketchup	kitchen	latch
match	notch	patch
pitch	satchel	scratch
snatch	sketch	stitch
stretch	switch	thatch
twitch	watch	witch
wretch		

Silent Letters

6. Silent 'w'

wrangle	wrap	wreath
wreck	wren	wrestle
wretch	wriggle	wring
wrinkle	wrist	write
wrong		

1. Silent 'p'

pneumatic	pneumonia	psalm
psychiatrist	psychic	psychology
receipt		

2. Silent 'b'

bomb	climb	comb
crumb	debt	doubt
dumb	jamb	lamb
limb	numb	plumb
plumber	subtle	succumb
thumb	tomb	womb

3. Silent 'n'

column	condemn	damn
hymn	solemn	

4. Silent 'g'

campaign	champagne	deign
design	feign	foreign
gnarled	gnash	gnat
gnaw	gnome	gnu
malign	reign	resign
sign	sovereign	

5. Silent 'l'

balm	calm	embalm
palm	psalm	qualm
salmon	walk	yolk

More Suffixes

1. '-ic'

Lots of words end in '-ic'. Here is a list of some of them.

basic	characteristic	classic
comic	cosmetic	critic
domestic	dynamic	economic
elastic	electric	emphatic
fanatic	frantic	garlic
gigantic	hectic	heroic
magic	mimic	panic
pathetic	Olympic	organic
republic	romantic	sarcastic
scenic	scientific	specific
tactic	tonic	tragic
tunic		

a) When forming adverbs from words ending in '-ic' you add '-ally'.

Example

basic + ally = basically

b) Note that when *panic* is a verb you add 'k' before an ending beginning with a vowel, i.e.

panic	panicked	panicking

2. '-ist'/'-ism'

botanist	cellist	chemist
chiropodist	environmentalist	
evangelist	extremism	florist
machinist	naturalist	pacifist
perfectionist	pessimism	protagonist
oculist	optimist	royalist
sadism	scientist	stylist
tourism	ventriloquist	

3. '-logy'

anthology	anthropology	apology
biology	chronology	cosmology
ecology	etymology	geology
meteorology	mythology	physiology
psychology	sociology	technology
theology	zoology	

4. '-graphy'

autobiography	biography	choreography
geography	oceanography	orthography
photography	radiography	

Unusual Words

Here is a list of unusual words, many of them foreign.

abyss	aerobics	aerosol
algebra	baguette	biscuit
bizarre	blancmange	boutique
calorie	camouflage	chauffeur
chauffeuse	chauvinist	connoisseur
cygnet	dahlia	debris
decaffeinated	decathlon	deuce
dungeon	Fahrenheit	fiasco
goulash	gourmet	gymkhana
gypsy	gyroscope	haiku
hydrogen	hygiene	kayak
labyrinth	lacquer	liaison
lieutenant	lingerie	lozenge
lynch	lynx	martyr
medieval	mediocre	mistletoe
nymph	pygmy	pyjamas
python	quartz	restaurant
oyster	sandwich	scythe
sergeant	shampoo	silhouette
souvenir	spaghetti	stalactite
stalagmite	suede	surgeon
surveillance	sycamore	synagogue
sword	tandoori	theatre
thyme	toupee	tuition
turquoise	vacuum	vehicle
venue	versatile	violin
virtue	waltz	witch
yacht	zebra	zinc
zither		